The Long and Winding Road

www.penguin.co.uk

Also by Alan Johnson

This Boy
Please, Mister Postman

The Long and Winding Road

Alan Johnson

BANTAM PRESS

LONDON · NEW YORK · TORONTO · SYDNEY · AUCKLAND

TRANSWORLD PUBLISHERS
61–63 Uxbridge Road, London W5 5SA
www.penguin.co.uk

Transworld is part of the Penguin Random House group of companies
whose addresses can be found at global.penguinrandomhouse.com

First published in Great Britain in 2016 by Bantam Press
an imprint of Transworld Publishers

A CIP catalogue record for this book
is available from the British Library.

ISBN 9780593076033

Typeset in 11.5/15 pt Minion
by Jouve (UK), Milton Keynes
Printed and bound in Great Britain by Clays Ltd, Bungay, Suffolk

Penguin Random House is committed to a sustainable
future for our business, our readers and our planet. This book
is made from Forest Stewardship Council® certified paper.

1 3 5 7 9 10 8 6 4 2

For Natalie, Emma, Jamie and Oliver

Chapter 1

I KNEW I shouldn't have gone. It was my sister Linda who persuaded me. Seven years after emigrating to Australia, she and her husband Chas were returning to England for the first time, to attend the wedding of our half-sister Sandra on 25 August 1990.

Sandra's father would be 'giving her away'. The problem was that Sandra's father, Stephen Johnson, was also my father. He was, of course, Linda's father, too, but while she had re-established contact with him, I had not. In a different context I suppose he gave us away, or at least left us to our own devices. I was eight when he walked out and thirteen on the only other occasion I'd seen him since, at my mother's funeral, where he'd hovered on the periphery. It seems over-dramatic to say that, as far as I was concerned, I didn't have a father; as if I'd grown up emotionally damaged by his departure, by his rejection of my mother, Lily, and of us. But I bore no shoulder chips, carried no burden; there were no scars on my body, or on my soul. I was completely and entirely at ease with being fatherless. I accepted it as my natural state, like having blue eyes and dark chestnut hair – the colour of Lily's. Steve's was ginger.

It wasn't as if Steve had broken some kind of bond between us when he left. We'd never been close. And Linda had always said that she hated our father. Indeed, she'd once tried to stab him with her Girl Guide's penknife. He was a boozing, gambling womanizer who abused our mother physically as well as mentally. If he hadn't been so feckless she wouldn't have had to ruin her already fragile health by scrubbing and cleaning other people's houses for a pittance. Yet hatred was not an emotion I ever felt capable of summoning up. Lily had ensured that the misery in her life didn't transfer to mine. She and my sister absorbed it. They'd kept things from me so that I wouldn't be aware of the full extent of Steve's behaviour. Still, I knew enough to feel elated when he left. No more shouting matches that could be heard by all the other families living around us in our west London slum. No more attacks on my mother. No more creeping around in silence on a Saturday morning while he slept off the excesses of the night before.

At that time, in the 1950s, the Home Service would broadcast appeals for information about missing people. Every morning our big, old wireless, hired from Radio Rentals, would solemnly urge the likes of 'Mr Gerald Smith, formerly of Sunbury-on-Thames', to please 'get in touch with his mother, Gladys Smith, who is seriously ill'. I remember wondering if, one of those mornings, just after 'Lift Up Your Hearts' and before the eight o'clock news, would come the plea: 'Will Mr Stephen Arthur Johnson, of Southam Street, North Kensington, London W10, return home, where his wife, Lilian May Johnson, is waiting to hear from him.' Steve had slipped away on a Saturday morning in 1958 while the three of us were 'down the lane' in Portobello Road market. My mother had no idea where he'd gone.

In the end, he was tracked down to Upland Road, East Dulwich, the home of Vera, the barmaid at the Lads of the Village, one of the various pubs across Kensal Town where Steve played piano to an appreciative audience. It was always a mystery to me how Vera managed to get to and from work in North Kensington from East Dulwich, which must have been at least ten miles away. Aged eleven, and an avid collector of football programmes, I once made the journey to a shop in Dulwich where, I was reliably informed by *Charles Buchan's Football Monthly*, there were thousands for sale. The bus ride took so long that I was amazed to find I was still in London. Having no understanding of population density or the vastness of the city south of the river, the whole time I was there I was nervous I might bump into Steve.

And now the wedding invitation arrived from that same house in Upland Road. 'Mr and Mrs Stephen Johnson request the pleasure of the company of . . .' After thirty-two years he wanted the pleasure of my company. Linda was coming all the way from Perth, Western Australia for Sandra's special day – and she had been so afraid of flying that even when she and Chas emigrated she'd insisted on going by sea. Apparently, she had conquered her phobia on several holiday flights to Bali, but this was a gruelling journey just to attend a wedding.

'Sandra's our sister,' Linda reiterated needlessly over the phone. 'Our flesh and blood. It would make her day if we could be there for her.' She was as determined and as persuasive as ever. I was cornered. Against my better judgement, for Sandra's sake, I would have to go.

~

I wouldn't have as far to travel. By 1990 I was living and working in south London myself. My job with the Union of Communication Workers was based in Clapham, and home was a flat in the urban sprawl of Thornton Heath, at St Christopher's Gardens, a new development bordering the A23, the Brighton Road. I was a forty-year-old divorcee and grandfather, my daughter Natalie having given birth to her own daughter, Carmel, in 1987. If I could summon up hatred for anything it was that word 'grandfather'. It made me feel like an ancient clock, or a grey-haired pensioner in a misshapen cardigan pottering in his garden.

I didn't tell my children, Natalie, Emma and Jamie, now aged twenty-four, twenty-two and (almost) twenty, about the wedding invitation. They had shown no curiosity about their family history. In truth neither their mother, Judy, nor I had encouraged it. We'd never been keen to talk about our childhoods. We had created a new family, far from the deprivation of North Kensington. Why would we want to dwell on the snapped branches of our family tree?

Now one of those branches had blown back from a world of gaslit streets and damp, crumbling houses. I was about to be reunited with my father. Were there any fond memories I could dredge up to help me to prepare myself for the ordeal? One scene constantly recurred. We are in the kitchen at Southam Street. I am sitting on the cracked lino as Steve stands talking to my mother. From my perspective, he seems tall. For once they are not arguing, but talking; discussing something face-to-face, close to one another. He has come home from his intermittent work as a painter and decorator, his red hair flecked with paint. Wearing a crumpled brown gabardine mac boasting more buttons than are strictly necessary, he is smoking a cigarette and speaking earnestly. I can smell Steve's familiar musk – a mixture of putty, tobacco and alcohol – but he isn't drunk, or angry. Perhaps it is the rare civility of this encounter that imprinted the image on to my memory, me with my head tilted towards the flyblown ceiling on that evening long ago, gazing at a father I could for once look up to.

Could I disinter any other benign images? Yes. There was the trip to Walton-on-the-Naze. A friend of Steve's had hired a car. Lily, Linda, Steve and I squeezed into its leather interior with Steve's friend and his wife to be driven to the Essex coast. I could recall the excitement of anticipating the treat as much as the treat itself. It was my first journey in a car and only my second visit to the seaside. Snapshots from that outing floated up from the depths of my memory. Linda and Steve eating cockles and whelks while I devoured an ice-cream wafer, a large block of ice cream sandwiched between two brittle biscuits; the men removing the elasticated armbands that held their overlong sleeves in place in order to roll them up to catch the sun.

At the end of that hot day, on the road home, Linda and I were left in the back of the car outside a pub while the four adults went inside. Lily came out with bottles of lemonade and bags of crisps for us. There was only one brand of crisps in my childhood: Smith's. A factory in our part of west London gave local women a chance to earn some money putting salt into little pieces of blue waxed paper and twisting them into tiny sacks to be dropped into the packets of crisps as optional seasoning.

Yes, that was a good day at Walton-on-the-Naze – a pleasant memory; something to savour (literally, in the case of the crisps). And surely it must have been Steve who gave me the little plastic submarine, fuelled by baking soda, that I so cherished. You put the plug in the butler sink, filled it with water and the submarine would sink, gradually dispelling bubbles from its hold.

Then there was the trip to the barber's. Perhaps my first. The barber's was a man's world. I knew this instinctively, sensing that the whispered conversations, like the masculine soapy fragrance, were the hallmarks of a male domain. A plank of wood would be placed across the thickly padded black leather arms of the barber's chair to bring small boys up to the required height for hair-cutting. Steve sat smoking and reading the newspaper, probably picking out the horses he would bet on, as he did every single day that horses anywhere were running races.

And there was that word Steve would use in jest when adopting a mock upper-crust tone. What was it? Invariably? No, it wasn't that. Indefinitely? Indubitably? That was it. On a Sunday Lily might say, 'Aren't you going to see your mother this morning?' and Steve, in a good mood as he prepared to embark on his meticulous weekend toilette (he always liked to look smart), would reply: 'Indubitably, my dear.' A posh word uttered lightheartedly as a dig at those who led a very different life from ours. Indubitably.

I would run these childhood scenes through my head as the reunion approached, trying to dispel any negative thoughts. Sure, Steve had left us, but I was a grown man now who understood how relationships could break down. Steve would have been about thirty-seven when he'd decamped – the same age I'd been when I drove away from the Britwell estate in Slough and my marriage to Judy. It was true that I'd retained a close relationship with my kids and that the divorce had been as amicable and as painless as we were able to make it. But hadn't my mother tried hard to encourage me to stay in touch with Steve? She'd even gone to the extraordinary lengths of offering to accompany me on a visit to Dulwich; to humiliate herself by entering the comfortable domesticity of Steve's new life with Vera just to ensure that I maintained contact. 'A boy needs a father,' she would insist. But to no avail. So the fault, if fault there was, for my fatherless state was mine as much as his.

I said nothing about this DIY cognitive therapy to Linda in the phone calls from Australia that became increasingly frequent as she pressed her case. I'd already surrendered and said I'd go but she was suspicious that I'd cry off with a late excuse. I said nothing, either, to my girlfriend, Laura.

I'd met Laura when she worked at UCW House as a personal assistant to the general secretary of the union, Alan Tuffin. Laura was tall, attractive and the funniest woman I'd ever met. She lived in Herne Hill, a south London girl from a family dominated by women. She was one of two sisters and her glamorous mother was one of three. They all loved a wedding. Laura would be coming with me, while the rest of the matriarchy planned to attend the church in Dulwich to see the show.

Laura had been born the year before my mother died. She was looking forward to meeting Linda for the first time and thought it wonderful that I'd see my half-sister at last and my father after such a long separation. I had neither the inclination nor the emotional vocabulary to explain the trauma that was creeping up on me as the day grew nearer.

~

Linda looked thin and drawn. In the seven years since she had left for Australia she had sent me the odd photograph but I hadn't realized how much weight she'd lost. We wrote to one another regularly, long letters on flimsy, blue airmail paper, folded inwards and sealed to form an envelope. I'd written of Natalie's marriage, Carmel's birth, Jamie and Emma's exploits, the end of my marriage. She related the success of her Magic Moon nursery, the Australianization of her children, Renay, Tara and Dean, and Chas's immersion in the local community of Armadale in the Perth suburbs.

Now she was back in London, speaking with a slight Aussie twang. She and Chas came to stay with me in my two-bedroomed flat in St Christopher's Gardens the night before the wedding. Jamie joined us. He was a student at Roehampton Institute and lived with some fellow undergraduates in a former council house on the vast Roehampton estate. When Laura arrived at 8pm we all walked round to a nearby Italian restaurant. Over dinner the five of us talked about everything under the sun except the next day's event. Linda was as voluble as ever, making sure that the conversation didn't flag and that everyone in turn was properly interrogated – she wanted to be fully informed about our lives. She also planned to visit her old friend Judy, my ex-wife. It was through Linda that I'd met Judy – they had studied and worked together as nursery nurses. Judy was also about to be married. Jamie was going to be best man. Everything, we agreed, had turned out fine – in the end.

Linda touched only once on the subject we were all avoiding when she asked Jamie if he didn't feel the urge to come to the church the next day to see his grandfather. I was relieved when he said he felt no draw or obligation whatsoever. He and his sisters had lived a life devoid of grandparents as neither their mother nor father could produce a parent between them. Jamie had better things to do the following day. For a start, Queens Park Rangers were playing at Nottingham Forest. Two of the passions I had inherited from Steve – support for Rangers and love of music – had been passed on in turn to Jamie but neither of us had any desire to follow the river back to its source.

Linda didn't comment, or make any reference to our childhood, confining herself tactfully to some general remarks about how happy Sandra had been when she'd told her we'd be there. Laura went home and Jamie, Linda, Chas and I returned to St Christopher's Gardens, where I spent a sleepless night on the sofa while my sister and her husband occupied the master bedroom and Jamie slept on a Postman Pat Z bed, provided for his comfort in the tiny spare room.

Sandra had a fine day for her marriage to Eamman Horgan. As the church organ thundered out 'Here Comes the Bride' and we all stood up, she passed me on the arm of her father. It was the first time I had ever seen her. I couldn't discern much of a family resemblance, though she did have Linda's eyes, through which an equally vivacious personality shone out. As for Steve, I'm ashamed to say that the first thing I noticed about him was his full head of hair. At sixty-nine years of age, the ginger had turned grey but it was Brylcreem-slicked into the same style he'd always worn, combed back from the forehead. Given the hereditary nature of baldness (and my vanity), this was the happiest possible revelation. I could live with being a grandfather as long as I wasn't destined to be a bald one.

Looking on from the congregation, I was able to scrutinize him while remaining unobserved. I was already suppressing emotions that had welled up with an almost overwhelming suddenness. Swirling among them was self-pity, for sure, and a deeper anger than I ever thought I could harbour at this stranger who was said to be my father. I couldn't help but think of Lily and her longing for a stable marriage, reasonable health and a house with her own front door. Most of all I felt a compelling urge to avoid the embarrassment of meeting a man I'd be expected to call 'Dad' but who meant nothing to me. Of one thing I was certain: in the midst of all this angst there was not a smidgen of regret that I had never followed Lily's advice to forge a bond with my father.

Linda was standing on the other side of Chas, one place away. Every so often during the ceremony she'd lean forward to smile at me and, I think, to check how I was coping. I wondered how she could look so cheery. Why weren't we marching out together, hand in hand, publicly refusing to have anything to do with our father's glowing pride at crowning the achievements of his life without us by offering his youngest daughter's hand in marriage?

I decided that I had three options. Leave now and spoil Sandra's day. Stay and be sucked into a family relationship that repelled me. Or get through the wedding and the reception afterwards with as little contact with Steve as possible.

I would never have Linda's maturity or magnanimity and I couldn't find the words to talk to her or to Laura about how I felt. Fortunately, we had to leave the reception early anyway as I'd agreed to drive Linda and Chas to Essex, where they were to stay with Chas's daughter. So I went for option three and steeled myself to endure the next few hours with a smiling face masking the utter detachment I felt inside.

Outside the church, in the late summer sunshine, guests and

onlookers stood around as the wedding photographer earned his fee. Laura's mother, grandmother, sister and aunt were there, dressed up in their late-1980s fashionable gear, all wide shoulders and big jewellery. I was sporting a pale blue suit that I couldn't have worn three years earlier or three years later. It had shoulder pads, a single-button jacket, turn-ups and no vents. If the Mod police had arrived I'd have been arrested, if not for the suit for the wide, patterned silk tie around my neck and the brogues on my feet.

Steve stood in a family circle with his wife, Vera, her son Michael from a previous liaison and two of Steve's brothers, my uncles. The three Johnson men were all short, about five foot four, I'd guess. One of them, Uncle Jim, lived with his wife Betty in the Peabody Buildings on Dalgarno Gardens in the flat originally occupied by my paternal grandmother when she was alive. Uncle Jim and Auntie Betty had always been kind to my mother, and it was Jim who'd agreed to act as guarantor for Linda and me when our social worker somehow managed to secure a council flat for us in Battersea after Lily died.

The same could not be said for the other brother, Wally, from whom Lily had sought help when Steve abandoned us. He had told my mother that 'we all have our problems' and shut the door in her face.

I learned later from Linda that I'd had to be pointed out to Steve amid the milling throng outside the church. She suggested a couple of times that we go and say hello. On each occasion I managed to find an excuse, diverting the conversation as we stood in the shade of a large oak tree chatting to Laura's family.

Eventually the radiant Sandra came across with Eamman

and insisted on taking us over so that I could be introduced to my father. She had me firmly by the arm, and suddenly I was face to face with Steve. I noticed the thick, black frames of his glasses for the first time. He was impeccably turned out, as he had always been on Sundays and holidays, or when playing the piano in the pubs and clubs of west London, right down to the highly polished shoes. His suit was early 1950s demob style, so we were each sartorially representative of our different eras.

He said, 'Hello, son.'

I said 'Hi,' but we didn't shake hands and, thankfully, at almost that precise moment, the photographer shouted, 'Bride's family!' and began to muster us for a photograph.

Linda grabbed my hand, perhaps fearing I'd make a run for it. She was right to force me into that photograph. This, after all, was what we had come for – to be together for Sandra's special day. We lined up as directed and the photographer captured the scene: the day I met my father for the last time.

I escaped as quickly as I could. Linda was alert to the radio waves transmitted by my suppressed emotions. At the reception we'd sat with Uncle Jim and Auntie Betty and I'd managed to avoid any further close encounters with my father.

It was only when I departed that we made any physical contact, shaking hands in the functional way one does when saying goodbye. Vera said: 'Now that we've got together again, we need to stay in touch.' I nodded and smiled. Nod and smile, that was me. I recognized deep emotions but refused to articulate them. At least I could have left Steve in no doubt about my hostility. I could have been honest with him, told him man-to-man what I thought of him; forced him to regret in some way his treatment of Lily. But instead we shook hands limply.

He was aware that I was divorced. Maybe there was a knowing look in his green eyes that said, 'Now you know about relationships, and how they can wax and wane, you can understand why I left Lily, exactly as you left Judy.' Perhaps he expected his forty-year-old son to demonstrate the same maturity as his eldest child. But here's the thing about Steve: I don't believe he actually thought about it very much at all. He'd settled with the woman he loved and that woman wasn't Lily. I could take it or leave it. Just as I never wanted any kind of relationship with him, he didn't particularly want one with me. Just as he was a stranger to me, so I was to him and building any kind of father-and-son relationship now was anathema to us both.

So the problem wasn't him, it was Sandra. I really liked my half-sister and she was keen for me to stay in close touch – 'now that you live nearby'. As an only child she'd sought out her half-siblings. She had made contact with Linda, and it was for Sandra's sake that Linda had re-established contact with Steve.

Now Sandra wanted contact with me. But Sandra and her husband lived with Steve and Vera. They planned to move out when they could get a mortgage to buy a place of their own, but regardless of where they lived, any kind of relationship with Sandra meant engaging with Steve. Even if we managed to avoid each other physically, his presence would permeate Sandra's conversation. She loved her father and couldn't be expected to treat him as a non-person in deference to me.

I pointed this out to Linda as I drove her and Chas along the

A13. Laura had gone home to Herne Hill and Chas was dozing in the passenger seat. Linda was in the back of my Ford Fiesta, catching my eye in the rear-view mirror as we chatted. She told me how pleased she'd be to reach her forty-third birthday the following month.

Three generations of women in our maternal family had died at forty-two, the age Linda was now: our mother, grandmother and great-grandmother. Lily had lived her life under this shadow. She had a debilitating heart disease, mitral stenosis, which required frequent and lengthy stays in hospital. As a result, Linda had looked after me since long before our mother died.

When the consultant at Hammersmith hospital, a world-renowned cardiac centre local to us in west London, told Lily that her life could be extended if she was prepared to be a guinea pig for a revolutionary new operation to replace the mitral valve, she had only recently turned forty-two. A sense of foreboding was undoubtedly one of the reasons why she turned down this opportunity. Later that year she became so desperately ill that she no longer had a choice. She had the operation and died afterwards in hospital. Aged forty-two.

My sister had inherited our mother's fascination with spiritualism, astrology, destiny and fate. I suppose it wasn't superstition – though they were both superstitious, too – so much as a preoccupation with karma, the Hindu and Buddhist principle of cause and effect whereby people's actions in their current lives affect their future in both this existence and their lives to come.

Whatever it was, it was instilled into Linda by Lily in much the same way as an appreciation of Emmeline Pankhurst's campaign to get women the vote. These were beliefs and values to be passed down the female line; things that Lily and Linda discussed in the big double bed they shared after Steve had gone. Linda learned to be pleased if a black cat crossed her path and never to walk under a ladder or step on cracks in the pavement (walking anywhere in town with Linda is a challenge). I've never seen my sister wear opals or the colour green and she never trusted a man with a dimple in his chin, all as instructed by our mother. She was convinced that Lily's spirit was guiding us through life, but that didn't ease her trepidation at reaching the dreaded age of forty-two – particularly when she, too, had to face the prospect of surgery.

We've both enjoyed good health, Linda and I. Her theory was that we'd been exposed to so many germs in our childhood that we'd become immune to most diseases. Our only spells in hospital were for the youthful afflictions to which most children of our generation succumbed: tonsillitis and appendicitis. I can remember Linda's face at the window of St Charles hospital, gazing mournfully after Lily and me as we walked away after visiting time. It was a Sunday afternoon in, I think, 1954. Seven-year-old Linda had been admitted to have her tonsils removed and in those austere and joyless days children could be visited only during set hours on a Sunday. Visiting Wormwood Scrubs prison would probably have been a more welcoming experience.

Thirty-five years later, in a different hemisphere, Linda had been told that she needed a hysterectomy. I had been informed of this in one of the flimsy blue missives from Western Australia but I'd failed to make the connection with her age. She hadn't referred to it herself so as not to worry me.

Linda admitted now how utterly terrified she had been. But

happily the operation had been a complete success and, having recovered, she was convinced that she had broken the curse and would live to be a hundred.

Changing the subject, Linda voiced the hope that, having met Sandra at last, I would stay in touch with our half-sister. She gave me a little lecture about how I'd failed to go and see any of our relatives in our mother's home city of Liverpool. Five of Lily's seven surviving siblings still lived there and we had more cousins than I could keep track of, though Linda – our collective memory bank – managed it. Before she and Chas flew back to Australia the following week, they planned to go up to Liverpool. The least I could do, as her ambassador, was to keep relationships ticking over in between the visits she intended to make every few years.

I'm afraid I let her down badly. For nineteen years I'd been focused on raising a family on a council estate in Slough. And now I was focused on something else: becoming general secretary of the Union of Communication Workers.

Chapter 2

My official job title at the union was outdoor secretary, which conjured images of John Cleese reading the news from a desk on the beach in *Monty Python's Flying Circus*. Fortunately, my office, on the first floor of the magnificent, purpose-built UCW House in Crescent Lane, Clapham, had four walls and a ceiling.

UCW House had turrets and a stuccoed mock-Tudor entrance. At my end of the long corridor were the operational officers who grappled with the issues affecting the terms and conditions of delivery staff, indoor sorters, clerks, cleaners, drivers; the men on the travelling post offices immortalized in W. H. Auden's poem 'The Night Mail' ('This is the night mail crossing the border, bringing the cheque and the postal order') and in John Grierson's 1930s documentary of the same name; the doorkeepers in the major post offices and the élite liftmen who worked in a few principal sorting offices. (When I included them in the national productivity scheme I warned that their bonuses would go up and down. I laughed; they didn't.)

My job was to look after the interests of the bulk of Britain's

200,000-odd postal workers: those who delivered the mail. Hence the 'outdoor' bit of my job title.

You could smell the cordite from the battlefields in our corner of UCW House as we fought to retain and improve our members' working lives through the traumas of the Thatcher years.

At the other end of the corridor sat my rival for the UCW crown: the organizing secretary, Derek Hodgson. Down in his domain all was peaceful. Far behind the front line all that could be heard was the gentle click of typewriters and the odd subdued 'brrrp brrrp' from those slim telephones we used then that looked like exclamation marks.

The Organizing Department dealt with, among other things, branch rules, the union's training programme and the district organizers, lay officials who relied on the patronage of the organizing secretary for some of the plum jobs like administrating at the week-long residential schools.

Those typewriters would not be clicking for much longer. The days of carbon paper and Tippex were coming to an end, victims of the computer revolution. But in 1990 there was still a typing pool, as well as two secretaries per national officer. One of these secretaries would take dictation in shorthand, sitting patiently, legs crossed, on the other side of the officer's large desk, remaining alert through the long pauses that punctuated the pearls of wisdom that fell from his lips.

We officers were just coming to terms with a stunning piece of new technology called a Dictaphone, into which we could pontificate while the secretary got on with other things. This was a solitary pursuit for the officer, and some were more reluctant than others to adopt it. The clarity of my diction into the machine wasn't great. I recall 'pillar box' coming back typed as 'pillow box' and 'Ashton-under-Lyne' as 'Ashton', thickly underlined by my diligent secretary.

Every morning at 10am and every afternoon at 3pm, a tea trolley trundled the full length of the corridor, starting out in the tranquillity of the Organizing Department before heading towards the worker bees at our end. Alice and Jean, the 'tea ladies', would dispense cheery gossip along with the all-milk coffee or builder's tea on offer. Their counterparts on the ground and top floors would move in perfect formation along the corridors there at exactly the same time. Irrespective of what was happening in the world outside, you could set your watch by those tea trolleys and they stopped for nothing and no one – not even royalty.

UCW House once received a visit from HRH the Princess Royal, who had become the first member of the royal family to attend a union conference. After we agreed to deliver fund-raising leaflets for the charity Save the Children, of which she was patron, free of charge, she had taken the podium at the UCW conference to thank our members for their efforts. She was given a warm reception, despite the potential for confusion created by my old friend Derek Walsh, that year's national chairman, who, flustered by having to explain the protocol to our 1,300 delegates before her appearance, instructed them that when she entered they must stand up and remain in their seats. Fortunately, they knew what he meant.

Later she came to UCW House, where security was tight. Everything had to be coordinated to perfection, every movement on every floor meticulously programmed. And it was – until, as we reached the top of the staircase to the first floor on our way to the boardroom, where her Royal Highness was to address the Executive Council, we heard the ominous sound of rattling cups and saucers. It was 3pm. The security guards were forced to shrink back against the wall as Alice and Jean made their way along the corridor with the tea trolley.

Derek Hodgson was always keen to know what was happening in the Postal Department. He was a diligent, hard-working national officer, albeit one operating in a stress-free environment. Just as I recognized him as my main rival for the top job, he knew that I was probably the only person who could beat him when the current general secretary, our unassuming but extremely effective boss, Alan Tuffin, retired. Indeed, Derek was the favourite. Not only did he have the district organizers on his payroll, but in his current position it was impossible for him to be tainted with failure. At every conference our branches mandated us occupational officers to achieve improvements to their terms and conditions. Every day we grappled with the changes that were necessary to ensure that the Post Office was relevant in the rapidly changing world of communications. There were disputes to settle, strikes to prevent, discipline cases to defend. In the Postal Department we walked across minefields; in Organizing they skipped over meadows.

Derek had an additional point in his favour. He was nearly ten years older than me. All national officers were required by the rigidity of the rule book to retire at sixty. Alan Tuffin would reach that age in 1992 just as Derek would be ripening into his early fifties, the traditional vintage for an incoming general secretary.

For now we each toiled in our offices at opposite ends of the first floor, like two boxers in their separate corners waiting to step into the centre of the ring. I would glean intelligence from the enemy camp every time I used the gents', which was at Derek's end of the corridor. He was at a disadvantage on this front as he had to find excuses to visit our quarters. And it was impossible for him to arrive unannounced, since Derek didn't so much walk as bustle. Well-built and stocky, he walked as fast as some people could run. And his habit of having steel caps put on the toes and heels of all his shoes meant that his approach along the parquet floors of the corridor sounded like a horse trotting towards us.

A horse towing a Gypsy caravan, come to think of it, for he was also one of those men who insist on attaching their important accoutrements to their person. He wore his steel-framed glasses on a chain around his neck and an array of fountain pens clipped to the pocket of his short-sleeved shirts. But the biggest inhibitor to any attempt he made to move surreptitiously was his keys. Derek carried more keys than a Beefeater at the Tower of London. They accompanied him everywhere on a series of substantial rings clipped together on his thick, buckled belt. It's a wonder he didn't keel over from the weight. So no matter what was going on in the Postal Department, however much noise there was from the typewriters, the photocopier or low-flying aircraft circling over Clapham, we never failed to hear him coming.

The 1980s had been an awful time for trade unionism. Having begun the decade with 13 million members, British trade unions ended it with half that number. It felt as if we were some kind of underground movement, fearful of survival as successive blocks of legislation restricted our activities and diluted our influence.

Some of the fault lay with us. During what I suppose could be called the glam-rock era of trade unionism in the 1970s we had failed to use our power to build a durable legacy that could withstand a hostile government. The union movement preferred to defend unballoted strikes than to pursue industrial democracy. It was complicit in perpetuating long hours of overtime but neglected to establish, or even to seek, a statutory minimum entitlement to paid holidays; it championed the closed shop rather than the minimum wage.

It is of course easy to say all this in hindsight, but there were plenty of voices much more influential than mine trying at the time to convince the trade-union movement to reform itself before somebody did it for us.

In other parts of Europe trade unions were becoming part of the fabric of the ways companies operated, helping to lay down basic minimum standards that were legally enforceable: caps on working hours, entitlement to paid holidays, a national minimum wage. We in Britain were not only against this so-called European social model, we were against Europe full stop. As a TUC (Trades Union Congress) delegate to conference after conference, I'd sit there in my tank top and flares as any proposition calling for a national minimum wage was debated and defeated. Such a measure was best left to those deluded trade unionists in Scandinavia, the argument ran. It would distort our precious 'differentials' (the higher pay negotiated for those with more skills or longer service). Rights at work came with your union card, and if minimum standards were available by law, what incentive was there to join a union?

This was a terrible miscalculation but it didn't on its own account for the battering the trade-union movement took in that decade. By the time the approach to Europe was effectively reversed in the late 1980s our numbers had diminished and what little influence we'd had on government policy had been destroyed.

A series of momentous and bitter disputes had seen the steel workers, miners, print workers and train drivers defeated. Coal, gas, electricity and water (all heavily unionized) had been privatized, Britain's 'smokestack' manufacturing and heavy industry had shrunk and unemployment had risen to over 3 million.

The Post Office hadn't succumbed to privatization, deindustrialization or any major dispute but things were changing. The avuncular chairman, Ron Dearing, had moved on and power and influence had passed to Bill Cockburn, the firebrand head of the Letters Division (basically what is today Royal Mail), who took a more confrontational approach to industrial relations.

He it was who had introduced the productivity scheme – Improved Working Methods (IWM) – that had helped to elevate me to a national officer. I had acquired a certain expertise in the nuts and bolts of what was then a voluntary scheme, which our local branches could decide whether or not to enter. In essence it allowed the union locally to sell back working hours they thought they could do without in exchange for a weekly bonus. It was fiercely controversial within the union because it encouraged the 'sale' of jobs and because the most inefficient offices gained the most from it.

IWM's defenders pointed out that if the hours were genuinely unnecessary they would be winkled out and abolished eventually with nothing to show for them in the pay packets of postal workers. Under IWM the local workforce received 75 per cent of the savings.

The scheme had become compulsory in the mid-1980s but it had done nothing to solve Royal Mail's chronic recruitment problem in south-east England. This swathe of the country outside London (where 'London weighting' was paid) routinely had 10,000 vacancies. Little had changed since I'd transferred as a postman from London to Slough, where Judy and I had raised three children on my earnings from long hours of overtime made available by this staff shortage. The IWM bonus couldn't be advertised as part of the wages in order to attract applicants because it could fluctuate and might well disappear altogether if too many hours were used.

Bill Cockburn decided to try to resolve the problem by introducing a pay supplement in the most severely affected offices, on the reasonable assumption that the union wouldn't take industrial action to stop their members being paid more money. He was wrong.

The union saw these payments as eroding its ability to address the serious problems of low pay and long hours that affected all its members. We feared that these Difficult Recruitment Area Supplements (DRAS) would herald the end of national pay bargaining.

We balloted our members, receiving a strong mandate for a twenty-four-hour strike. It would be the first national dispute in the Post Office since 1971 when, as a twenty-year-old postman, I'd participated in the seven-week all-out strike that had almost bankrupted the union. We had lost badly back then and the cost had severely inhibited our ability to take industrial action for a long period. Even now, seventeen years later, veterans of 1971 would relive their memories of seven weeks with no income and no strike pay, warning against any attempt to resort to a measure that the union had in any case traditionally rejected as a way to resolve disputes. Historically, we had always been more in favour of arbitration than confrontation. The strike was scheduled for 31 August 1988. Responsibility for sorting all this out fell squarely on my shoulders.

Laura had an early indication of what life with a thoughtless union negotiator would be like. As the day of the strike loomed we were heading to Bournemouth for a week at the TUC conference. On the way it was arranged that I should meet senior Post Office managers at a hotel in Winchester for a brief conversation to try to establish some grounds for compromise.

I parked the car on Winchester's main road, where Laura decided to do some shopping. The 'brief conversation' lasted seven hours. We had no mobile phones then, of course, and I couldn't contact Laura, who had shopped, walked up and down, sat in the car, gone for a coffee, gone for something to eat – anything to fill the long hours while I searched fruitlessly for a resolution. She no longer worked for the union but she must have felt as if she did.

On the day of the strike the entire network shut down. In those pre-internet days, the postal service remained crucial to communications and indeed to commerce, but Bill Cockburn decided that when our members returned to work the following day overtime would not be authorized to clear the backlog. He knew that postmen and women could recoup the day's pay they'd lost by working an extra shift. So instead he attempted to bring in casuals at cheap rates to clear the millions of items stacked in dusty mail sacks across the British Isles.

Laura had to drive back from Bournemouth alone while I embarked on a series of meetings with the Post Office, held in remote New Forest hotels to avoid media intrusion. As we negotiated in our various rural retreats the dispute worsened. Our members stayed on strike and the backlog grew. The Post Office withdrew the DRAS payments and agreed to negotiate on the whole question of high staff turnover and unfilled vacancies in London and the south-east.

The problem, as so often in the hundreds of local disputes I dealt with over the years, was the arrangements for returning to work, made worse in this national altercation by Bill Cockburn's 'no overtime' edict. This was gradually and subtly softened during the course of our negotiations to 'a certain level' of overtime, which managers were authorized to offer in the thousand or so offices between John O'Groats and Land's End where local negotiations were to take place.

After ten days in the New Forest we'd thrashed out a template for local negotiations and were finally able to come out of hibernation. My next job was to oversee the multiplicity of negotiations to make sure our efforts at national level translated into local agreements for an orderly return to work. Given the interconnectivity of the network, it was vital that this was properly coordinated so that everyone returned at the same time on the same date. I felt like a composer who'd helped to write a chorus for a thousand choirs to learn and sing note-perfect in complete synchronization.

Amazingly, the choirs sang, but not before I and my trusty assistant, a gutsy Glaswegian by the name of Mike Hogan, had sweated over the orchestration. Often described as a bear of a man, Mike had appropriately begun his Post Office career as a telegram boy in Bearsden. He'd transferred to King Edward Building in Holborn (the Eastern Central District Office) as a young man and become a formidable figure on the union's powerful London District Council. His tough and unsentimental demeanour was a façade. Beneath the hard shell dwelled a sensitive, cultured polymath. Mike was difficult to get to know but nobody who took the trouble to break through the carapace ever regretted the effort. And he was totally loyal to me. Through all the trials and tribulations I encountered in the union, Mike Hogan was always there fighting beside me.

At this time he was pulling off the difficult trick of getting London back while I travelled to the Midlands and the north-west to personally negotiate the return-to-work agreements in the most recalcitrant offices. These included the big beasts of Manchester, Liverpool and Coventry but, strangely enough, the last office to agree was little Stratford-upon-Avon. I liked to imagine that, steeped in the words of the Bard, their townsman, they had stiffened their sinews, summoned up the blood and disguised fair nature with hard-favoured rage.

All our members across the country had been standing like greyhounds in the slips waiting for Stratford-upon-Avon to settle before all 160,000 of them could return to work together. The twenty-four-hour strike had lasted two weeks.

With the DRAS payments withdrawn, the union and the Post Office allowed things to settle down before returning to the negotiating table and hammering out a perfectly sensible agreement under which these pay supplements essentially became an extension of London weighting, spreading out into the Thames Valley and other parts of the Home Counties. I coined the phrase 'no ponds or islands' to direct the union's approach and ensured that all offices within the borders of this newly defined area received the weekly supplements.

At the same time, we improved a number of terms and conditions for our members nationally, such as establishing a better system for paying overtime and additional annual leave. This package was accepted overwhelmingly, the Post Office secured their additional recruitment tool and a totally unnecessary dispute was resolved.

Derek Hodgson wasn't entirely helpful during the two-week DRAS strike. He made a point of turning up on the picket line at Liverpool and Manchester while I was ensconced in the New Forest negotiations and every time I reported back to the full Executive Council I'd have to listen to his little homilies about the importance of standing up to the supposed tyrant Bill Cockburn. I followed the sage advice of my mentor, the previous UCW general secretary Tom Jackson – the man who'd encouraged me to stand for the Executive Council and was still urging me on to greater things from his home in Ilkley, where he was now a successful dealer in antiquarian books.

'Never insult today the man you'll be negotiating with tomorrow,' he'd once told me in his soft Yorkshire accent. However difficult Bill could be, it was hardly likely that whoever came next would be Mother Teresa.

Derek had a colourful way of expressing himself. I remember him telling the executive that Cockburn would be 'as happy as a dog with two cocks in a forest full of lampposts' about the way the dispute was going. But our enmity rarely led to open hostility. We were both too professional for that. Derek had been a postman in Cardiff and while we were completely different personalities, throughout our years on the UCW Executive Council we'd always rubbed along. He'd had the satisfaction of beating me in the ballot for organizing secretary in 1985. I'd been persuaded to stand against him for the vacant position and was comprehensively defeated – a fate that Derek was confident awaited me when the top job came up.

He had plenty of opportunities for Schadenfreude during my time as the union's principal national officer for postmen and women. The IWM local productivity scheme had become too expensive for the business to bear. The total hours saved had now been exceeded by the hours discounted from the scheme as 'authorized variations' – the work hours local officials managed to convince their managers should be treated as if they had never existed. I could take some satisfaction for this as the person who wrote the handbook, devised the training scheme and spent years travelling the country helping local branches to be more adept than management at manipulating the system.

In 1988 the Post Office began the process of abandoning IWM, which ended with me and Bill Cockburn sitting in a room together having been given an hour by our bosses (the chairman of the Post Office and the UCW general secretary) to come up with a solution.

The deadline had been set because, in a typically skilful bit of brinkmanship, Alan Tuffin had said he would announce a strike ballot via the media if the issue wasn't resolved quickly. This had been such a tumultuous period for industrial relations in the Post Office that the prospect of another strike would undoubtedly mean the loss of significant contracts, particularly on Datapost, a guaranteed same-day/overnight service outside the statutory monopoly.

IWM had by then been going for nine years and while some offices had built up a weekly bonus for their staff as high as £60, many still earned nothing, despite the scheme now being compulsory. The deal Bill and I came up with in that intensive hour of rapid negotiation was to transfer the bonus to basic pay as a supplement, ranging between £10 and £20 a week. Those on a bonus above £20 would see it reduced over three years, with a lump-sum buy-out of the excess amount; people who made below £10, including those earning nothing, would be brought up to the new minimum level. Those on bonuses of between £10 and £20 remained as they were, except that the bonus would be crystallized into a permanent weekly payment, regardless of productivity.

This caused much consternation (and led to my first television appearance, when a delegation of disgruntled members from a London parcels office marched on UCW House) but it also gave thousands of postmen and women the biggest increase in pay they'd ever received. Those on high bonuses would receive lump sums of many thousands of pounds and overall, a fragile and fluctuating productivity payment would now be channelled into boosting the regular wage.

The constant dilemma for negotiators is gauging if and when they have reached or exceeded the 'bottom line' of the person on the other side of the negotiating table. But if the hurried way in which this deal was made was less than perfect, I was satisfied with the outcome and happy to put myself in front of some very angry members, mainly in the London offices, to defend it. Derek, I suspected, wasn't entirely unhappy about my predicament.

His next opportunity to profit from my discomfort came with the return of Sunday collections, which the Post Office had cancelled in the early 1970s as part of a cuts programme, resulting in an unacceptable delay in the delivery of mail posted over the weekend.

It was my driving passion to consign to history the six-day week worked by almost all of our delivery staff, and which I'd had to work myself for so long as a postman. Strangely enough, I didn't have many allies on the Executive Council, but one thing that did unite us was a refusal to even contemplate abandoning the Saturday delivery as well. That would have been the easy route to a five-day week but the union had a proud record of defending service standards and it would have meant that mail posted on a Friday wouldn't even be processed until Monday and not delivered until Tuesday – an even more unacceptable reduction in a service built around next-day delivery for letters carrying a first-class stamp.

Mike Hogan and I spent many hours in negotiation to arrive at an agreement that restored Sunday collections (and all the associated processing work) without reinstating the obligation for a postal worker to be on duty on a Sunday if he or she didn't want to. We succeeded. All the work associated with Sunday collections would be voluntary. It would be paid at double the hourly rate and, in accordance with our superannuation agreement, a Sunday attendance would be pensionable – perfect for somebody coming up to retirement who wanted to boost his or her occupational pension.

I put this deal to a special conference of the union held over a June weekend in Bournemouth. The sun was shining in a cloudless blue sky, the birds sang, waves lapped against the shore on the beach outside as my carefully constructed agreement was massacred on the conference floor.

In that rarefied atmosphere speaker after speaker poured out impassioned oration on a single theme: they expected the union to negotiate a shorter working week for its members, not a longer one; fewer hours, not more; better, not worse terms and conditions. It was all over by lunchtime. The hall emptied, leaving only the carcass of an agreement, a distraught outdoor secretary and a quietly smiling Derek Hodgson.

While Derek and I played out our own tiny drama, developments of epic proportions were taking place on the world stage. As the 1980s gave way to the 1990s, the Berlin Wall was demolished, Nelson Mandela was released after twenty-seven years in prison, Margaret Thatcher was toppled.

I listened to a lot of Billy Bragg in the 1980s. His masterpiece 'Between The Wars' finishes with the lines:

Sweet moderation
Heart of this nation
Desert us not, we are
Between the wars.

And it was 'sweet moderation' rather than violent revolution that seemed to be in the ascendancy.

The Berlin Wall (or, as the Communists called it, the 'anti-Fascist Protection Rampart') was dismantled brick by brick, along with the totalitarianism that had kept it in place.

Apartheid in South Africa was destroyed by Mandela's quiet magnanimity. The fearsome Mrs T. was unseated by the unassuming leader of the House of Commons, Geoffrey Howe, her longest-serving Cabinet minister. Within a few years there would even be the prospect of a lasting solution in the Middle East through the Oslo Accord.

The trade-union movement was an important voice in this swirl of events. As Enzo Friso, then the head of the International Confederation of Free Trade Unions, remarked at the time: 'Free trade unions were the main architects of the fall of totalitarianism in the East. They are the motor of democratization in Africa and have been the only opposition to the dictatorships of Latin America.'

The ousting of the Iron Lady, by her own party, after eleven and a half years as prime minister sent shockwaves around the country and beyond. Although Howe's departure, ostensibly over the European Exchange Rate Mechanism, and his devastating resignation speech triggered the event, it was Michael Heseltine who eventually wielded the knife, sharpened on the unpopularity of the community charge, better known as the poll tax.

The poll tax, a fixed charge per head on every citizen, had been brought in to replace the previous system of local government taxation, whereby rates were paid by residents based on the value of their property, regardless of how many people lived there. It was widely viewed as unfair and unnecessarily punitive to the less well off.

Mike Hogan and I had had a taste of the bitter harvest it would reap at the AGM of our Edinburgh branch. We'd been involved in settling a dispute there and had been invited to receive the formal thanks of the branch for the work we'd done. But an earlier item on the agenda concerned the effects of the poll tax, which the Thatcher government had inflicted on Scotland in 1989 as a gruesome prelude to its national implementation the following year. Speaker after speaker came to the platform in the huge hall where the meeting was held. We were struck by the contrast between the courtesy of the welcome extended to us by each speaker as they smiled and said good morning and the anger they were venting within seconds into the microphone positioned directly in front of where we were sitting. There were tales of warrant sales (the arrival of the bailiffs), evictions, desperation and defiance.

I listened with mounting horror as a succession of postal workers told of the chaotic implementation of this charge, particularly in shared accommodation where landlords had no accurate information about exactly who was living in their properties. These outraged postal workers were employed men and women who had to pay 100 per cent of the tax (students and the registered unemployed paid a lower figure). One

Edinburgh postman, Brian Fallon, was a Labour councillor. A decent and principled man, he was obliged to stand in for Margaret Thatcher in receiving the collective venom of his colleagues at the meeting. The local authority had the unenviable task of collecting the tax that provided the major source of funding for local services – one that would prove as impossible to carry out effectively in England and Wales as it was then in Scotland. Brian had shown the courage to come to the meeting to explain the dilemma facing the council but it would be fair to say that he wasn't the most popular person in the hall. Mike and I left that meeting better educated about what was heading our way and more convinced than ever that the Thatcher government was on its last legs. As things turned out, she was but the Conservative government wasn't.

In fact, such was the resistance to the hated tax that large numbers of people refused to pay it and some decided not to add their names to the electoral register in an attempt to evade collection, thus losing their right to vote. There were suggestions that this could have helped the Tories to hang on to power for as long as they did.

As 1990 ended and 1991 began I proposed to Laura. We were seeing in the New Year at a restaurant in Herne Hill with her parents and her sister and at midnight I asked her if she'd marry me. I'd written the proposal in a letter to her which I had in the inside pocket of my new blue suit. I was worried that without this evidence of intent she might think I was drunk and insincere. In fact, as the clock struck midnight, I was sober and as serious as I had ever been in my life. I'd been seventeen when I proposed to Judy and working as a shelf-stacker at Anthony Jackson's supermarket in the Upper Richmond Road. By the time we married six months later I was a postman and beginning to realize that what I really wanted to do was going to prove beyond my grasp.

My nascent musical career, which had been abruptly curtailed by the theft of my Höfner Verithin guitar – along with every musical instrument, amp, speaker and microphone that had once belonged to the In-Betweens, the semi-professional band with whom I played rhythm guitar and sang backing vocals – was not to be revived. When our bass guitarist, a postman, asked me to form another group with him I decided to follow him not on to the seductive stages of London's pubs and clubs but into the Post Office, exchanging wistful hope for a steady job.

I could never have foreseen then that at forty I would be a union officer and what I would be dreaming of was becoming UCW general secretary.

In the first few minutes of 1991 Laura accepted my verbal proposal before she'd even read the written one. We set a date for a summer wedding.

Chapter 3

I TOOK A risk early in 1991 by absenting myself during a crucial period in the run-up to the election of the general secretary when Alan Tuffin convinced me to spend a month in America on something called the International Visitors Programme. This scheme encouraged young(ish) British journalists, politicians and trade-union officials to go to the USA to learn more about the American way of life. Funded by the US taxpayer, visitors were obliged to spend the first week in Washington, after which they could draw up their own itinerary and pass the next three weeks going wherever they wanted. This was, of course, a thrilling opportunity, but the election was only months away. My trusty defender, Mike Hogan, agreed to place his sturdy frame behind my desk, deputizing for me as outdoor secretary. He would cover my back and provide a reliable account of what had gone on while I was out of the country.

I had never been to America – I'd been in my thirties before I even set foot on a plane, and that was only to go to Dundee to resolve a dispute for the union. Now I would be flying to another continent to spend a month virtually alone, quietly observing a country whose culture had so pervaded British society that I naïvely believed it could hold few surprises.

I encountered much anti-US prejudice among some of my fellow activists in the UCW. One colleague never missed a chance to describe America as 'the land of bullshit'. The activities of trade unionists there were treated with suspicion on the grounds that, like most US institutions, they probably supported repressive regimes around the world so long as they had the necessary virtue of being anti-Communist. Now, in February 1991, the US was leading the military coalition in the first Gulf War. The objective of Operation Desert Shield was to end the Iraqi invasion of Kuwait and restore that country's monarchy to power.

As I flew to America on a Pan Am jumbo jet, I began reading *The Bonfire of the Vanities*, Tom Wolfe's novel about ambition, racism, social class and greed in 1980s New York. As an example of American literature it was in the wonderful tradition of Mark Twain, Philip Roth, John Steinbeck, John Updike and many other brilliant US authors I'd read. However, it probably wasn't the introduction to America that the International Visitors Programme would have recommended.

What I wasn't prepared for was the diversity of that vast country. After my week in Washington talking to government agencies, the AFL-CIO (the American Federation of Labor and Congress of Industrial Organizations, the US counterpart of the Trades Union Congress) and the three main postal and telecoms unions, I travelled alone to Columbus, Ohio; Denver, Colorado; San Francisco, Las Vegas and Orlando, Florida, ending my odyssey in New York.

Each city and state was like a different country, the contrasts more pronounced than the similarities. By the time I arrived in New York I'd finished *The Bonfire of the Vanities* and while it hadn't made me frightened to walk the streets, I didn't ride the subway as I had in Washington and I was cautious about wandering around after dark.

On the penultimate day of my programme a stretch limousine was sent to transport me to the AT&T (American Telephone and Telegraph) worldwide international centre. The US telecommunications giant, although by now obliged by US regulators to divest itself of its regional operations and turn them into individual companies, still enjoyed a virtual monopoly on phone services.

The centre was in New Jersey, just eighty minutes' drive from my hotel in Manhattan (the famous Barbizon – originally built as a 'club residence for professional women' – which had only begun admitting men ten years earlier) on the corner of Lexington Avenue and East 63rd Street. This ridiculously elongated vehicle carried me through New York, past turn-offs to districts that had featured heavily in *The Bonfire of the Vanities*. Brooklyn, the Bronx, Harlem . . . every place name familiar and suggestive of the brooding undercurrent of 1980s violence I'd just been reading about.

Within forty minutes we were driving through small towns lined by clapboard houses in verdant countryside reminiscent of rural Berkshire. Over lunch at AT&T I was told that nobody in this New Jersey community locked their front doors or their cars, day or night. The only thing that New Jersey seemed to have in common with New York was the apparently obligatory Stars and Stripes that fluttered from every porch.

I observed many things in America, both profound and

trivial, that made my month in that incredible country one of the most enriching experiences of my life. On the odd occasion I'd have the company of an IVP host who'd agreed to welcome visitors to his or her particular neck of the woods, but mostly I travelled alone. I drove a left-hand-drive car on the right (or wrong, if you're British) side of the road in Florida, and wondered at the sedate speed of American drivers. In Washington I noted the phenomenon of people on their way to work drinking coffee from polystyrene cups as they walked along the street – a habit I was convinced would never catch on at home. I visited the Phillips Collection just around the corner from my Georgetown hotel to gaze at my favourite painting – Renoir's *Luncheon of the Boating Party*. I attended my first-ever breakfast meeting and vowed never to repeat the experience if I could help it. In San Francisco I wandered around the Tenderloin District alone after dark and was told the next morning that I was lucky to be alive.

In Las Vegas I spent an entire evening walking up and down the strip, studying my surroundings like a naturalist in a neon jungle. Amazed at how cheap food and drink were in the cafés and restaurants, I was told that the people who ran Las Vegas (and the implication was that this included gangsters as well as politicians) kept prices down to ensure that visitors had plenty of money left to spend on gambling. I parted with only $10 in one of the vast casinos where there was roulette, pontoon, baccarat and the novel phenomenon of video games.

As for the American trade-union movement, here I found inspiration as well as diversity. US Mail was a protected species under the constitution (Benjamin Franklin was apparently a postmaster) and privatization wasn't remotely in prospect.

However, it was illegal for postal workers to strike. Disagreements and grievances were dealt with in a complex process of conciliation and arbitration. Contracts setting out improvements to terms and conditions were negotiated every few years or so and the pay of a letter-carrier was around three times higher than that of a postman or woman in the UK.

With no age discrimination, senior US trade-union officials were considered still to be up and coming when they hit sixty. The general secretaries were in their seventies and, in one case, eighties. I certainly felt younger when I left America than I did when I arrived.

Inspiration and astonishment came in equal measure at the International Ladies' Garment Workers' Union (ILGWU) on Seventh Avenue in New York, formed by European Jewish immigrants in 1900. All clothes made by their members had by law to carry a tag showing that the garment had been produced by American unionized labour. Eighty-five per cent of their members were women fighting to preserve decent standards in an industry notorious for sweatshops and exploitation. The union provided legal representation to workers who'd entered the US illegally to help them gain citizenship. They saw illegality as the ally of that exploitation but they were engaged in a lonely battle.

In a country where 32 million workers had no medical insurance at all and millions of others were under-insured, the union provided a miniature national health service for its members. The ILGWU health centre I visited occupied four floors and dealt with 800 patients every day. Its 150 staff included twelve doctors, with consultants also available under contract. The centre covered everything from eye care to cancer treatment;

from chiropody to AIDS; from smear tests to major surgery. All union members had access to this amazing facility for a nominal fee of $8.

The most profound and moving moment of my visit to America came on 25 February, as American ground troops advanced on Kuwait. The night before, the impending launch of Operation Desert Storm had been announced on the TV news channels, whose reports reflected the controversy of the invasion and the anxiety of a nation still scarred by the long and ultimately futile battle with the Vietcong that had ended sixteen years earlier in defeat with 58,000 American soldiers killed and over 300,000 wounded.

It was a hot, humid day and I was looking round the 'World Showcase' section of the Epcot Center in Orlando. As it was out of season, the other visitors to this Disneyland for grown-ups were mainly Americans. A series of themed pavilions dedicated to different countries around the world recreated architecture and landscapes intended to represent their culture. Thus the piece of Florida soil that Epcot had decided would be for ever England boasted red telephone boxes, a fish-and-chip shop, the inevitable pub and various mock-Tudor buildings, including a replica of Hampton Court palace.

At the entrance to the 'American Adventure' pavilion a large crowd had gathered round a barbershop quartet which would, on an ordinary day, have been providing a cheery welcome. This was, though, no ordinary day. The ground war had begun, young US citizens were already dying and this a cappella performance had taken on a new and melancholy significance. As I watched the Americans alongside me adding their voices to a slow and melodious rendition of 'Home On The Range', tears began to flow and sobs could be heard above the singing. By the time we reached a gentle arrangement of 'John Brown's Body' there wasn't a dry eye in the crowd, held together and rooted to the spot by pathos.

On my last night in the States I switched on the news in my New York hotel to hear the president's live broadcast. His message to the nation was that the Allies had been victorious: Saddam's troops had been forced out of Kuwait and the Gulf War would end at midnight. So this was not to be a repeat of Vietnam, as so many Americans had feared. There were those who argued that Desert Storm should have continued, that the Allies should have pursued the retreating invaders into Iraq and deposed Saddam Hussain for good. Others maintained that this defeat already spelled the end of his despotic regime. Few expected this first Gulf War to be followed by a second.

The cab driver taking me to JFK airport was a verbose New Yorker who steered with one hand and devoted the other permanently to the horn. He tooted everything. A car on his side of the road and well within his forward vision was there to be tooted at, as was any vehicle that dared to emerge from a side street. As for any drivers that were waiting patiently in queues of traffic, they received the loudest toot of all. This klaxon concert never once interrupted the rhythm of his conversation. I wondered how he'd get on as a London cabbie. He'd probably gravitate towards Tooting.

We got to talking about politics. He was a Democrat. I asked who he thought was likely to get the nomination to stand against George Bush in the presidential election the following year. He declared that, after the success in Kuwait, Bush was now unbeatable. The Democrats would put up somebody like Jesse Jackson, a 'poseur', he said, who they needed to get out of their hair. Let him take the inevitable fall and focus on a proper candidate for when Bush stepped down in 1996.

There was no mention of Bill Clinton, the candidate who was to make George Bush a one-term president. It was a lesson in how rapidly political fortunes can change and how incumbents can take nothing for granted.

The cab driver dropped me off at the Pan Am gate and my month in the USA was over. It had been an important part of my continuing education. As I pushed my luggage through the terminal I felt sure I could hear the sound of a car horn tooting in the distance.

That summer, on 3 August, Laura and I were married in a Methodist chapel. Although I was a confirmed atheist, lightning didn't strike and there were no claps of thunder.

Jamie was my best man. By now he was the age I'd been when he was born – twenty – and financing himself through his university course in politics and local government by working part-time at the House of Commons for my friend Kate Hoey, the Labour MP for Vauxhall, whom I'd got to know through my trade-union work and Labour party activities.

Natalie came with her husband and daughter, Emma with her partner and their son. All three of my children had now left the Britwell estate in Slough, where they'd had as happy a childhood as Judy and I were able to provide for them, although I have to acknowledge that I had been a largely absent father, initially through the long hours I worked as a postman and subsequently as a result of so much time spent travelling the country as a national union representative.

There was a UCW presence at the wedding which included Mike Hogan and the general secretary, Alan Tuffin, for whom Laura had worked as a personal assistant. Derek Hodgson would have been surprised to be invited and he wasn't. We both knew where we stood: we were colleagues rather than friends; rivals, not bosom buddies.

Laura's family matriarchy was out in force – impeccably dressed and fabulous as ever. They called me Mr Kite after Fred Kite, the Communist shop steward played by Peter Sellers in the 1959 Boulting Brothers satirical comedy *I'm All Right Jack*. Laura's maternal grandfather, who'd died before I met her, had been a Communist and one of the founders of the print union NATSOPA. He would certainly have sympathized with Fred Kite's famous line about life in the Soviet Union: 'Ah, Russia. All them cornfields and ballet in the evening.' Laura and her older sister, Lisa, retained union membership wherever they worked in tribute to their grandfather. Given that they then worked in the City (for Reuters financial services) the benefits of union membership were not immediately apparent.

My father-in-law, John Patient, was a lugubrious character who dutifully accepted the various nicknames bestowed upon him by his wickedly witty wife, daughters and sisters-in-law. When I met Laura he was known as 'Old P.', and by the time we were married it was 'Chips', after the husband in the film *Shirley Valentine*, who complained if he didn't get 'chips and egg' for his tea on the same day every week.

The women may have poked fun at John but they were all beneficiaries of his incredible range of skills. Plumbing, electrics, building, woodwork, painting, decorating – there was nothing John couldn't turn his hand to and no complex practical problem he couldn't solve. His quiet, understated genius constantly amazed me while he perpetually wondered why anybody should consider his abilities to be anything particularly special.

We were all proud of him on that sunny August day when he loped into the chapel with his daughter on his arm to the strains of the wedding march. When she made the return trip back up the aisle with me an hour later, looking incredibly beautiful in her ivory dress, it was to the theme from *The Dambusters*.

The childhoods of both my new in-laws had been affected by the Second World War. John had lost his sister in the Blitz. Maureen – Mo – Laura's mum, had been evacuated and then brought back to Kennington in south-east London by a mother who was convinced her children would be safer in the city. I often wondered how Mo's fierce intelligence would have blossomed if, like that of so many others, her education hadn't been completely disrupted by the war. She often told me about the terror that engulfed her as the bombs fell on London. I can't remember my mother – who had served in the NAAFI in London after leaving Liverpool at the age of eighteen – ever talking about the war. Like most of my generation, I'd grown up with an image of those days that was based on old black-and-white films: cheerful, stoical Londoners defying the Luftwaffe with singalongs in their cosy air-raid shelters. In reality lives had been scarred. There had been no counselling for the traumatized, no escape from the carnage they saw every day.

A few years later we visited an exhibition at the Imperial War Museum that focused on the civilian experience. There John saw his sister's name inscribed alongside those of all the other civilian victims of the London Blitz. There was a re-creation of a bomb shelter in which you could sit and experience what it would actually have been like when the bombs fell. Mo and I went in. As we sat in the dark the simulated air raid began, complete with tremors, flashes of light and the sounds of low-flying planes. Mo gripped my hand, began to shake and within minutes we had to leave, pushing past other visitors, as I shepherded Mo, now sobbing uncontrollably, out into the fresh air. Decades of buried anguish had erupted like a volcano. It brought home to me just how lucky I was to have been born into postwar rather than prewar Britain.

As London rebuilt in peacetime, Mo's family were allocated a new council house in Brixton, where she married John, the boy next door, who drove flash cars and was a wizard at electronics. He and a business partner invented the first device that could photograph, time and date betting slips, a godsend to the growing number of betting shops in combating the various scams for placing bets after a race had been won.

Up until our marriage I'd had eleven addresses in my life. Now I moved to the twelfth. I'd lived in rented accommodation until the age of thirty-seven, for half that time in the same council house on the Britwell estate where Judy and I had resisted the temptations of Margaret Thatcher's 'right to buy' scheme. I'd taken out my first mortgage on the flat in Thornton Heath. The union had long ago realized that if they expected postmen and women, telephonists and counter clerks to stand for national officer positions based in London, they needed to provide help with housing for successful candidates. Thus it was that, having already been responsible for my first stay in a hotel, my first flight on an aeroplane and my first visits to Scotland, Wales and Northern Ireland, the UCW had also arranged my first mortgage.

Laura and I now acquired a detached, three-bedroomed house in Upper Norwood, again on a mortgage organized by my employer. The benefit was that you didn't have to pay a deposit. The disadvantage was that interest was fixed at the rate of inflation pertaining at the time. It was in double figures when we moved into our new home. I signed on the dotted line committing me to pay off what I owed by 2025, when I would be seventy-five years old.

Although I'd swapped my blue collar for a white one, working by brain rather than by hand, I could still hardly be described as a man who moved with the times. In many ways I was bemused by the modern world, always the last to adapt to a new trend or the latest advance in technology.

Some of my colleagues were by this time walking around weighed down by bulky contraptions known as 'mobile phones', a bandwagon I had no intention of jumping on. I hadn't gone 'on the phone' at home (got a landline, in the modern parlance) until the early eighties and being accessible to others wasn't a priority for me. I didn't think of myself as an introvert but I was a bit of a loner, never happier than when I was working in splendid isolation. It was a weakness in my battle to become general secretary. Derek Hodgson had a mobile phone.

Apart from not seeing any need for them, I noticed the horrible way this big, heavy hardware – which bore no relation to the lightweight, slimline phones we use nowadays – distorted a suit jacket when plunged into a side or inside pocket. Needless to say, Derek avoided this problem by finding a way to clip his mobile phone to his belt, where it joined the collection of accessories dangling from his person.

One of the joys of being elected to the Executive Council of the union and later becoming an officer was that I could go to work in a suit. Some men have to be forced into a 'whistle'. I had to be forced out of one. For me, donning suit, collar and tie was second nature. Ever since becoming a Mod in my early teens I'd dressed according to the maxim 'You may be poor, but don't show poor,' and taken a pride in my appearance.

One of the fringe benefits that had attracted me to the Post Office was the blue serge uniform postmen wore at the time. We were given tokens to have it dry-cleaned four times a year but I happily paid for more frequent laundering and asked Judy to sew a permanent crease into the front of the trousers. In the seventies, when three-piece suits came into fashion, I'd wear the waistcoat issued with the uniform, which was ignored by most of my colleagues.

The one part of the uniform there wasn't the slightest chance of me wearing was the cap. It was a generational thing. When I became a postman all the old stagers (roughly defined as anyone over thirty) wore a cap, just as most of them had done in the forces. The baby boomers, however, remained hatless, even in the pouring rain.

As outdoor secretary I was consulted by the Post Office about their plans to change the uniform. The relentless drift from the smart towards the utilitarian, from the substantial serge trousers with the red stripe down the side to shorts, was delayed by my refusal to accept the end of the tunic jacket during my five-year stint. It was one of my proudest achievements.

As for my civilian wardrobe, I'd only ever had one suit made for me. It was a double-breasted grey chalk pinstripe, purchased for £47 from Burton's in Slough High Street in 1978. It was the one time I've ever been ahead of a fashion trend. I badly wanted a double-breasted suit. I can't now remember why. Maybe I'd seen Bowie wearing one, or perhaps Bryan Ferry. One thing's for sure, they had been out of fashion for so long that the only way to acquire one was to have it made. But I was never happy with that suit. The only time I recall actually wearing it was for a fancy-dress party on the Britwell to which Judy and I took the kids in the early eighties. I put on the Burton's suit with a black shirt and co-respondent's shoes and went as Al Capone.

However, I like to think that I started something. By the mid-1980s it was impossible to buy an off-the-peg suit that wasn't double-breasted – shapeless things with padded shoulders and ventless jackets. That blue suit I'd worn the New Year's Eve I proposed to Laura was the beginning of a return to the sanity and elegance of the single-breasted suit.

If I was able for many years to resist carrying a mobile phone, on the grounds, among other reasons, of the damage they did to the line of a suit, other changes weren't so easy to hold at bay. Pay day at the Post Office used to involve us postmen queuing at a grille every week on a Thursday evening to receive our wages in cash. It was handed over in a stubby brown envelope which, on weeks where plenty of overtime had been worked, would be reassuringly fat. Typically I'd do twenty-five hours' overtime, a sixty-eight-hour week, but it wasn't unusual for postmen to work thirty-five or even forty extra hours on top of our stipulated forty-three-hour week.

The wages envelope had holes in the side and the cash would be partially exposed at the top. The holes were to demonstrate that the cash was in fact inside and the exposed notes allowed for a quick check before you signed to confirm that the money due had been safely received. When I was a local union rep I advised all my colleagues to keep a check on how much 'docket' they'd done at the various rates (time and a quarter, time and a half, etc.), factoring in the night-duty allowance, Saturday premium payments, driving allowance and so on, to ensure they had been paid the correct sum. We postal workers welcomed the arrival of the calculator with even more enthusiasm than the general population.

I still worked long hours, but now it was as a salaried employee with no paid overtime and no allowances. Pay had long been 'cashless' for my members and my salary, too, arrived in the bank account that had once been Girobank but was now Alliance & Leicester (Post Office Girobank having been sold off for a pittance by the Thatcher government in 1990 when mutualization was under attack).

Hole-in-the-wall cash dispensers had made it unnecessary to queue at the bank to draw out money and the credit card was helping to remove the need to carry much cash at all. I'd applied for my first such card in the late 1980s, long after everybody else. It came from Access, based in Southend, along with the free gift of a bedside radio alarm clock with a liquid-crystal display.

I had an ingrained antipathy to buying anything 'on tick'. Linda and I had grown up dodging the various 'tallymen' who knocked on our door, usually identifiable by their distinctive raincoats and the thick payment ledgers tucked under their arms. I have never forgotten the humiliation of having to ask kindly Mr Berriman, who ran the corner shop, if the cost of the goods on my mother's shopping list, which he'd just packed into a cardboard box, could be added to our already extensive bill.

I might have left that poverty far behind me now but I could still feel its cold embrace. So I resolved to use my newly acquired Access card as a convenience rather than a way of obtaining credit. From that day to this I have never incurred interest charges, always meticulously paying the monthly bill to the penny by the required date. The mortgage didn't feel like a debt. The repayments were taken directly from my salary and in the more prosperous circumstances that came with my union position, I was confident of being able to keep them up provided I was able to avoid the dangerous obstacle that was built into my white-collar job: the need to be re-elected every five years. My first re-election was due in 1992, by which time I hoped to be general secretary.

The final round of the heavyweight contest between Alan (Skinny) Johnson and Derek (Bruiser) Hodgson began on Wednesday 13 November 1991, when nominations closed in the ballot to determine the next general secretary of the Union of Communication Workers. Derek and I were the only candidates.

I was as ready as I'd ever be. The industrial upheaval within Royal Mail had eased. Agreements on recruitment supplements, the end of IWM and a new industrial-relations framework were having a positive effect. Even Sunday collections, the cause of a near knockout for Derek in an earlier round of the fight for the UCW championship belt, had bedded in nicely after Mike Hogan and I tweaked the agreement, leading to a branch ballot and overwhelming acceptance.

The UCW had an eccentric way of electing its general officers. Their approach was not unlike the attitude of the Victorians to sex: they knew it was necessary – enjoyable, even – but it mustn't be allowed to frighten the horses. The entire process was devoid of anything remotely resembling excitement. There were no hustings. There was not even any provision for branches to put forward supporting nominations.

Candidates were to have one nomination only, that of their own branch. For Derek and me that was no problem. We were in the UCW officers' branch, which consisted of thirteen members, us and the other full-time officers, and which, by tradition, never refused a nomination. What the union described as our 'biographical details' – age, union history, political affiliation, if any, union schools attended – were published to the membership along with a 300-word statement that was to be our only official communication. To put out any other literature would have been to risk expulsion from the contest.

This suited me. I was no campaigner. The whole concept was alien to me and I was useless at it. In the Slough sorting office I would simply put my name forward for a branch position and then carry on as usual, delivering mail and waiting for the AGM, where the result would be announced. My election to the Executive Council hadn't been accompanied by any horse-trading for votes with other branches. Slough was too small to have any horses to trade. As for my current national officer position, it had just fallen into my lap after my predecessor was medically retired.

So throughout the three months of the election I simply got on with my job as outdoor secretary. I can't recall doing anything or going anywhere with the express aim of garnering votes in the election for which I was one of only two choices.

Derek, on the other hand, was a natural campaigner. He and his close allies were out on manoeuvres. He rattled and tap-danced his way along the corridor at UCW House more often than usual to find out what was going on at our end. His organizing empire, meanwhile, remained immune to my charms. Down at his end, no opportunity was missed to influence a branch secretary or a district organizer with a quiet enquiry as to how they saw the future, with the offer of a favour or the arrangement of a visit. I say this with admiration: Derek Hodgson was running a proper, grown-up campaign within the constraints imposed by our union.

For my part, all I had was an arrogant expectation that the membership would recognize the qualities I considered to be perfectly self-evident without there being any need for me to draw them to anyone's attention. While Derek never missed an opportunity, I never missed an opportunity to miss an opportunity.

I had an exaggerated faith in those precious 300 words circulated with the ballot paper to every member. I remember using mine to say pointedly that anyone could issue a recitation of the problems the union faced. What the membership needed to know was whether the person they were electing had the intelligence, skill and experience to deal with them. It was as close as I got to saying 'vote for me'.

But fortunately, they did vote for me – though only by the narrowest of margins. At 10.15 on the morning of 17 January 1992, Alan Tuffin called Derek and me up to his office. He handed us a folded piece of paper with the ballot result:

Hodgson D. G. 20,362
Johnson A. A. 20,732

An asterisk next to my name denoted that I'd been elected, by just 370 votes, as the seventh general secretary of the union: the youngest in its history and the first to be elected by one member, one vote and to be subject to re-election every five years. My ambition realized, I felt a curious sense of anti-climax as the yoke of office descended.

Chapter 4

MOVING TO THE general secretary's office meant that I had physically as well as metaphorically reached the top at UCW House. Set at the point furthest from the entrance to the building, at the far end of the second floor, my well-furnished office looked out on to the sweeping entrance to our majestic premises and my designated parking space. The rest of the 150 or so staff had to park at the rear.

I could now drive my grey Vauxhall Astra into the coveted spot reserved for the general secretary. There was no union car, though. Instead there was an account for the general secretary with a local minicab firm called Mac Cabs.

Goodness knows why the union ever gave them its custom. Mac Cabs were not renowned for their fleet of luxury cars. Indeed, they seemed to have a company policy of only acquiring cars of ancient Eastern European origin. And they apparently recruited their drivers on the basis of their encyclopaedic knowledge of the *A to Z* – of Athens. I once had to direct one of their drivers to Trafalgar Square, which he'd never heard of.

Alan Tuffin told me about the time he'd attended a prestigious dinner with senior trade-union colleagues at the American

labour attaché's residence. As he stood in the porch chatting with other general secretaries at the end of the evening, a functionary would interrupt the conversation intermittently to announce the arrival of a guest's transport home.

'The car is here for Mr Todd,' came the call, and Ron Todd, the general secretary of the mighty Transport and General Workers' Union, bade everyone goodnight and strolled out to his chauffeur-driven limousine.

'The car is here for Mr Scargill.' And Arthur Scargill, general secretary of the National Union of Mineworkers, got into his chauffeur-driven Jaguar and purred off to his union-funded flat in the Barbican.

Alan was the last to be picked up. The functionary waited with him politely for the Mac Cab booked to take him home to his modest semi in Bromley. As Alan gazed anxiously out into the posh London street, he heard a piercing whistle and the cry: 'Oi, Al! Over 'ere!'

Turning in the direction of the voice, he realized that Len, a Mac Cabs driver so huge that he probably weighed more than his rusting Moskvitch car, was beckoning him to come to his aid. The car had stalled and he needed a push. The last thing the US attaché's functionary saw as he closed the elegant double doors for the night was the general secretary of the Union of Communication Workers, jacketless and with his shirtsleeves rolled up, pushing a battered Russian saloon through an exclusive London street while receiving shouted instructions from Len in the driver's seat.

As a commemoration of Alan Tuffin's ten years as our general secretary, a decade in which his unassuming, low-profile approach had taken the UCW unscathed through headwinds and hurricanes in which other unions had foundered, I convinced the Post Office to provide us with a pillar box to be positioned at the front of the building, next to the general secretary's parking space. Instead of listing the collection times, the plaque beneath the mouth of the postbox recorded Alan's contribution to postal services in general and to the union in particular. While all of his more extrovert contemporaries were awarded peerages or knighthoods, Alan was awarded a pillar box.

I inherited Alan's staff. The two personal assistants were ex-union activists. Peter Curtis, a big, handsome country boy with hands like joints of ham, had been a postman at Andover. His rich Hampshire accent had been a feature of our conference debates in 1976 when I was first a delegate. Subsequently elected to the Executive Council, he'd opted to become part of the union's civil service rather than run for a national officer position. He commuted in each day from Middle Wallop, enjoying what I always considered to be the perfect combination of an idyllic rural existence and a job in London.

The other, Mick Stoner, was another bright guy who'd chosen the steady life of an office worker over the less certain future of an elected official. Mick had been an international telephonist, a job that required linguistic qualifications. His Essex accent was invariably prominent, irrespective of the language he was speaking. One of his party pieces was a rendition of 'La Bamba' in its original Spanish – Barcelona meets Basildon. A constant source of conspiratorial gossip, Mick had always had his enemies but I'd never been one of them.

Peter and Mick occupied separate offices in the general secretary's department. Mine could be accessed only via an outer office where my secretary, Dorothy Lovett, reigned supreme. Dot was probably among the last of that overworked, under-appreciated species of office life, the boss's secretary. I was the third general secretary she'd worked for and while new technology was reducing the need for her shorthand skills, the added responsibility she carried made her more of a personal assistant than a secretary. Indeed, I'd promoted her to that role by the time I left.

Dot was the only person I've ever known who actually wafted. She would waft into the office, her quick, small steps giving the impression that she was borne around by a tiny hovercraft cushion under her high heels. Always immaculately dressed, she was the kind of woman who would spend an hour applying make-up before leaving the house just to put the bins out. And she would wear little chiffon scarves that seemed to float behind her on the breeze trailing Chanel No. 9. A south London working-class girl, she had perfected an accent that was more Knightsbridge than Wandsworth. She spoke as quickly as she walked, firing off information like an elegant, scented auctioneer, lapsing occasionally into costermonger when the need arose. As far as I know Dot had left school at the first opportunity, married, had children and worked all hours for the union throughout, developing her extraordinary skills for organization, communication, conciliation and problem-solving along the way.

She had never been a member of our union (all employees, apart from the thirteen national officers, had to be members of a different trade union) but her dedication was absolute. She loved the UCW and the UCW loved Dorothy.

So there we were, Dot, Peter, Mick and me, in the prow of the good ship UCW. Alongside us on the top floor, in offices that opened on to a common typing pool, was the deputy general secretary's department.

My vanquished opponent, Derek Hodgson, had been the victor in the ballot for the number two position and so we were transformed from rivals at opposite ends of the first-floor corridor to allies on the next floor up. The position of deputy was viewed as either the consolation prize for a failed bid for the top job or a springboard for an assault on the leadership. For Derek it must have felt like the former. He still yearned to be general secretary but, given our respective ages, probably his only chance of achieving that goal would be to stand against me when I was up for re-election after five years. I considered such a challenge to be unlikely. Derek might have been ambitious, but he wasn't disloyal.

On taking up his new post, he'd immediately pledged his solidarity. 'You and me, bach,' he said in the exaggerated Welsh accent he reserved for solemn occasions, 'no one will be able to put a cigarette paper between us.' And they couldn't. We never became great friends, but Derek was trustworthy and hardworking.

He might not have been odds-on to succeed me but, even at that early stage, I was interested in who would. Inspired by Tom Jackson, my predecessor but one, I was keen to engage in succession planning; to discover those flowers born to blush unseen and prevent them from wasting their sweetness on the desert air. As a twenty-year-old postman with three kids living on a council estate in Slough, I'd watched Tom on the television news when he'd led us through the devastating defeat of the 1971 strike. During the seven weeks the strike lasted he, and his trademark handlebar moustache, became better known than most Cabinet ministers. Seven years later, as an official of my local union branch, I made a hash of moving a proposition from the conference rostrum. Tom left the platform and followed me into the dark outer reaches of the Winter Gardens in Blackpool to offer words of encouragement.

It was the first time I'd ever spoken to him. By then he was a BBC governor, a regular panellist on Radio 4's *Any Questions?* and a hugely respected voice on the moderate wing of the trade-union movement, where in those days all the leaders of the principal unions were acting as necessary ballast for the hot-air balloon that the Labour movement could often become. On that day in 1978, in front of my delegation (whose nomination I would need), he advised me to stand for the National Executive and thus ensured that I would.

Following Tom's example, and accompanied by my friend Derek Walsh, who was by now the union's general treasurer, I had taken the young Liverpool branch secretary, Billy Hayes, out to dinner during a Labour party conference with the single aim of persuading him to stand for my position of outdoor secretary when I vacated it.

Billy had been a Bennite, one of a new breed of UCW representatives keen to see activists organize into political caucuses and to end the union's traditional abhorrence of things like conference fringe meetings and overt electioneering. I was unashamedly old school regarding élitist cliques such as the Broad Left, Mainstream, Workers' Voice and so on, considering them to be at best a distraction and at worst a corrosive force that was bound to become a self-appointed internal opposition to the elected leadership.

Billy was bright and firmly rooted in the Labour party, albeit further to the left than Derek and me. Unlike many of his compatriots, he wasn't frightened of taking responsibility and I'd witnessed his courage at first hand when he had joined with me in convincing striking Liverpool members to return to work after the DRAS dispute. He could have left it to me and avoided a clash with his more militant activists. But he didn't. He took responsibility, and that had impressed me.

Whether our conversation that evening helped to win him over or whether he had already made up his mind to stand for the position I'll never know, but he did succeed me as outdoor secretary and, later, as general secretary of the bigger, merged union, which he led for fifteen years.

Mike Hogan and I kept our eyes open for emerging talent before and after my elevation. Mike had by now become indoor secretary, responsible for those who processed the mail – the sorters, coders and parcel workers whose work patterns and very existence faced the biggest challenge from the development of new technology.

Ever since the early days of IWM I'd been watching a twenty-something union official in south-west London. Dave Ward was a big man with a broad, smiling face and a substantial brain in search of something to sharpen itself on. He had taken the IWM scheme to new heights in his delivery office, making imaginative changes with the help of an equally enlightened local manager.

In Edinburgh, where we'd witnessed the savage reaction to the poll tax, there was an equally talented young prospect by the name of John Keggie. A blond, slim lad with roots in the wrong side of the tracks, John was as tough as nails and had the added advantage of being an eloquent and persuasive speaker.

Mike and I considered these two to be leadership material, although neither of them was particularly political. Unlike Billy Hayes, Dave and John took little interest in current affairs, preferring to focus their attention on the industrial aspects of trade-union work. But so impressed were we with these two precious assets (and others, such as Peter Dodd at Manchester, Paul Kennedy at Birmingham and Carl Webb in Blackpool) that we took a personal interest in their development, arranging a union school at the UCW's hotel in Bournemouth so that we could discuss the developments we foresaw in postal services and their potential impact on industrial relations.

We knew that the Post Office badly wanted to end the second delivery which only existed in towns and cities. Indeed, this intention had been expressed as far back as the mid-sixties, by Tony Benn when he was postmaster general. I had always thought it nonsensical to send delivery staff round the same streets twice in one day. The second delivery accounted for only 1 per cent of the mail but 20 per cent of the delivery costs. Residents of no other towns or cities across the developed world received two deliveries a day, apart from a few districts in central Paris. We wanted to prepare the union for the inevitable and to convince our most talented and influential activists that the union's role would be not to fight a futile battle to defend the indefensible but to extract the best possible quid pro quo.

Key to our strategy was my long-held goal to put an end to what I regarded as the now totally anomalous six-day week imposed on our delivery postmen and women. Most of British industry had been gradually switching to a five-day week since the early 1930s. There were plenty of industries that operated over six or seven days without requiring their employees to work more than five.

Abolishing this iniquitous practice was one of the four objectives I had set for my five years as general secretary. The others were to lift significantly the basic pay of postmen and women, ending their dependence on long hours of overtime; to carry through the long-mooted merger with the National Communications Union (NCU) and, finally, to defend the Post Office against privatization. The last objective, though, was one I believed would become irrelevant once Labour had been swept to victory by an enthusiastic electorate at the general election to be held in the spring of 1992.

Friday 10 April 1992. A gloriously sunny day, but Black Friday as far as the Labour party was concerned. The Conservatives, under the considerably milder-mannered John Major, who had replaced Thatcher, had won an unprecedented fourth term with a twenty-one-seat majority. It had been one of the most dramatic elections since the Second World War. Almost every poll had predicted that Labour would either triumph, albeit narrowly, or become the largest party in a hung Parliament, and the result came as a horrible shock.

At lunchtime, Alan Tuffin, Mike Hogan and I trudged across Clapham Common to an Italian restaurant where we stayed too long and drank too much to drown our sorrows.

Alan, having handed the reins of the UCW to me, was

seeing out his year as president of the TUC. He had been utterly convinced that Neil Kinnock would be the next prime minister and that I would enjoy what he always desired but never experienced in his ten years as general secretary: a Labour government to work with. I, too, had been optimistic. I'd done my bit the previous day to help the election of Malcolm Wicks as the new Labour MP for my home turf, Croydon North West. Malcolm, an academic whose life's work was the improvement of social policy, was a self-deprecating politician with a huge intellect and a bone-dry sense of humour. I liked him from the moment we met and I had been confident that his gain from the Tories would be replicated in enough constituencies to give us victory.

As we three compatriots swilled Chianti we discussed the future, concluding that John Smith, the shadow chancellor, should be the next leader of the Labour party and that Post Office privatization would be back on the agenda. We knew that the management viewed this as the only way to acquire the commercial freedom the business needed to compete in an increasingly aggressive international market. Postal privatization had already happened in New Zealand, and now Germany and most of Scandinavia were moving in that direction, too. Our old adversary, Bill Cockburn, was its principal advocate in the UK and he would see the re-election of the Conservatives as a green light. We thought it highly likely that John Major would now attempt to do what even his predecessor, the Iron Lady, had refused to contemplate: to end 476 years of public ownership and privatize the Royal Mail.

We didn't have long to wait for the fuse to be lit. In July, John Smith was duly elected as leader of the Labour party. That same month, Michael Heseltine – who used the grand, ancient and essentially meaningless title of president of the Board of Trade (the Board of Trade had last met in 1781), but who should more accurately, if prosaically, have been described as the secretary of state for trade and industry – gave notice of the government's intentions.

I was out of town at the time, having been persuaded by Alan Tuffin to participate in a Duke of Edinburgh Commonwealth study conference, as he had done in the late 1950s. These were gatherings of hundreds of men and women from business, the trade unions, the legal profession, the voluntary sector and public services, which took place every four years in a Commonwealth country. Alan had gone to somewhere exotic (the Bahamas, I believe) for a fortnight. I was less fortunate in terms of the opportunity for foreign travel, it being Britain's turn to host the event. I went only as far as Oxford, and from there on a study tour of East Anglia.

I had for some time resisted and ridiculed Alan's pleading insistence that this conference would broaden my horizons, but he was absolutely right. The participants were split into groups of sixteen to be sent to different parts of the UK. In my East Anglia party was a harbourmaster from Ghana, a banker from Canada, a Brit from the UK nuclear industry, a local authority chief executive from Newcastle and an employment law barrister from Australia, Tony North, who became a lifelong friend. (Tony is now a senior judge but as funny and lacking in pomposity as ever.)

I imagine that the time we all spent together was as close to the experience of being a university student as I would ever get. That atmosphere was intensified by our lodgings in university accommodation, at Keble College, Oxford and then at the University of East Anglia. We were mature students, certainly, but we were doing proper study and mixing with people from vastly different backgrounds.

Three important events occurred in that fortnight. First, on a quiet Sunday morning in Oxford, having arrived the previous evening, I strolled into a free concert being given by a string quartet and sat mesmerized by a beautiful performance of Dvořák's 'Serenade for Strings'. Music, along with football and books, had been the cornerstone of my life since I was at primary school, but while I was steeped in pop music, my knowledge of the classics was sketchier. The piece took my breath away and was preserved for ever in my memory as the soundtrack to that beautiful morning.

The second came a few days later, when Michael Heseltine gave a televised press conference alongside Sir Bryan Nicholson, the chairman of the Post Office, announcing that the government were to consult on a proposal to privatize postal services. The third was that, as we sixteen putative students toured Suffolk and Norfolk, I began to think seriously about how the union could lead an effective campaign to defeat the government. I'd witnessed other anti-privatization campaigns (not least our own against the British Telecom sell-off) fail comprehensively. There had been strikes, marches, rallies, petitions, all to no avail. They reminded me of a spoof slogan I had once read in one of those *New Statesman* competitions: 'Victory is a bourgeois concept; the only acceptable outcome for true socialists is glorious defeat.'

Our enormous network of 18,000 sub-post offices across the country was bigger than all banks, building societies and supermarkets put together and doubled. Surely we could harness the advantages of its huge size, together with the high regard in which the Royal Mail and the sub-offices were held, to generate a campaign that placed the public, rather than the union, at the forefront?

These were the thoughts that preoccupied me as I travelled home on the train, gazing out at the Oxfordshire countryside. By the time we pulled into Paddington, I had the vague outline of a plan. I knew I didn't possess the skills to fight this battle alone and that, for us to succeed, I would need a range of talents that my fellow national officers and I were not equipped to provide. The union had to be the instigators and founders of a campaign which was in essence led by the general public. Simply defending the status quo would be fruitless. We had to look forwards, not backwards. The UCW's position should be to set out an alternative plan for a publicly owned Post Office with full commercial freedom and the capacity to re-invest the profits it generated.

Royal Mail was producing a hefty annual surplus and its quality of service was the best in the world. The government couldn't trade on public angst, as it had done in privatizing the railways. Industrial relations were peaceful. The constant stream of unballoted walkouts that had plagued the Post Office had dried up almost completely. There was an army of people who would become active in defence of their postal services. What they needed was organization, leadership and focus.

I wanted a small (but perfectly formed) campaign team able to make immediate decisions on my authority alone. I would, of course, report regularly to the executive and the membership, but we needed deftness to counteract the power of the government.

The Post Office had legions of press secretaries, policy officials and government-relations advisers working at Old Street to be summoned to the colours in the battle for hearts and minds. The government had the civil service, a huge media machine and the considerable resources of Whitehall at their disposal. We wouldn't be able to match all that, but we had one enormous advantage: over 100,000 of our members passed every one of Britain's 25 million addresses at least once a day.

They were our finest ambassadors, along with the subpostmasters in Britain's vast chain of post offices. They weren't UCW members, but their opposition to privatization would be better channelled through us than through the National Federation of Sub-Postmasters, whose leadership was being studiously courted by Heseltine. He refused even to meet me.

My little team was soon in place. It consisted of three extremely bright young union employees. Mario Dunn, the son of an Italian mother and an Irish father, had, at only twenty-five, taken over from Peter Hain as the union's head of research after Peter was elected as MP for Neath in 1991. Peter had been working in the union's research department for fifteen years and had been a national figure through his high-profile anti-apartheid campaigning even before he became a parliamentarian. Stepping into those large shoes at such a young age was a challenge, and Mario had proved himself a great acquisition from the Transport and General Workers' Union, where he'd started his career. He was also a political soulmate, enormously knowledgeable, active in his local party and scathing about the delusional left and its corrosive influence on the Labour party.

What I really valued about him, though, was his readiness to tell me things I didn't want to hear. His would be the voice of caution, sometimes even derision, that tempered a few of the more bizarre and fanciful suggestions I came up with.

Daniel Harris, another engaging lad in his twenties, with bags of energy and a brain that overflowed with ideas, had been appointed by Alan Tuffin as head of campaigns. I asked him to drop everything else he was doing to dedicate himself entirely to the most important campaign in the union's history.

The final member of this inner circle had come to the union as part of a reform I'd planned before getting the job and had to implement in the glow of my honeymoon period if it was to succeed.

Ever since the formation of the union in 1920, one of its thirteen national officers had been the editor of its journal, *The Post*. Assigning a post office worker to this role may have been sustainable in an age when news was something that appeared only in slabs of print every morning. By the 1990s, however, the Union of Communication Workers had the most outdated and amateurish approach to communications of any major trade union. The editor had the cushiest position imaginable. The union's printers did all the production work there was to do, and the editor's staff did the rest. The resulting drab publication was like a slightly less readable version of *Pravda*. Few members even turned its pages, but most read *The Courier*, the Post Office's slickly produced house magazine, from cover to cover.

Apart from our journal, and publishing a few branch circulars and bulletins written by the various officers, the editor had no other responsibilities. No negotiations to lead, no debates at conference, not even any responsibility for dealing with the media. I had resolved that, when the incumbent retired (helpfully, soon after I assumed the role of general secretary), I would attempt to convince the Executive Council that this elected officer position should be scrapped and replaced with an appointed head of communications, with all the necessary qualifications, to take charge not just of *The Post* but of the full range of the union's communications across broadcast and print media.

My problem was that when officer vacancies were filled it was usually by lay members of the Executive Council. As all union officers had to retire at sixty, lay members would be planning their possible elevation well in advance. I now needed to convince those lay members to ditch the post that many would have been coveting. So it was now or never. If I missed my moment, a new editor would be elected and the issue shelved for twenty years until he or she retired.

To their eternal credit the executive agreed to the change. The union advertised the position and was inundated with applications – from journalists, broadcasters and people with so many qualifications that they struggled to confine them to a single sheet of paper. There were editors of other union journals, including the award-winning GMB magazine; even well-known industrial correspondents of major national newspapers.

I demonstrated my naïveté and inexperience by shortlisting twenty of them. This was by any standards a long list, not a short list, and on a sweltering day in the summer of 1993 all twenty turned up at UCW House to be shepherded into the hottest room in the building for a day of tests and interviews. It's a wonder they didn't all walk out straight away, especially as

I was dealing with a dispute in London at the time and had to leave them to stew while I did television interviews on the front lawn.

I was joined on the interview panel by Mick Stoner, Derek Hodgson and another close ally, Ernie Dudley, the national officer responsible for our clerical grades. Ernie has a special place in my affections, primarily because of his skill, dedication, loyalty and because he was such a thoroughly decent man. But also because of a hilarious incident at a union conference in Bournemouth.

A motion was being debated concerning an issue on which there had already been a ballot resulting in an embarrassing 'no' vote. Now conference was pushing to go through exactly the same expensive process when all the signs were that it would be lost again, only more heavily. It was a cracking debate to which Ernie had the right of reply – the all-important final word. He was a very good speaker and before long he had the audience in the palm of his hand, including those of us on the platform. You could have heard a pin drop as Ernie reached the end of his peroration and issued his final plea.

'Conference,' he said, leaving a precisely timed pause. 'If you carry this motion you'll place this union in a Catch 69 situation.' There was a hiatus of about two seconds before laughter began to ripple round the hall, increasing in volume as awareness of what he had said dawned. I will never forget the look on Ernie's face as he gazed imploringly at his colleagues for a clue as to what had caused this outbreak of hilarity. Needless to say conference carried the proposition. They quite liked the idea of being in a Catch 69, as opposed to a Catch 22, situation.

The interview panel, then, was one I knew would indulge me

if there was a difference of opinion. We cut the twenty down to ten before starting the interviews. It was still too many, but at least we now had a shorter long list, or was it a longer short list?

The heat hung over Clapham like a thick blanket as we interviewed applicants whose understandable tetchiness was suppressed only by their ambition to be offered the job. It was 6pm before the final interview took place. Into the room came a bouncing ball of positivity called Julia Simpson. Small and dark, with a dancer's poise, Julia was working on the journal of a small civil-service union. Her CV was the least impressive of the ten we'd shortlisted but at the interview she raised our jaded spirits with her energy and enthusiasm. She'd read great chunks of the union's virtually unreadable annual report and told us exactly how we should be communicating some of the esoteric issues it contained. Julia was one of only two women in the original twenty and the only one to make it to the final cut. The panel was split two each between her and one of the illustrious industrial correspondents. I pulled rank and chose Julia.

Having created the worst possible selection process, I managed to make the best possible appointment. The department was modernized, with young talent promoted, and deals more favourable to the union were negotiated with printers and suppliers as Julia's charm offensive (backed by the tank regiment of her determination) swept all before it. Under its new editor, the union's journal was transformed into a vibrant magazine and went from never even being considered for best trade-union publication in the annual awards organized by the TUC to carrying off the top prize three years in succession.

Now I and my campaign team, Mario, Daniel and Julia,

set about our task of defeating a government which, despite being weakened in September 1992 by Black Wednesday – when sterling was forced out of the European Exchange Rate Mechanism – seemed even more determined to privatize the postal service.

My new role gave me an automatic seat on the TUC General Council, where a newly elected leader was exerting his influence. The UCW was practically the only major trade union not to have nominated John Monks. It was nothing personal. My concern was the practice of the Congress House treadmill to serve up successive TUC general secretaries from within, which had previously produced a turkey in Norman Willis. Lovely man, lousy leader had been the almost universal view of Norman. Now we were being asked to elect his successor on the same basis. I suppose I had hoped that somebody like Rodney Bickerstaffe, a charismatic leader of the health-service union, would put his hat in the ring. He never did so we didn't nominate anybody.

I was immediately aware of how wrong I'd been. John was that rarity, a leader devoid of ego who thought deeply and wore his considerable wisdom lightly. He was modernizing the TUC, amending the archaic structure whereby it had mirrored every government department, and attempting to plug the gushing leak in union membership.

A colleague on the General Council of the TUC was Tony Young, the leader of our sister union, the NCU. We would need the TUC's help in our efforts to merge our two unions, streamline our services and take advantage of the economies of scale that joining forces would make possible. While some other unions seemed to be merging for the sake of it, this combination made absolute sense. We both represented members in the Post Office and British Telecom (BT). We were strongest in the Post Office, where the NCU had only a small number of engineers and garage mechanics. Within BT, where NCU membership predominated, we represented only telephonists and cleaners, whose numbers were declining rapidly.

Merger had been discussed intermittently for decades. Tony's predecessor, John Golding, who'd been an MP before becoming general secretary, had broken off talks with Alan Tuffin, who had himself made merger a priority during his period of office. Now it was very much on the cards again.

Tony and I were friends. He was a small man with an Asiatic look to his thickly bespectacled eyes, which once led me to introduce him teasingly at a Labour party reception as Kim Il-Young. Tony could take a joke and neither of us was able to muster the level of solemnity and self-importance shown by some of our colleagues on the General Council.

Tony had left school at fifteen to become a General Post Office (GPO) telephone engineer, climbing telegraph poles and connecting lines. In Wichita it may be a romantic occupation – in Ealing, where Tony is from, less so. A fellow autodidact, Tony must by now have read the complete works of Dickens, Tolstoy and Trollope, having been well on the way to that objective when we first met.

He had been the original creator of the Broad Left in his union. As I've mentioned, the UCW had largely escaped the faction-fighting that turned some unions into ill-tempered debating societies and their conferences into the rhetorical equivalent of the conflict between Mods and Rockers at seaside locations in the 1960s. And while it wasn't by any means the worst, the NCU had become difficult to lead. Having once tried to convince me to start a Broad Left movement in the UCW, Tony now admitted he'd been wrong. His Broad Left had denounced him as a class traitor as soon as he made his first negotiating compromise. These idiotic dogmatists would have condemned Nelson Mandela as having sold out.

The very different culture within the NCU made some of my fellow officers nervous about the wisdom of a merger. But as we would be bringing a substantially greater number of members to the show, it was felt that our more moderate culture ought to prevail. And the ranks of the NCU had now been swelled by 30,000 CPSA (Civil and Public Services Association) telecoms clerical workers, who were already diluting the influence of the fractious engineers. So during the course of 1993 we did everything necessary to move the merger forward while still remaining separate unions.

In essence the NCU's membership was politically mad but industrially sound (strike action at BT was rare), whereas our union could have been fairly described as industrially mad but politically sound. These differences are perhaps best illustrated by the extraordinary fuss made over some mildly radical proposals that John Smith made a year into his leadership of the Labour party. I liked John very much, as did Derek Hodgson, who was on the party National Executive Committee (NEC) and thus well placed to observe him closely at their monthly meetings. Smith was a brilliant debater with a sharp intellect but above all he was a pragmatist and sought to extend the path

Neil Kinnock had begun to carve away from the anarchy of the early eighties, when Labour's motto might as well have been 'No compromise with the electorate.'

The issue John made his own was reform of the way the party took its decisions – something on which Neil had been defeated in 1984 at his first conference as leader. There were multiple elements to this but the main thrust was twofold. The trade unions wielded 90 per cent of the total vote at conference. In other words, the constituency delegates – who represented actual party members, those good people who slaved away knocking on doors and stuffing envelopes to get Labour candidates elected – had only 10 per cent. This was a hangover from the days before the party became a membership organization in 1918. As a first step to changing it, Smith proposed that the voting split between affiliated unions and the membership should be 50–50.

The second proposal was that prospective parliamentary candidates should be elected on the basis of one member, one vote at local party meetings. This would end the farcical situation of local branch officers of affiliated trade unions turning up with a pocketful of votes based on the number of their members who paid the political levy in that constituency. Some unions may have consulted their members about how that block vote would be cast, but such a process would have been vanishingly rare. In any case there was no moral justification for using the fundamentally undemocratic block vote in this way.

From the reaction of some of my union colleagues to these modest proposals, you'd have thought John Smith had decreed the slaughter of the first-born. It was, they said, an outrageous attack on the historic role of the trade unions, a betrayal of our history, an attempt to break the link between the party and the unions which had founded it.

At a meeting I had with him soon after he took over from Neil Kinnock, John told me that this would be the first step in a process that needed to be finalized over a longer timescale and which must eventually result in one member, one vote for the election of the leader of the party as well. Tony Young and I were both supporters. The difference between us was that I had an executive that was by and large constructive. Tony had an executive that was by and large disruptive – never happier, in the case of the dominant Broad Left, than when they could splatter their general secretary's face with large quantities of egg.

John Smith's problem was that his proposals to reform the Labour party had to be passed by an unreformed Labour party conference. In the warped view of some of my ultra-conservative colleagues at the TUC, turkeys were being asked to vote for Christmas. Big unions such as the Transport and General Workers and the GMB were implacable, as was Tony's NCU, despite his best efforts. They were oblivious to John Smith's central message that if Labour was the party of change it had to be prepared to change itself.

By lunchtime at conference that September, it looked as if Smith had been defeated and that his leadership would be over before it had properly begun. In a last desperate throw of the dice, John Prescott, then shadow secretary of state for transport, was drafted in to make an unscheduled speech just after lunch and an hour or so before the vote was taken. His impassioned oration and the decision of the white-collar MSF

(Manufacturing, Science and Finance) union to abstain gave John Smith victory by 47.5 per cent to 44.3.

He sent me a handwritten note thanking me for my help. That farcical fuss over a mild piece of modernization and indeed democratization had a lasting impact on me. There was so much to be modernized in a party that clung on to shibboleths as if they were life-support machines. A good man almost had his leadership destroyed by proposing a change that nobody in their right mind will ever suggest reversing. There were so many more important changes that John Smith could now move on to with me in his vanguard, burnishing my Mod credentials.

Chapter 5

At UCW House our campaign against privatization was by now in full swing. It had a name, 'Stand By Your Post', a logo and already a series of successes. Most notably we had set up and funded a body called Protecting Postal Services (PPS), which became an umbrella organization for all those non-political groups that were opposed to privatization, particularly charities focused on the protection of rural communities and helping the disabled. The former were worried about the preservation of the universal service at a single price and the cross-subsidy that would be required from easy-to-deliver town mail to fund the more expensive deliveries to remote areas. The latter were concerned about Royal Mail services such as Articles for the Blind, which delivered hefty braille items free of charge. Once Daniel Harris had come up with the concept, we funded an office for PPS, appointed a chief executive and then made sure the UCW played no further part in its activities. We were reassured that it was successfully performing the function for which it was designed when the Women's Institute applied to join.

In the meantime, Julia Simpson accosted her own postman

on her doorstep and measured the depth of the outside top pocket of his uniform jacket. The poor chap must have thought he was dealing with someone who needed urgent medical assistance, but Julia had a plan. She produced a crib card, which would fit neatly into the uniform pocket, listing the union's arguments against privatization and for commercial freedom in the public sector. It was distributed to every delivery postman and postwoman to help them spread the word on their walks.

Julia aimed to get at least one news story a month sympathetic to our cause into the national press. For instance, there was one concerning a Swedish toy manufacturer which, we discovered, had offered to pay for the hundreds of thousands of cards from Santa (postmarked 'Greenland') that the Post Office's Philatelic Bureau in Edinburgh sent out during the festive season to every child who posted a stamped letter to Father Christmas. In return this firm wanted one of their toy catalogues to be enclosed with the reply, highlighting the gift – or, more probably, gifts – the child had asked for so that little Jack or Jodie could helpfully point Mummy and Daddy in the right direction.

The Post Office had refused to contemplate this crass commercialization of Christmas but how long would it be, we argued loftily, before such a cynical offer was accepted by a privatized company driven by the need to maximize returns to shareholders?

The parliamentary Labour party was waiting eagerly for the government to publish a privatization bill so that they could take up the popular cause and oppose it on the floor of the House. I spent a good deal of time with Robin Cook, Labour's shadow secretary of state for trade and industry, and far too much at sessions of the Trade and Industry Select Committee, whose chairman, the Labour MP Dick Caborne, was a great ally and had the committee engaged almost permanently on the various ramifications of Post Office privatization.

Robin and I hit it off. He was a difficult man to get to know and I'm not sure I ever succeeded, but we shared an interest in electoral reform and he was a source of sound advice and political inspiration. I'd become convinced of the need for some kind of proportional representation way back in my twenties, when I first become aware of the terrible discrepancy between the way the country votes and the composition of the House of Commons. Robin put the most eloquent case for reform I had ever heard but getting rid of the first-past-the-post system was a task for the future. For now the job to be done was to defeat the government's privatization plan. Aside from his easy articulacy, I was impressed by the fastidiousness of Robin's research. It was he who told me that Anthony Trollope, who'd written his chronicles of Barsetshire while working as a Post Office surveyor (and introducing the pillar box), had married a woman named Rose Heseltine. I used this nugget in my speeches, remarking that when my members called Heseltine a trollop, it wasn't an insult, it was a historical fact.

Despite my regard for Robin, in truth our campaign wasn't at all interested in wasting time on a Labour party whose support was assured. Our unrelenting, microscopic attention was focused on the Tories. We'd already ascertained that the Ulster Unionists were supportive of Stand By Your Post. In addition to the skilful lobbying by our activists in Northern Ireland, the arguments about whether the Queen's head could still appear on our postage stamps if Royal Mail were privatized and the loss of synergy with Republic of Ireland postal services, which would continue to be publicly owned, meant the prime minister couldn't rely on the Unionists to bolster his numbers. He was already struggling with a small majority being reduced by the Grim Reaper.

I personally spent hours in the House of Commons talking to Conservative MPs. We had identified an A list of twelve who we considered to be certain to vote against privatization and a further eighteen who were still to be convinced and might either oppose or abstain in a Second Reading vote.

The official position of the government after Heseltine's announcement in late 1992 was that they were continuing to consult and they held to this throughout the following year. This delay was crucial to our campaign. Julia's briefing card, which all our Royal Mail members carried, provided advice to customers on the most effective action they could take to object to the privatization that most of them opposed (99 per cent, according to opinion surveys near the end of our campaign). If the local MP was a Conservative they should write to him or her expressing their opposition strongly but politely. Daniel insisted that we shouldn't provide a template. He argued that duplicated letters carried little weight. Members of the public should send personal letters, typed if necessary, although handwritten would be better.

If MPs received three or four such letters a week it worried them; nine or ten would flag up a major problem and nineteen or twenty suggested that a revolution was in prospect. With the help of PPS, its constituent parts and our own membership across the whole country, by the end of the year the MPs on our hit list were being deluged with letters. The Tory member for Horsham, Sir Peter Hordern, told the press: 'In thirty-four years in Parliament, I have never had so many handwritten complaints on one subject.'

We'd also commissioned a report from London Economics, a specialist policy and economics consultancy, which demonstrated that privatization was unnecessary since all the commercial freedoms the Post Office needed and desired could be provided within the public sector. The reason we commissioned London Economics to produce this report was that it would be authored by Bill Robinson, a leading economist who worked for them at the time. Robinson was a former adviser to Norman Lamont as chancellor of the exchequer and a man of impeccable right-wing credentials. The report duly resulted in a huge news story which Julia and Daniel ensured was seen by every one of the thirty Tories we were targeting. Also on our circulation list were the government whips, who we knew would be crucial in deciding if the legislation would be announced in the next Queen's speech.

The impact of our campaign was so forceful that on 19 May 1994 a cartoon in *The Times* depicted Michael Heseltine, in a postman's uniform, being attacked by a dog with my face. Such was my obscurity that the dog's collar had a disc bearing the initials 'AJ' to make sure readers knew who it was supposed to be.

The cartoon was shown to me by Derek Hodgson as we sat on a shuttle flight to Edinburgh that morning. I was, of course, thrilled to be caricatured in this way but my joy was tempered by the sadness of the occasion. We were on our way to John Smith's funeral.

~

It had all happened so quickly. On 11 May Laura and I had attended a Labour party European gala dinner to raise funds for the forthcoming elections to the European Parliament. The date held a personal significance for me. It was my mother's birthday. Had she lived, Lily would have been seventy-three. As it was, this May day in 1994 marked the thirtieth anniversary of her death. As I did every year, I dedicated a moment of quiet reflection to my mother on her birthday. As a child I used to run up the Portobello Road to buy a cheap piece of crockery as a present from one of the many barrows where stallholders would hold crowds spellbound by balancing sets of dinner plates along one arm as they auctioned their wares. ''Ere you are, darling, you can 'ave this lot for seven and six – and I'll throw in a teapot for nuffink.'

In between performances I'd quietly purchase a cup or saucer from the popular blue-and-white hooped range that matched the colours of Queens Park Rangers. Lily would always express delight as I handed over her unwrapped present. My intention was that she'd eventually have a full set. By the time of her death I think there were two cups and two saucers. Lily was for ever young in my memory although the clear image of her physical presence had faded over the years. All that was left now were a few sepia-tinted photographs.

The gala dinner was in a wonderful location – the ballroom of the Park Lane Hotel – and it would provide Laura with an opportunity to meet John Smith for the first time. Since his 'one member, one vote' victory the previous September John had consolidated his position in the party and the country with the recent local government elections producing significant Labour gains. There was something about this Scotsman with the plainest of names that was winning over a public previously immune to Neil Kinnock's more charismatic Celtic charm. 'Integrity' was the word most closely associated with John's character. He oozed dependability. And unlike John Major, who had also earned public respect, he led a united party.

That evening he had been on top form, giving an excellent speech and undertaking the chore of touring the tables as if it were the one thing he really wanted to do. The jazz singer George Melly and the American harmonica player Larry Adler entertained an appreciative audience convinced that, with John as our leader, the long, hard slog of opposition could soon be over.

Laura and I left at 10.30pm. Twelve hours later Derek Hodgson came into my office to tell me that John Smith had died of a heart attack during the night.

There was an outpouring of genuine public grief but we in the Labour party had no option but to mix mourning with manoeuvring. Derek and I agreed that Gordon Brown, the shadow chancellor, should be our next leader but then I spoke to Robin Cook, who told me he was backing shadow home secretary Tony Blair and thought it unlikely that Gordon and Tony would both stand.

I had first met Tony Blair as Alan Tuffin and I were walking back to our hotel one lunchtime during a Labour party conference in Blackpool. Tony, then shadow employment secretary, had been heading for the Winter Gardens on his own, struggling against a fierce wind. Alan shouted the introductions over the noise of the gale and, after exchanging a few brief words, we went our separate ways.

I wasn't the first member of my family he'd encountered.

About ten years earlier, during a by-election, my son Jamie, aged eleven, had come across the Labour leader Michael Foot walking round our estate, part of which lay in the safe Tory seat of Beaconsfield. Foot was out on the stump with the Labour candidate. Jamie went to say hello to him and had a chat with the young hopeful, whose name he had forgotten by the time he rushed home, so excited was he to have met the leader of the Labour party. Tony Blair had stood no chance of winning Beaconsfield but was now the latest contender for the job of the man who'd walked beside him that day.

The leadership election took place on 21 July 1994 – the first to be held under the new rules brought in by John Smith. As Robin Cook had predicted, Gordon Brown did not stand, choosing to give his fellow modernizer Tony Blair a clear run. It is widely believed, and was later acknowledged, that there was a gentlemen's agreement between Blair and Brown whereby, if Blair became prime minister, he would in due course step down and lend his support to Brown's succession.

The other candidates were Margaret Beckett, the acting leader, and John Prescott. Tony Blair was the decisive winner, and Labour had a new leader.

Between John Smith's tragic death and his funeral, the most important development in our campaign against privatization had occurred. We'd heard that Michael Heseltine would be making a statement to the House on 19 May. The expectation was that he would announce the publication of a White Paper setting out the government's plans. We'd been lobbying heavily for a Green Paper – the first step in changing a law which offers proposals for discussion without any commitment to action. This would involve a public consultation we could use to demonstrate the absence of any support at all for privatization beyond the Post Office and Her Majesty's Treasury.

Mario, Daniel and Julia were in my office as we pored over Heseltine's statement, which had been faxed over by Robin Cook's office. We now know that Heseltine had been forced to rewrite his statement to change the paper from white to green by the Cabinet, who had been spooked by the whips about the success of our campaign. It was a wonderful day. Not only did we have a Green Paper but one of the three options to be consulted on was commercial freedom in the public sector (albeit with several pages of the document devoted to pointing out the impossibility of that aim).

In order to privatize Royal Mail, the government was suggesting that it be ripped away from Post Office Counters completely. While there were precedents in other countries for privatization, a split of this kind had never been attempted anywhere in the world. Heseltine must have reckoned that by pursuing such a separation he could dilute public opposition and get the sub-postmasters on his side.

For us it opened up a whole new argument. This was now privatization *and* break-up of the Post Office. If anybody thought the break-up bit was immaterial we were there to tell them that the natural synergy between Royal Mail and the counters network would be destroyed, to the detriment of both.

Our euphoria was kept in check by the realization that the show wouldn't be over until the fat lady sang. Or, to put it more politely, since the lady in question would be Her Majesty, the slim lady spoke. For not until the Queen's speech in November would we know if our campaign had been entirely successful, given that our aim wasn't just to stop the legislation gaining the approval of the Houses of Parliament but to prevent it from being included in the government's programme in the first place.

The fact that the Green Paper consultation period covered the summer recess was seen by many commentators as a blow to our campaign. We considered it to be helpful. As Daniel pointed out, MPs spent most of the recess at home, which was usually in their constituencies. Wherever they were, their mail would be delivered by a UCW member and they could not ignore the local carnivals and family events in support of the Post Office and against privatization, complete with inflated 'Postman Pat' balloon effigies, that were being organized by our branches in Tory constituencies. For this final four-month push we decided that the campaign would benefit from some professional assistance. There was a vast array of lobbyists and public-relations experts to choose from. It was Mario who suggested that we hire Lowe Bell.

'Lowe Bell?' I exclaimed. 'Tim Bell's company? Thatcher's friend? Her favourite lobbyist? The one that helped her win all those elections?'

'That's right. The ones with unrivalled influence and reach into the Conservative party,' Mario replied calmly.

The more I thought about it, the more attractive the proposition seemed. Just as Lowe Bell were known for their right-of-centre leanings there were plenty of lobbyists renowned for their connections to Labour and the unions. But the latter knew little about the party that would decide the fate of the Post Office. Daniel and Julia agreed that while hiring Lowe Bell would raise eyebrows in the Labour movement, our whole campaign had been counter-intuitive and risking disapproval was something we could live with. We decided to invite three companies to tender for the contract, two with impeccable Labour credentials and Lowe Bell.

Each firm came to Clapham to a make a presentation. Lowe Bell fielded a team of three: Kevin Bell (no relation), Neal Lawson, a Labour man who'd worked with Mario at the Transport and General Workers' Union, and Guy Black, a former special adviser to John Wakeham, the secretary of state who had spearheaded the privatization of the electricity industry in the late 1980s. Their presentation was by far the strongest and they were by no means the most expensive, either. We hired them and embarked on an exhilarating period of high-adrenaline campaigning.

Lowe Bell were impressed with what we'd done already and had made it clear that they wanted to work alongside Mario, Julia and Daniel, not replace them. Their clearly defined role was to get behind enemy lines; to ensure we were aware of the government's plans, to brief us on which Cabinet members were for and against Heseltine's proposals, to nibble away at the Tory grass roots in the constituency parties and feed off the deep discontent we'd helped to foment.

The strokes we pulled together, my team and Lowe Bell, were many and varied but the most sensational was the meeting of Conservative party constituency chairmen at Conservative

Central Office in Smith Square, Westminster. These men (and a few women) were the most powerful figures in a party whose members had little involvement with policy, but could cut up very rough indeed when the policy they were happy not to be involved in devising met with their disapproval. They also had a jealously guarded monopoly on selecting local candidates.

Lowe Bell organized this meeting covertly through intermediaries. The purpose was to hear Tim Eggar, one of Heseltine's junior ministers, discuss privatization with 'a senior Post Office executive'. This was actually the recently departed David Laine, with whom I'd become friendly when he was managing director of the Post Office's in-house catering company, Quadrant. He'd resigned after a bust-up with Bill Cockburn.

Young and ambitious, David was tall, angular and very posh – a bit like the actor Simon Williams in his *Upstairs, Downstairs* persona. He walked like a Tory, talked like a Tory, dressed like a Tory and for all I knew was a Tory, but he was against privatization, and I recruited him to work for us on a consultancy basis. It was his modulated tones to which the Conservative party constituency chairmen warmed as he explained, in a reasonable and rational way, why break-up and privatization would be a disaster for postal services and the nation.

Poor Tim Eggar had been expecting the support of his fellow speaker. Instead, by the time it was his turn to speak, his audience had had all their fears confirmed. Mario was in the audience and remains convinced that Eggar recognized him from the many meetings he'd attended with me at the Department of Trade and Industry (DTI). It was when their eyes met that Eggar realized it had been a set-up. We had a close relationship with the DTI officials responsible for Post Office policy, one of whom told us that Eggar returned from the meeting convinced that the Conservative party would never accept Post Office privatization.

Lowe Bell were working assiduously on the government whips' office to reinforce that very message and to spread it further among Tory MPs. By the time of the Conservative party conference in Bournemouth that year, Heseltine was reeling from the effects of our campaign but the old stager came out fighting.

Lowe Bell managed to get me into the event. It was my first experience not only of a Tory party conference, but also of a conference of a party in government in the modern age, with all the attendant security. It had been a long time since Labour party conferences warranted any protection at all.

In the run-up to Bournemouth, through the frantic period since the publication of the Green Paper in June, I'd been busy taking on the duties of a role to which I had no entitlement. The National Federation of Sub-Postmasters (NFSP) was a powerful force that used its muscle sparingly. Unaffiliated to the TUC, let alone the Labour party, it prided itself on its good relationship with the Conservative government and had kept a very low profile throughout our campaign.

At that time the network of sub-offices, privately owned businesses where local traders such as grocers and newsagents were paid to provide Post Office counter services, must have numbered around 18,000 – still vast, but in decline, as it had been for twenty years. The post office had once been the only place where people could buy a stamp, post a parcel or collect their pension. All that had changed. Since the early 1980s it had been possible to have pensions paid directly into individuals' bank accounts and this was the single biggest factor reducing custom at the sub-offices. Not only did fewer government transactions mean lower revenue for these sub-postmasters, but their village and corner shops lost footfall, too, with fewer customers coming in to collect their money and then spending it on other goods.

The general secretary of the NFSP, Colin Baker, was a shrewd ex-copper. We got on very well but Colin was reluctant to pick a fight with the government, even though he saw the danger of tearing the counters network away from Royal Mail and was aware that his members were deeply concerned about it.

Colin felt that keeping the counters in the public sector was a victory in itself and that through his links with the Tory party, and in particular with the chair of the 1922 Committee, he could extract something meaningful in pay and conditions as his price for going along with the legislation. It was an entirely reasonable position. The general public could be forgiven for not knowing the intricate details of Post Office trade unionism or the difference between crown offices, where our members worked, and the much more numerous sub-offices, where they didn't. They assumed that the UCW represented all postal workers so we simply acted as if we did.

I wrote individually to every single sub-postmaster enclosing posters to pin up in their shops and leaflets to place on their counters, thus reaching the 22 million people who visited a post office every week. We weren't allowed to display such anti-privatization material on Post Office premises but these shops were owned by the sub-postmasters, and they could display what they wanted.

Whenever I appeared in the media as the figurehead of the campaign I emphasized the threat to counter services without making any attempt to clarify who represented their staff.

Colin Baker had nothing to say to the press or the broadcasters but I did, and I knew I was speaking for the vast majority of NFSP members when I voiced opposition to break-up and privatization.

The morning of the big debate at the Conservative conference arrived. I use the word 'debate' in its loosest sense. Conservative party conferences do not debate issues. They are stage-managed to an extent that shocked even me, someone who recognized the need to make televised conferences a showcase rather than a bloodbath, as Labour's had been in the recent past. Basically, this was the Michael Heseltine show; an opportunity for the 'president of the Board of Trade' to do his end-of-the-pier act, wowing the Tory faithful as he did every year.

That morning's *Daily Telegraph* carried a front-page story centred on an opinion poll that yet again underlined the huge public opposition to privatization. The union had commissioned this and many other opinion polls throughout the campaign. Daniel had briefed the journalist who wrote the article and Lowe Bell had helped to make the *Telegraph* aware of the level of disquiet in the government whips' office. But we couldn't rig the outcome. The anti-privatization mood was genuine. I don't know how he did it, but Daniel managed to have a copy of the *Telegraph* slipped under the hotel-room door of every Cabinet minister, whether they'd ordered it or not.

We had organized a lobby of delegates as they arrived at the conference that morning. I'd asked our Bournemouth branch secretary to hand-pick about ten postmen and women to come to the conference hall and distribute leaflets. I specified that they must be 'avuncular', and whatever the female equivalent was, and watched with pride as they enthusiastically carried out their task. Every one of them must have been someone's favourite postie. They probably earned a fortune in Christmas boxes, such was their cheery demeanour. Dressed smartly in full uniform, complete with collar and tie, the only thing they lacked was a robin perched on their shoulder. As well as the leaflets they were carrying sheets of blue stickers bearing the message 'Stand By Your Post' printed in large type, which they were helpfully fixing to the lapels of appreciative delegates. Some delegates were coming back for more to pass around to their colleagues.

On this occasion I had no seat in the Bournemouth International Centre, where I'd attended more union conferences than I cared to remember over the years. But I had the pass Lowe Bell had secured for me and stood with Kevin Bell, Guy Black and Mario in a perfect spot, sideways on to the stage.

There were many propositions submitted by local Conservative associations opposing the government's policy but these were cheerfully ignored. The proposition 'selected' for debate was a few paragraphs of drivel congratulating the government on undertaking extensive consultation on the future of the Post Office and reminding conference about their successful record on privatization.

Thanks to the efforts of our lobbyists, when Michael Heseltine took the stage to make his speech he found himself looking out on a sea of blue stickers opposing his policy. He gave a magnificent performance. This was the famous address in which he teased Gordon Brown for using the phrase 'post-neoclassical endogenous growth theory' in a speech written for him by his young special adviser Ed Balls. Having derided the speech, Heseltine delivered the perfectly timed punchline: 'It's not Brown's, it's Balls.'

He went on to tell delegates that they shouldn't listen to the politically motivated criticism orchestrated by the Union of Communication Workers but should instead speak to the National Federation of Postmasters, which supported his plans. This went down like a lead balloon with the people who had been picking up anti-privatization literature from their local post offices for months. Heseltine made no reference to pressing ahead with privatization. The consultation period was over; the Queen's speech less than a month away. This was the secretary of state's opportunity to issue a defiant message about finishing what he'd begun two years earlier. The fact that he didn't suggested that we were on the verge of a great victory.

The fat lady sang on 3 November, when the government announced that the Post Office would be neither split up nor privatized. Heseltine had apparently tried valiantly to salvage something from the wreckage over the preceding days. He had offered to sell a minority rather than a majority share, suggested turning Post Office Counters into a workers' trust and held meetings with recalcitrant backbenchers in a frantic effort to convert them. His internal opponents were implacable. The more marginal their seats, the more obstinate they'd become. We know from the answer to a written parliamentary question that the response to the Green Paper consultation was 15,400 submissions, of which only sixty supported privatization.

This is how the Cabinet minute recorded the decision of the Major government to abandon the cause:

> The process of driving through such legislation would create serious divisions within the Conservative party and be a source of long-running political difficulty for the government . . . It

> was not in the interests of the government that it should suffer a humiliating defeat. To press ahead now with the near certain prospect of defeat would be to put courage ahead of calculation and risk creating an unprecedented embarrassment for the government which would severely damage its reputation and standing.

The *Sun* called it the end of Thatcherism. Robert Taylor in the *Financial Times* described it as 'the most effective and professional campaign by a British union'. Peter Kellner in the *Observer*, seeking to explain 'why Heseltine's face is plastered with egg', declared that 'the UCW ran a blinder of a campaign. In doing so it exposed the futility of many campaigns against the Conservatives over the past fifteen years. If the right lessons are learned, we could see the birth of a new era of political combat.'

Many other commentators reached similar conclusions. I'd tasted glory but I knew I couldn't have achieved it without that army of delivery staff and the ever-improving postal service for which they were responsible. I also knew how fortunate I was to have Mario, Julia and Daniel working alongside me.

There was an understandable interest from many quarters in their future employment and eventually Daniel was poached by Clare Short to become her special adviser, Julia went on to many other triumphs at Education, the Home Office, 10 Downing Street and, latterly, on the board of British Airways and Mario went into public affairs. We've never lost touch and I continue to follow their progress like a proud parent after a graduation.

Chapter 6

If I was expecting some kind of breather after our victory I was mistaken. The daily grind hardly paused. I felt like an athlete who'd just breasted the tape in the 10,000 metres only to be told he had another race to run straight away.

There was a new merged union to be created with my friend Tony Young from the NCU; meetings of the TUC General Council to be participated in; the lead role that the general secretary played at the time in four different sets of annual pay negotiations – in Telecoms, Royal Mail, Parcelforce and Post Office Counters – to be taken. Still, as I was fond of reflecting, this job was better than pedalling uphill early on a cold morning in the pouring rain, with the wind against you and 35lb of mail strapped to the front of your pushbike.

It was a disingenuous comparison given that I'd only ever spent a couple of months as a cycling postman during my thirteen years on delivery. What I'd actually left behind to become an employee of the UCW were the rural delights of Littleworth Common in Buckinghamshire, where I drove a van, and delivered newspapers, coal, eggs and anything else my customers wanted, usually finding time to park in a country lane to read a chapter or two of a novel in the interlude between finishing the delivery and starting the collection.

I was still an avid reader, although the number of books I was getting through had declined to around one a month now that so many other things were eating into my reading time. I found leadership an absorbing, fulfilling but lonely occupation. Still, as I've said, I am by nature a loner, preferring my own company to the networking and glad-handing that leadership demands. I enjoyed spending time with good colleagues like Mike Hogan and Billy Hayes. In fact, all my national officer colleagues were strong and loyal supporters. But in the end, as is the case with all positions of ultimate leadership, the proverbial buck stopped with me. I no longer had Alan Tuffin to talk to when I encountered a particularly difficult problem, as I had occasionally done as outdoor secretary, knowing that I'd receive helpful advice. I'd always tried not to rely on him to resolve any difficulties. Indeed, more than once I'd refused his offers to become involved. But it was always comforting to know that he was there if the buck got too heavy.

Now I felt that every problem being grappled with by any of my national officers was my problem, whether it was the outsourcing of telephone operator jobs to India and elsewhere, the downgrading of crown post offices or, above all, local disputes in Royal Mail, which had sparked up again. Leadership for its own sake was never something I enjoyed in the way Alan had, revelling in the position and the authority and power it brought.

This discomfort with leadership may well have been a factor in the smoothness with which Tony Young and I were able to sort out the vexed question of our respective positions after we'd merged the two unions. In many other union mergers there had been rancour and retribution over such matters. Tony and I quickly agreed that, subject to the union's approval, we'd be joint general secretaries for a while and then let the members decide who should be the leader, with no special protection or compensation for the loser. In the meantime we'd manage the union in tandem until our respective five-year periods of office (which ran roughly parallel) were up. This would give the merger time to bed in properly.

Vesting day was to be early in the following year, 1995. The new union needed a name and the memberships of both unions were invited to choose one from a selection of shortlisted suggestions. In a burst of stunning innovation my members (the substantial majority) decided that instead of the Union of Communication Workers we should become the Communication Workers Union.

Among the NCU's cohort of officers the new union would inherit was the finest trade-union official I've ever worked with. Jeannie Drake had plumped for a career in the unions from a wealth of other options she could have pursued on leaving university. Having cut her teeth in the civil-service union she was currently the deputy general secretary of the NCU. She had the special gift of being able to harness her formidable intellect to an admirable eloquence and capacity for empathy – all great attributes in their own right but rarely, in my experience, so successfully combined in one individual. Now she would become one of our three deputy general secretaries. It was enough of a reason in itself for merger.

I once asked Jeannie why she'd so often been second in command but never a leader. She told me how inhibited she'd always felt as a woman in a profession of strong egos and a cult of machismo. The deputy position simply felt more comfortable. I'm sure she was reflecting what many women feel as they hover around the pinnacle of the organizations where they work. So although she was the most talented trade-union officer I've ever met – not just the most talented woman officer – hardly anybody in the union world, let alone the wider one, will have heard of her. Which I suspect suits Jeannie down to the ground.

Tony and I agreed that rather than integrate the unions before merging, the merger should drive the integration. In this we mirrored the mistakes that the EU was to make in constructing the single currency. Far from bringing very different economies closer together, the euro highlighted the differences between them. This merge now, decide later approach took its most tangible form in our reluctance to construct a rule book and instead to pencil in a delegate conference for this purpose a few months after vesting day.

With the NCU already the product of a recent merger between engineering and clerical workers, the two tribes – the oilies and the inkies, as they called themselves – maintained all manner of processes from their previous unions and had yet to find a formula for peace and harmony together in the NCU. Now they were being spatchcocked into our much larger union. To force the two bodies together in a conference venue was like shoving Take That on stage with the Traveling Wilburys. In our defence, I should make it clear that the membership had voted overwhelmingly for merger in a referendum and while it would have been politically incorrect to oppose the process, activists in our respective unions could always find a host of reasons for delay. Prevaricating amendments littered our conference agendas until Tony and I forced the issue by carrying a proposition at each of our respective union conferences which set the date for the merger.

The rules revision conference, where the inkies and the oilies were joined by the posties, was a disaster. All three factions fell out. There were even reports of violent altercations between delegates from different sections outside the conference hall.

Tony and I had achieved the longstanding ambition of forming a single union in Posts and Telecoms but we couldn't claim to have done so successfully. We were now joint general secretaries of a strange institution that continued to function as before at branch level while being fused together at national level. It had resulted in representatives being pushed into each other's company at a conference where the mood was at best one of mutual toleration.

As well as my professional objectives, I had three very important ambitions on my personal agenda: to learn to swim, to play the piano and to speak another language (not necessarily all at the same time).

I'd tackled the first challenge several years earlier, having been a staunch non-swimmer since the age of eight, when Mr Gemmill, our omnipotent primary school headmaster, had taken all the boys in my year to Lancaster Road baths for a swimming lesson and started off by telling us to throw ourselves one by one into the pool, where he stood ready to catch us. It was, he explained, the best way to overcome any fear of water. I suppose as a teaching method it was similar to pushing a novice parachutist out of an aeroplane. In my case the parachute didn't open. For some reason Mr Gemmill failed to catch me and I sank to the bottom of the pool. I don't remember my life flashing before me, but if it did it would have been a very short film and we'd have been standing for the national anthem before Mr Gemmill's huge hands clasped my shoulders and pulled me to the surface. Instead of curing my fear of water, he had succeeded only in entrenching it.

As Natalie, Emma and Jamie grew up, it was Judy who taught them to swim while I sat on various Cornish beaches on our annual holidays squeezed into whatever shade I could find, fully clothed, with my nose in a book.

I was forty and engaged to Laura before I resolved to erase this blot on my manliness. I recruited my resourceful mother-in-law-to-be to help me. Mo discovered that evening swimming lessons for adult beginners were on offer at the Elephant and Castle baths just down the road from Laura's family home in Herne Hill. So every Tuesday evening for six weeks, I drove my little Ford Fiesta down to the Elephant. The instructor was one of those gay men who revelled in playing to the stereotype. He never once dipped so much as a toe in the water himself. He hated getting his hair wet, he told us. Instead he'd stand at the side of the pool as we students clung to the rail looking up at him for instructions.

Having given an elaborate demonstration of breaststroke movements for arms and legs, he made us walk further and further into the middle of the pool before ordering us to plunge in and swim as best we could towards him and the safety of the rail. His method of getting us accustomed to water was different from Mr Gemmill's. We were to complete these early strokes with our faces in it. This, he insisted, would teach us to breathe properly as well as to confront and banish the fear of submersion.

After a couple of weeks, we were kicking off from one side of the pool ('Tuck your little legs up under you, Alan, so that you *push* against the side for momentum. *Oooh*, that's perfect! You'll be mistaken for a dolphin if you're not careful!') and surfacing on the other having swum a width without raising our heads from the water. Now I needed to practise. John and Mo's next-door neighbours had a full-sized heated swimming pool in their back garden, transformed from outdoor to indoor pool by an inflatable enclosure. Mo negotiated access for Laura and me when the neighbours were away, as they often were. The problem was that having learned to swim face-down I found it difficult to do it any other way. I wasn't going to get very far if I had to stop every time I needed to come up for air. Eventually, I managed to lift my head and breathe at the same time as kicking out my legs, as I'd been taught ('Like a frog, Alan! Like a frog!'), and paddling frantically until I found that I could actually swim – after a fashion.

But I never really got over the fear and for me going for a swim involves much preliminary faffing around. There are photographs taken by Laura of me swimming on holiday (always when nobody else was around) that show the worried look on my face as I navigate the pool. I still only do widths, never lengths. The deep end represents a terror I've never conquered.

The second goal ought, I felt, to be easier given that my sister Linda and I carried a smidgen of our father's musical genius in our genes. I'd taught myself to play the guitar as a kid, been part of a semi-professional band in my youth and had messed about on keyboards on and off all my life. My father could reproduce a tune on the piano almost note-perfect after hearing it once. When he first met my mother, he played the piano at army concerts, resplendent in his uniform and white gloves. There was always an old 'joanna' in whatever slum we lived in for him to practise on. But he kept the keyboard locked so that Linda and I could never use it. After Steve left in 1958, my determined sister wrenched open the piano lid with a screwdriver. I taught myself some chords and did a bit of vamping but for me the piano couldn't compete with the guitar.

In my early twenties I'd taken evening classes at Slough college to try to learn the piano and reached Level 2 (the second grade in music, which measures proficiency on a scale of 1 to 8) before going off to study other things on becoming a union branch official. In my early forties, having ticked swimming off my list, I decided to revisit ambition number two. I signed up for more evening classes one September, this time at a college in Croydon, along with my sister-in-law's boyfriend.

Lisa, herself an accomplished pianist, was living at the time with Christian Petite, a mercurial Frenchman she'd met at work at Reuters. He was straight from central casting. Thin and wiry, with bulging eyes and a handsome nose, all he was missing was the beret, the matelot shirt and a string of onions round his neck. Christian smoked Gauloises incessantly. He introduced me to pastis, Sauternes and the joys of cooking. He served the rarest meat I'd ever eaten. In fact it was sometimes doubtful whether the animal on our plates had actually breathed its last. Come to think of it, his cuisine might well have been a factor in Laura and me deciding to turn vegetarian for a few years around that time.

We all loved Christian and his crazy French ways. One morning he told Lisa he had a later start than her at the office that day and would lie in for a while longer. She got up, dressed for work and left to catch the train. As soon as he heard the front door close behind her he leaped out of bed, threw on some clothes, jumped on his powerful motorbike and roared up to Reuters at St Katharine's Dock, next to the Tower of London, where Lisa found him sitting at his desk, calmly reading the newspaper with a cup of coffee beside him, when she arrived at the office.

He brought a similar quirky approach to learning the piano. After our class on a Monday evening, I'd go back to Lisa's with Christian to practise on her piano the simple little pieces set for beginners by our patient tutor. Christian didn't bother practising the set pieces. Instead he was obsessed with learning the fast and complex piano theme to the BBC's long-running *Ski Sunday* programme, instantly recognizable to Sunday evening television viewers.

He bought the sheet music and asked Lisa to show him the finger movements for both hands. He had no interest in knowing which notes he was playing or indeed in learning to read music at all. All he wanted to do was to play this one piece and he laboured over the keyboard on it throughout the week, returning to the easy pieces he was supposed to be learning only at our evening class. Not surprisingly, he struggled more with these than the rest of us who'd taken the trouble to practise them.

By December most of the ten people in the group had

mastered our simple pieces – except Christian, who was no doubt perceived by everyone, including the teacher, as the slowest pupil in the class. Our tutor decided that the final lesson before Christmas should take the form of a concert. We'd all bring in wine and snacks and one by one we'd sit down at the piano and play something of our choice, which in almost every case was likely to be the beginners' exercise piece we were best at. When we arrived that evening there was no sign of Christian, but at the last moment he appeared, bearing an expensive bottle of Châteauneuf-du-Pape and some exquisite mushroom vol-au-vents.

Having fortified ourselves with some refreshments and the festive atmosphere, we all sat in courteous silence as each pupil went up to do their party piece. One chose 'Frère Jacques', and I remember playing 'The Song of the Volga Boatmen', picking out the notes uncertainly and earning the respectful support of my fellow students. Christian's insistence on going last was put down to nervousness. When everyone else had had their turn, the group offered indulgent smiles and encouraging nods as our struggling classmate was coaxed towards the piano.

He settled himself on the stool and produced a note-perfect rendition of the theme from *Ski Sunday* at breakneck speed, both hands a blur across the keyboard. Everyone in the room – except me, as I knew what was coming – sat open-mouthed in amazement. When he had finished he rose from the piano stool to loud applause and directed a Gallic shrug towards me as he lifted his glass to propose a toast to our bemused tutor.

My third ambition is one that has, sadly, defeated me. I have tried to learn French. I've taken lessons, purchased an array of tapes and CDs, read the books and perused the dictionaries.

What little I've learned I've forgotten. Whatever else I achieve in life, my inability to grasp another language will always be a regret. Although even if I'd managed to become fluent in French I doubt that I'd ever have understood Christian Petite.

By my mid-forties, then, I was the monolingual joint general secretary of a newly merged communication workers' union, able to get by in a swimming pool and at the piano.

It is hard to identify the precise moment when the direction of my life began to change. It was Tony Young who introduced me to the poems of Robert Frost and 'The Road Not Taken' is the one I reread most often. Soon I would arrive at the point where 'two roads diverged in a yellow wood' but before I reached it I would encounter many smaller byways, some no more than barely discernible trails, where less significant choices were made by me or for me. As Frost observes in his poem: 'Yet knowing how way leads on to way, I doubted if I should ever come back.'

The merged union had to make some decisions as to who was to sit on the TUC General Council and the National Executive Committee of the Labour party. Trade unions above a certain size had automatic representation on the General Council, roles that were traditionally filled by general secretaries. Tony and I had both sat on that body on behalf of our pre-merged unions.

The Communication Workers Union (CWU) was now large enough to qualify for two seats and we proposed to our Executive Council that these be taken by Tony and me as joint general secretaries. The executive disagreed. They argued that since we had an embarrassment of riches when it came to general secretaries, one of us could guard our interests at the TUC while the other occupied our seat on the NEC of the Labour party.

This would mean displacing Derek Hodgson from the part of his job that he enjoyed the most. The deputy general secretary of the UCW had for as long as anyone could remember been on Labour's NEC. The position corresponded with his wider role as the political officer of the union.

Derek had played virtually no part in the merger. In the run-up he'd been one of those who could find no argument against the logic but didn't really want to see it happen. He was a conservative with a small 'c' where the union was concerned but had never been a destructive influence as I pursued what he knew was one of my major objectives.

As the merger took place Derek was on a long period of leave visiting his relatives in New Zealand and so had missed the important phase where the two executive bodies came together and got to know one another. So large was this new combined executive that its meetings had to be held in the boardroom at Congress House in Great Russell Street, which was also, helpfully, a neutral space. With UCW headquarters in Clapham and the NCU's in Ealing, we were constantly seeking to avoid giving grist to the mill of those of our activists keen to find evidence of a takeover rather than a merger.

Derek returned from his sojourn abroad to find his Labour party position under threat. Tony and I worked together to keep Derek where he was. We refused to accept our initial defeat at the hands of the executive and worked up another proposal which gave the joint general secretaries new functions while leaving Derek's position untouched. We were defeated again. The executive were adamant that it would be a waste of our influence to have both general secretaries on the TUC General Council. As Tony was senior (he was about a decade older than me) he qualified for a place in the inner circle of the TUC and should remain there. It should be me who replaced my old rival on the Labour party's ruling body. Having beaten Derek to the job of general secretary he had so coveted, I was now being forced to remove him from a role he already held and which he loved.

The new executive was unanimous – old NCU and old UCW together – in its insistence that I be drafted immediately into the union's position on the Labour party's ruling body. As was mentioned several times during the debate, it wasn't as if I would be a stranger to this environment. I'd had a close association with the Labour leadership ever since being elected as UCW general secretary. Indeed, I had been the only leader of an affiliated union to back Tony Blair in his efforts to reform Clause IV of the Labour party constitution.

I had never been in any doubt about the need to revise Clause IV, or the hostile reaction that any attempt to touch what had become, for some, the Labour party version of the Dead Sea scrolls would ignite. Clause IV was the paragraph in our constitution which set out the Labour party's aims and objectives and it was hopelessly out of date in its commitment to the public ownership of everything.

The Clause IV debate, which began in October 1994 and ended in April 1995, spanned the period of the merger. Victory in the battle over Post Office privatization and the way it had been achieved had given the UCW a certain cachet. There was an air of invincibility around us that was difficult to live up to. The reputation we had earned for innovation and modernity, on the other hand, I was determined to maintain. I had always seen the infighting within the Labour movement as Mods versus Rockers and a political equivalent of those Bank Holiday clashes on Brighton's pebbled beaches now seemed to be happening on a weekly basis. To flog this metaphor to death, I suppose that when Clause IV came along, hot on the heels of Stand By Your Post and John Smith's one member, one vote battle, I was itching to ride my Lambretta straight into the massed ranks of vintage motorbikes and the leather-jacketed traditionalists who sat astride them.

I was aware that the old Union of Post Office Workers had been supportive of Hugh Gaitskell's attempt to rid the party of its shibboleth in 1959. Moreover, I was increasingly interested in the constitutional reforms articulated by a movement known as Charter 88, which advocated replacing the first-past-the-post electoral system with proportional representation, devolving power to Scotland, Wales and the English regions, establishing a written constitution and abolishing the House of Lords in favour of an elected second chamber. I wanted Labour to implement these changes and felt that the public was unlikely to trust us to revise the British constitution if we were incapable of revising our own.

I'd read an influential 1993 pamphlet written by Jack Straw on the need to reform Clause IV and by the time the issue came to a head the following year I was well versed in the arguments. I'd discussed them with my friend and political mentor, Robin Cook, who was initially sceptical. He felt that the clause was best left alone. He quoted the beautiful final lines of W. B. Yeats's poem 'He Wishes for the Cloths of Heaven', which I've always loved:

> I have spread my dreams under your feet;
> Tread softly because you tread on my dreams.

Like it or not, he was suggesting, this chimed with the emotional investment many of our members had made in the Labour party. I agreed that we had to tread softly. Clause IV needed to be revised, not simply scrapped. But, I complained to Robin, I'd joined a political party, not a religion.

The wording of Clause IV was a creature of its time; 1917, to be precise, just after the Bolshevik Revolution, when a command economy held a brief attraction for a Labour movement that had yet to become a party of government. Now it was a dated and unattainable creed. To retain it among our revised objectives would be to enshrine a constitution that resembled a rock formation. Worse than that, it contradicted every election manifesto the Labour party had ever produced. It wasn't just that we no longer wished to bring all aspects of our economy under public control. The truth was that we never had. There was nothing sacred about these fifty-six words. They hadn't been handed down from the heavens in a shaft of light. Neither were they etched from coal and glazed in workers' sweat.

I discovered a pithy and revealing report of the adoption of the clause in a contemporary journal of the Postmen's Federation (a founding father of the Labour party and a grandparent of the UCW): 'Delegates to the adjourned Conference of the Labour Party were looking forward to a day's arduous work devoted almost exclusively to a discussion of details, instead of which they found themselves at liberty before lunch. Labour's constitution had been revised in less than two and half hours.' It was clear that the people who cobbled together the clause would not have expected it to remain unamended, let alone unamendable.

My view was that Labour's socialist values were about working collectively to ensure a more equal society where all citizens were free from ignorance and poverty. Now our new young leader was determined to set out these values in a revised constitution and I resolved to support him.

There weren't many chiefs of the major affiliated unions who felt as warmly as Tony Young and I did about Tony Blair. John Monks was excluded from the debate within the party by the TUC's political neutrality. But I knew that he, too, felt positive about a man who was capable not just of securing power but of retaining it for long enough to introduce the social change that the Tories were incapable of even contemplating. John had been a calm voice of reason in the frenetic debates of the late 1980s as the British trade-union movement abandoned its strange position of being not only anti-Europe, but anti the European model of social protection for workers. Back then we'd been pro the closed shop and anti the minimum wage. Now the pro and anti had been swapped and were the right way round.

Chapter 7

THE 1994 LABOUR party conference had taken place in October, before the merger, when I was still in total control of the sixth-biggest affiliated union. The UCW always held its reception on the Tuesday evening of the conference and, since the leader's speech was on the Tuesday afternoon and the leader was obliged to appear at every reception, it was invariably a well-attended event. The residual excitement from the afternoon's set piece permeated the atmosphere and would be refuelled by alcohol and the obligatory sausage rolls and coleslaw.

That evening the room was buzzing. At the end of his speech a few hours earlier, Tony Blair had announced a review of Clause IV of the party constitution, to be concluded at a special conference the following spring.

It so happened that a proposition had been placed on the conference agenda by several constituency parties and trade unions seeking to defend every word of the existing clause. While the sponsors had been unaware of the plan Tony Blair would unveil in concluding his address, there had been sufficient speculation on the subject to generate these motions which, in the normal course of events, would not have attracted much attention.

By the wet Wednesday morning after the leader's speech, they had assumed a new significance. Several propositions had been welded together as a 'composite'. This couldn't stop the Clause IV review but it would provide a platform for its defenders to demonstrate how important it was to maintain every dot and comma of the sacred text.

All the same, as I entered the red velvet splendour of Blackpool's Winter Gardens, having arrived late after a leisurely breakfast, bleary-eyed and intent on a quiet morning in the wake of the UCW reception, I wasn't expecting to find Derek Hodgson waiting for me in an advanced state of agitation.

The debate on the Clause IV composite had already begun. Robin Cook, as that year's chair of the Labour party, was presiding. Robin's initial scepticism about the review had dissipated and he was now a convert to the cause. He'd sent me a note via Derek, who sat with him on Labour's NEC. Would I step up to the rostrum to make the case for reform? If so, he would call me in as the final speaker from the floor. Although the note was from Robin it was probable that the suggestion had come from someone in Tony Blair's team.

I had about ten minutes to formulate something before being called. I racked my brains. That year marked the twentieth anniversary of the last time Labour had won a general election. In my short, hurriedly prepared contribution I used this milestone to emphasize how electorally unattractive we'd become and how important it was to take the difficult decisions that might just convince the British public we were worthy of their trust once again. The last time we'd been victorious Gary

Glitter had been topping the charts. I said that Clause IV of the party constitution was no more relevant to my members' lives today than one of his old LPs.

It wasn't great oratory but it led the news bulletins that night. Within the union, it unleashed one of those outbursts of manufactured outrage that I'd seen before, where the actual views of our members came to us at headquarters distorted through the prism of our activists. Over the coming weeks a whole series of resolutions would be passed up to union HQ from branches, district councils and regional committees expressing the disquiet, nay, disgust, of our members at this disgraceful attack on the fundamental socialist values of the Labour party.

No other trade union, so far as I was aware, voiced support for revising Clause IV. Some leaders were sympathetic but decided to maintain a discreet silence; others, like Tony Young's union, were so riven with factionalism as to be beyond the influence of the general secretary in any case.

My executive gave me the backing I needed to face down the criticism and turn the tables. Julia Simpson, who edited our journal, had a brainwave: when the revised Clause IV was eventually finalized, we should publish it alongside the original as a supplement to the journal and ask our members to decide which one they preferred.

I had some involvement in the process of redrafting Clause IV, making some minor suggestions for amendments to the text that was faxed to me at home by Sally Morgan from the leader's office. It was an excellent piece of work, reflecting the party's values in the modern age. We were, it proudly proclaimed, democratic socialists (the word 'socialist' had, incidentally, been completely absent from the old Clause IV).

The result of our union poll was astonishing – a 90 per cent majority for the revised Clause IV. End of argument. At the same time constituency parties were balloting their members up and down the country and also recording decisive votes for the new clause. All of those resolutions claiming to represent the disquiet of the membership were worthless. The only thing they represented was a mindset among the activists or, more accurately, I suspect, a lack of confidence among the wider membership to stand up to a small minority whose finger-jabbing certitudes had been part of the reason for Labour's long period languishing in opposition.

Although Militant had been driven out by now, many of their sympathizers still remained. For those people there would have been a simple explanation for the overwhelming support for the new clause – false consciousness. Or, to put it another way, the members' inability to appreciate the sophistication and sagacity of the arguments.

Shortly after it had been determined that I would replace Derek Hodgson on Labour's National Executive Committee, the final stage in the Clause IV process took place – the special conference to formally approve the new constitution. Tony Blair's huge and important success in ridding the party of its dated, unachievable and undesirable creed is often described as the Clause IV 'moment'. It was a very long moment. The one-day conference in London on 29 April 1995 would be the culmination of a protracted and meticulously planned campaign.

The CWU was one of only two unions that had balloted their members on the issue and I was guaranteed a speaking slot in the short, final debate. There were far too many speakers to fit into the time available, the vast majority seeking to speak in favour of the new clause before the ultimate decision was made. Derek argued that as he was still on the NEC until the changeover in September, he should deliver the CWU's contribution. Tony Young said that was ridiculous – at a conference such as this it would be union leaders who would speak, and I had been an important voice in this campaign from the start. In any case, as a member of the NEC, Derek was unlikely to be called into a debate that was principally designed to hear from delegates.

Derek wouldn't give in and so in the end I conceded. He had been unceremoniously shunted off the NEC and was desperate to sing his swansong. It was a speech I was keen to make, but what the hell? The battle had been won. I knew that if we put Derek's name forward as our speaker the CWU wouldn't be called, but that would make no difference to the outcome. Sure enough, Derek wasn't called, but Arthur Scargill was.

For years I'd looked on in amazement as, at conference after conference, Labour and TUC, Scargill was cheered by a section of the delegates all the way to the rostrum and back again. Even as the mineworkers' delegation shrank in size, it seemed, the applause for the architect of their defeat grew louder. This time there was no applause. I was sitting close enough to the rostrum to observe his features as, for the first time at a gathering of this kind, he encountered open hostility. He had led an organization pledged to defend the old Clause IV in its entirety. The booing and hissing that greeted his announcement that he would challenge the decision to adopt a revised clause in the courts had a visible effect on him. He was shaken.

Like David Owen and the rest of the Gang of Four who'd

left the Labour party in 1981 – if for very different reasons – Scargill would now flounce off to start his own political party designed in his image. Revising Clause IV had achieved more than I could possibly have imagined.

In the end it was the fight for better terms and conditions for postmen and women that indirectly led to my departure from the CWU. Buoyed up by success in achieving my other objectives – defeating privatization, merging with the NCU – I returned with renewed vigour to the task closest to my heart.

Most of those employed on the grades we represented in the CWU were on a good basic wage, working a five- or sometimes four-day week. However, because of the availability of overtime and a cornucopia of allowances, the grade on which the largest number of people worked – some 180,000 of them – carried a salary of just £10,000 a year and all delivery staff still worked Monday to Saturday. Overtime wasn't as ubiquitous as it had been, and where it existed it was declining, but the disparity between average earnings and basic pay was still huge.

I led for the union in the annual pay round with the various Post Office businesses – Royal Mail, Parcelforce and Post Office Counters. However, I knew that annual pay bargaining wouldn't get me the dramatic breakthrough I was seeking. For a start, the government kept a close eye on the ramifications any pay deal might have on the rest of the public sector. It was also the case that pay bargaining revolved around the level of inflation and the Retail Price Index (RPI). For many of the grades we represented the level of pay was about right and we needed to ensure that it wasn't eroded by increases in the cost of living.

But for postmen and women we needed a mechanism to turbo-charge the basic pay so that it formed a greater proportion of average earnings. I was perfectly prepared to throw overtime levels, allowances and bonuses into the mix in pursuit of higher basic pay and shorter hours, but I needed to tackle this outside the narrow parameters of the pay round.

By now the principal negotiator for Royal Mail was their director of human resources, Brian Thomson, a Geordie who'd come to Royal Mail from the shipbuilding industry and with whom I'd built a close rapport. Brian and I had put our heads together to resolve many problems including, when he was director of Royal Mail in London, a potentially calamitous dispute about the number of mail-processing centres in the capital which ended with an agreement that was almost perfect in its symmetry. Brian was expert in the science of what used to be called 'industrial relations' before the dreadful term 'human resources' replaced it.

The necessary components of success in negotiating a settlement are mutual respect, and indeed trust, between negotiators, the capacity to see the situation from the point of view of the other side of the table and confidence in the ability of the negotiators to deliver the eventual deal. I will not burden the reader with the detail of these complex talks. Suffice it to say that there was an opportunity to achieve my objective of putting delivery postmen and women on a five-day week with higher take-home pay that was no longer dependent on an abundance of unreliable and unsustainable overtime.

All the portents were good, the most important being that Royal Mail wanted something from the union. A negotiation of this kind could only succeed if there was something in it for both sides. They wanted to introduce a new way of working. Instead of the workforce being 'supervised' and 'inspected', much as they had been at the time of Rowland Hill's great reforms in 1840, staff would work in teams with uniformed 'team leaders' rather than suited supervisors. Individual postal workers would have career development plans, the Postman Higher Grade (PHG) would disappear and separate allowances for skills such as driving or operating a forklift truck would be consolidated into basic pay.

Portent number two was that Royal Mail agreed this whole project would be separate and distinct from the annual pay round.

Portent three was that the guy with whom I was negotiating was a skilled and tough negotiator but one I liked and trusted. Having initially described the exercise on which we were engaged as Opening Pandora's Box (which was perhaps unwise, given that in Greek mythology that box contained all the evils of the universe), we sensibly decided on a less fatalistic title: the Employee Agenda, which suggested a distinctive slant towards the wellbeing of the staff.

Despite the portents the negotiations ended in failure. They failed because I didn't do my job properly – it was as simple as that.

The bright young talents I'd nurtured and encouraged were now significant players in the union. Billy Hayes had replaced me as outdoor secretary; John Keggie from Edinburgh was now an influential member of my Executive Council and Dave

Ward, the clever young Tooting postman, was one of our leading officials in London. They recognized the opportunity that the Employee Agenda presented but they were also much more closely attuned to the legitimate concerns of the workforce about the nirvana towards which I was leading them.

Billy and my old comrade Mike Hogan were the officers negotiating with me. Through long hours of discussion, weekends away in bucolic isolation; through tortuous presentations and intricate calculations, we gradually inched our way towards an agreement. The problem was that I wasn't taking the union with me. Impatient with what I saw as the conservatism of activists who viewed 'teamworking' as a bid to undermine the influence of the union, I was relying too much on the destination and not enough on the route to be taken to get there. For me the six-day week was the real evil, not 'teamworking'. I would embark on ill-tempered rants to poor Mike and Billy about my vision of a postman in 2020 being obliged to leave his friends in the pub at 9pm on a Friday evening because, unlike them, he would still be having to work on a Saturday.

'What the hell are you doing still working a six-day week?' his friends would ask.

'Well,' replied my archetypal postman, 'I know the pay's lousy and I'm still doing long hours, but at least my union has protected me from teamworking!'

The negotiations, which began in earnest in the spring of 1996, ended in a marathon session at the headquarters of the Advisory, Conciliation and Arbitration Service (ACAS) in June. It was said that this final round was the longest single negotiating session in the history of industrial relations and would be enshrined in the *Guinness Book of Records*. I'm not sure if that was true. All I do know is that Mike, Billy and I embarked on it at 10.30am on a Thursday and concluded it at 9.30 the next morning.

This was the culmination of six months' toil. We painstakingly finalized each section of a mammoth agreement, sometimes face to face with Royal Mail, more often in separate rooms with ACAS officials ferrying words between us like ambassadors exchanging the gifts of potentates. And when this carefully constructed document, this product of a masterclass in negotiation – this veritable work of art – was presented to the Postal Executive of the CWU, it was rejected. Unanimously.

There are those in the trade-union movement who believe that strike action can achieve what meaningful talks cannot. The reality is that while the threat of a strike can help in the negotiation, once a strike takes place the stakes get higher for both sides and the chances of a successful outcome diminish. The union, conscious of the fact that the members have sacrificed earnings, will become less likely to accept a compromise; the employer, conscious that it will be perceived as having conceded to brute force, will be less likely to offer one.

On the Employee Agenda I'd used a strike ballot to maximum effect – announcing the overwhelming mandate at our annual conference as a prelude to the serious negotiation that was timed to begin directly afterwards. The legislation that made pre-industrial-action ballots a legal requirement had been introduced early in the Thatcher years. The result was that in any serious negotiation the union balloted to ensure that the nuclear option was available to them and the employer offered little in the way of concessions until they were sure that the union had sufficient support from their members. Thus the industrial-action ballot became a kind of barometer, measuring the atmosphere on both sides.

The Thatcher legislation contained a curious device that actually encouraged the response it was designed to prevent. After the ballot had been held it had to be acted upon within four weeks, otherwise it lost its legitimacy and the union would have to ballot all over again. However, once this initial industrial action had been taken there were no further limitations: the mandate lasted for as long as the dispute continued. To prevent being timed out we'd taken a bit of cursory industrial action after the ballot result had been announced and that had extended our mandate sufficiently to allow the long negotiations that had just ended in failure.

Things had changed since the great 1971 Post Office strike. They'd changed even since the DRAS dispute seventeen years later, when what was meant to be a one-day strike had been protracted by Royal Mail's provocative action as our members tried to return to work. There was no longer any appetite in my union – or, I suspect, in any union – for anything other than limited strike action such as a one- or two-day stoppage.

Following the comprehensive rejection of our carefully constructed agreement I was at a loss as to what to do next. I compounded my errors by stupidly expressing my frustration to a journalist in a late-night conversation which I believed was off the record. The subsequent coverage wasn't helpful. Fortunately, I just about maintained the goodwill of a sufficient number of activists to soldier on, although where we were soldiering on to wasn't apparent to anyone.

Royal Mail's insistence on a completely new way of working had been dismissed out of hand and without the 'pro quo' we couldn't extract the 'quid'. In the summer we began a series of weekly one-day strikes. We varied the day so that it was Monday one week and Tuesday the next, and so on, which, ironically, gave our delivery staff the rotating day off contained in the rejected agreement that had been designed to give them a five-day week. I suppose in theory we could have gone on like this for ever – indeed, it was already developing into something of a routine, albeit one that required our members to sacrifice a day's pay every week. We couldn't escalate the dispute because all the feedback from our activists indicated that they were just about holding the line as it was – to push for more than the weekly one-day strike would risk a membership rebellion.

Brian and I kept open our lines of communication both formally (through meetings at which Mike, Billy and I would troop along to Royal Mail headquarters in Old Street) and informally (in the Duke of Wellington pub opposite Waterloo station, where we'd try to construct a way out of the stalemate). In late August I had to wave off Laura and her family when they left without me for the villa we'd rented in Menorca. She'd ring to tell me how wonderful the weather was there as a deep depression set in over Upper Norwood, where I stayed behind alone with the cat.

And so the stalemate continued, and might well have continued to this day if not for a heavily disguised piece of serendipity. At the end of September, as I contemplated a timetable for the next round of one-day stoppages, Brian Thomson rang me to say that Royal Mail were preparing to challenge the industrial action we'd been taking. Apparently, we hadn't correctly declared the number of spoiled ballot papers. There were some nonsensical elements to the law pertaining to industrial-action ballots that could render them null and void for all kinds of ridiculously inconsequential reasons. Accurately declaring spoiled ballot papers was one of them. Brian had considered this to be a minor irrelevance when he'd first been told about it in July, and hadn't bothered to mention it to me. Now, with the dispute dragging on and with no end in sight, the hawks at Royal Mail were gaining the upper hand in pressing for a legal challenge.

I consulted the union's legal advisers and was told by an earnest young barrister named Simon that the discrepancy on spoiled ballot papers could indeed render the strike action we'd been taking for almost five months illegal. I asked what the ramifications were. He said that anyone who could demonstrate that they'd been adversely affected by the strike could seek compensation from the union.

Given the billions of letters and packets that would have been delayed as a result of each one-day strike (and by now we'd had about eight of them), the CWU could potentially be sued out of existence. The young barrister relayed this news to me like a doctor telling a patient he had a terminal illness. 'The union has no alternative,' he said gravely. 'This dispute has to end, forthwith.' I could quite understand the scepticism with which my Postal Executive would greet this information. Our relationship had remained cordial, but if I were them, I'd take any such analysis from me not so much with a pinch of salt as with a large chunk of Siberia.

So Simon, my radical young barrister, came with me to the Postal Executive meeting. By the time he'd finished explaining I could see, looking round the room at the drained, pale faces of my executive, that they appreciated the likely consequences of carrying on without a fresh mandate. If we balloted again, our exhausted members would in all probability vote against any continuation of the industrial action. And in any case, to do this would draw attention to the discrepancy in the first ballot and leave us open to devastation through the courts.

How could we regroup, extricate the union from its perilous position, retain the loyalty of our members and pursue our goal of higher pay and shorter hours for postmen and women? Our salvation was the annual pay round. Having studiously avoided incorporating the Employee Agenda into pay bargaining, both sides now saw the opportunity presented by the fast approaching date of 1 October, when increases from the normal pay round would take effect.

As far as the Employee Agenda was concerned, the Postal Executive voted unanimously for an outcome that we described as 'no victory, no defeat'. The entire kit and caboodle was shunted off into a series of joint working parties that would involve equal numbers of my Postal Executive colleagues and senior Royal Mail managers in a forensic examination of the new working methods that the business was keen to introduce. These would take months to conclude and were entered into without commitment on either side. It was the kind of project we should have commissioned before the negotiations started – except that I doubt Brian and I could have convinced our respective constituencies of this before they had fought each other to a standstill.

At the same time, we concluded a speedy pay agreement, above inflation with no strings attached. Usually the pay took months to finalize and the employer would want changes to working practices as part of the deal. So this was a welcome novelty, coming as it did alongside an end to the dispute and agreement on the way forward on the central issue of 'teamworking'.

All was well again. Except that I felt I'd lost credibility with Royal Mail as a negotiator and with my executive as their leader.

For me, it felt like a personal defeat.

Chapter 8

I WAS DRIVING up Gipsy Hill in south-east London when my newly acquired mobile phone rang and an unimagined future began to take shape.

It was Thursday 13 February 1997. My destination was a small Thai restaurant in South Norwood called the Mantanah, where we were gathering to celebrate my mother-in-law's birthday. I was late. I knew Mo would be wondering where 'Mr Kite' had got to and preparing to give me a good-natured ribbing when I arrived.

Taking the call would make me later still but, thinking it might be Laura, I pulled over, grabbed the phone, which was squatting on the passenger seat (mobiles may have been shrinking in size by now, but mine was still way too bulky to keep in a jacket pocket, unless you were prepared to put up with unsightly bulges), ready to berate my wife for delaying me by trying to hurry me up at the same time.

But it wasn't Laura, it was Anji Hunter, Tony Blair's formidable office manager. Tony wanted to talk to me, she said. Could she put me through?

I knew what this would be about. I'd recently written to the leader of Her Majesty's opposition regarding the selection of a candidate to fight the Newport by-election. There was a rumour that Alan Howarth, a Conservative MP who'd recently crossed the floor of the House, would be imposed on Newport, where the sitting Labour MP had died. I wanted to make certain that an excellent local councillor, Reg Kelly, who was a member of the CWU Telecoms Executive, would have a fair chance of selection in a membership ballot, and my letter sought an undertaking that Howarth would not be a shoo-in.

When Anji put me through Tony Blair reassured me that no candidate would be imposed and that the members would decide who would be their candidate in Newport. We exchanged a few pleasantries before I began to wind up the conversation so that I could rush off to the restaurant. But Tony had something else to say. He asked if I fancied being an MP.

'No,' I replied firmly – and honestly. 'I have never wanted to be an MP.' The truth was that I'd never remotely considered the possibility. What is more, for a general secretary of an affiliated union, hankering after a parliamentary seat would be diagnosed as a case of inverted ambition.

'Oh,' said Tony, slightly disconcerted. 'Somebody told me you were keen to come into Parliament.'

'I don't know who that was, but they obviously don't know me. I've never had any ambition to be a member of Parliament.'

There was a pause. Then Tony said: 'Well, I'd like you to be one.'

He told me that having his photograph taken with every Labour backbencher in preparation for the general election had brought home to him how many of them had 'done nothing but politics' their whole lives. He was concerned about this and wanted more people who'd had 'a proper job'. He felt I'd be ministerial material, although he made it clear he couldn't promise anything in that regard. It all depended on my ability to 'cut the mustard'.

I was stunned. I asked which constituency he envisaged me standing in but he ducked that question. First I needed to decide in principle whether I was prepared to take the leap.

Labour was preparing to table a motion of no confidence in the Major government over the handling of the Maastricht Treaty. There was a chance that it would be carried and trigger a general election a few months earlier than expected. Tony suggested that we speak again after the next monthly Labour party NEC meeting.

I sat for quite a while with the phone in my hand, gazing out at the shimmering yellow glow of a winter's evening reflected in the damp pavements of south London as commuters trudged out of Gipsy Hill station and up towards Crystal Palace. I must have sat transfixed for ten minutes, turning over in my mind the opportunity that had just been presented to me.

When I eventually arrived at the restaurant I was still dazed. But the prospect of a new career had taken root in my mind and I was already weighing up the pros and cons of abandoning the old one.

My stock in the union remained high, in spite of my sense of personal disappointment over the Employee Agenda debacle. The Postal Executive had unanimously agreed the methodology I had hammered out with Brian Thomson to take forward our claim for a better deal for delivery staff and the pay agreement had been overwhelmingly approved by the membership. My future in the new, merged union was pretty secure, Tony Young and I having already agreed that we wouldn't contest one another and that it would be me who stood for the position of CWU general secretary when our period of joint leadership ended the following year.

My reputation among the members had been greatly enhanced by a Michael Cockerell documentary about lobbying and lobbyists, *A Word in the Right Ear*, which had been aired by BBC2 in prime time on 9 January. Daniel Harris, who appeared in the film, had managed to interest Michael – then and now the doyen of political reporting – in featuring our Stand By Your Post campaign.

In the end, our action, described by Cockerell as the most ingenious and sophisticated campaign ever constructed against a government proposal, formed the centrepiece of the hour-long programme. The film quite rightly gave credit to the role played by Lowe Bell, with Sir Tim Bell himself participating, but I was pleased that it placed the lobbying company's involvement in its proper context – as a masterstroke that came near the end of an already successful campaign.

Julia Simpson distributed a videotape of this half-hour extract to every CWU branch, together with some glowing reviews, including one from *The Times* that pronounced the documentary 'the most fascinating television of the evening':

> The lobbying campaign was far too clever and elaborate to go into detail here, but what made the programme so watchable was the added subtext. Johnson casually adding that Bell (who reduced his fees for the union) was very much a Thatcherite and therefore just possibly had a vested interest in humbling Heseltine and Cockerill chipping in with a timely reminder that if this is what a modern, lobby-wise union could achieve

with the Conservatives in office, just think what they might be capable of under a Labour government.

We couldn't have been happier with the response. Branch officials were contacting headquarters to say how proud they felt, reporting that many more members now realized how well spent their subscriptions were; public affairs companies wanted us to talk about the campaign to their clients; the TUC was keen for us to run seminars for other unions. Maybe Tony Blair had been watching, too. The film was shown only a few weeks before our Gipsy Hill phone conversation.

The NEC meeting at which I was to discuss my future face to face with Tony Blair was one of the last to be held at John Smith House near the Elephant and Castle. The Labour party would soon move to Millbank Tower, which dominated the Westminster skyline along the Embankment from the Houses of Parliament. We were moving upmarket. Closer to the seat of power. Preparing for government.

The motion of no confidence had failed to dislodge the Tories early but they had run out of road. They would complete their full five-year term in May and there seemed little doubt that the electorate would finish the job when the people had their say in the general election.

The more I thought about it, the more I liked the idea of being elected to Parliament as part of a Labour majority. Tony Blair was the first Labour leader who was younger than me and he would steer the country into the next millennium, a prospect that held a deep, if abstract, significance. Social justice, greater equality and the eradication of poverty would be our governing principles. Policies such as the national minimum wage, devolution, measures to get young people into work and possibly electoral reform would be implemented; policies I cared about. I could contribute to that, be at the heart of an historic change in the country's fortunes. All this struck me as far more exciting than yet another round of pay bargaining and attending endless conferences.

The Employee Agenda dispute the previous year had been a defining moment in itself. Perhaps the fact that this opportunity to change careers had arisen so soon afterwards found me more ready to consider it than I might otherwise have been. I recognized that it provided an alternative I might well eventually have sought myself once the dust had settled. Instead the alternative was being presented to me.

Of course I would miss the union, but I had never been emotionally attached to it as an institution. It was the people I worked with who created the bond, and many of them had gone or would shortly be going. Added to that, the new union remained a strange beast to me and would become stranger still once we left our grand and familiar surroundings in Clapham, where postal unions had been based since the 1930s, to move to Wimbledon and a building empty of memories.

Laura was keen for me to make the change and I was soon committed in principle. But before taking the plunge I had to have that all-important discussion with Tony Blair on the crucial details: where, how and when? We hadn't spoken since the Gipsy Hill phone call a week or so earlier and for all I knew he might have changed his mind.

That NEC meeting was mundane compared to many I'd attended in the two years I'd been on the governing body of the Labour party. Naturally, I had been elected in the trade-union section, where most of my stablemates were deputies to general secretaries who sat on the TUC General Council, the body I'd left to take up this role, but I much preferred the political to the industrial. Colleagues from other sections of the party included Robin Cook, Mo Mowlam and Ian McCartney, who were all good friends and, of course, John Prescott, who was the deputy leader but someone with whom I'd had little contact.

We'd taken different sides in a bitter row over the school to which shadow Cabinet minister Harriet Harman sent her son. As a fellow resident of south-east London, I was well aware of the poor reputation of Harriet's local comprehensive (and indeed of most London schools in that terrible period of educational under-investment and shockingly low levels of attainment). The grant-maintained grammar to which Harriet's son would be going, along with many of his primary-school classmates, was a state school and it was ludicrous that the NEC of the Labour party should be discussing an issue that ought only to have been the concern of Harriet and her husband, the senior trade unionist Jack Dromey, a man I'd known and admired since the Grunwick dispute in the 1970s. John Prescott, who had taken a different view, had glared at me across the substantial NEC boardroom table when I spoke in support of Harriet.

That row was history now and today's meeting featured no such volatile issues. Tony Blair gave a report on preparations for the general election and engaged in some light banter with Dennis Skinner, renowned as an uncompromising figure from the hard-left Socialist Campaign Group. He and Tony should have been mortal enemies but there was a surprising level of affectionate respect between them. As I got to know Dennis better, I realized that behind the dogmatic image he'd created for himself lay an understanding better than most that while politics without principle was unethical, principles without power were futile.

Dennis saw Tony Blair as a winner, somebody who could acquire and retain power in the interests of the people he represented in the former coalfields of Derbyshire. Somebody who would knock the Tories for six on a regular basis. They always listened intently to each other's contributions and I think Tony viewed Dennis as an authentic voice of working-class communities, untainted by the perceived de haut en bas tendencies of the middle-class revolutionaries.

When the meeting finished I was summoned to a quiet room at the back of the building where Tony was waiting for me alone. He told me again that he was seeking a broader swathe of experience in the parliamentary Labour party; that the talented postwar trade-union intake had virtually all gone. He wanted me in the PLP and while he could guarantee nothing, there was every possibility that I'd be a minister. I'd have to serve my apprenticeship and prove my capability in the House. I wasn't bothered about that. I had no ambition to be a minister. I posed the question I'd put to him on the phone: precisely where would I contest a parliamentary seat?

He asked where I would like to stand. I told him that, since I was a Londoner, London would be the obvious place. There were, apparently, a number of seats that would become vacant in the period leading up to the election, but none in London, unless he could induce one particular MP to step down and accept a peerage. Seats were liable to be vacated further north that he felt I should consider.

There was one substantial problem weighing on my mind. I couldn't risk going for selection and failing. It would leave me swinging in the wind as far as my current job was concerned. If CWU members saw that I'd tried unsuccessfully to become a Labour MP, they were bound to conclude that I wasn't sufficiently dedicated to the job of general secretary to warrant re-election in 1998. I could, of course, be selected and then fail to be elected as an MP, but that was unlikely given that I would be standing in an existing Labour seat and all the signs were that we'd be gaining rather than losing seats in the general election. Tony said he understood my concern and told me not to worry about it. Sally Morgan in his private office would stay in touch with me.

We'd talked for fifteen minutes before somebody poked their head round the door to remind Tony that he had to leave for his next meeting. We shook hands. 'You've made the right decision,' he said. I hadn't actually given him any decision, although it is fair to say that all my reasonable objections had been removed. I was content for him to interpret my silence as affirmation.

And so began a strange but exhilarating six weeks of living one kind of life while preparing for another. I confided in only two people (beyond Laura's immediate family, who had been sworn to secrecy after I'd been unable to contain the reason for my lateness at the Mantanah Thai restaurant on Mo's birthday).

I was a great believer in the adage, originating from a remark of Abraham Lincoln's, that 'It's not me who can't keep a secret, it's the people I tell them to.' I told my PA, Dorothy Lovett, and Mario Dunn, who had switched from the research department to become head of policy in the new union. I had complete trust in both of them and I needed them to know to be able to liaise effectively with Sally Morgan.

I'm not sure what I was expecting from Sally, but what I got was radio silence. On 17 March the countdown to the general election began with the announcement by the prime minister, John Major, that it would be held on 1 May. He'd opted for the longest possible campaign – six weeks – in the forlorn hope that the opinion polls would turn in his favour.

The next day I travelled with Tony Young to Birmingham where, on the first day of campaigning, we were due to attend a CWU event in support of Gisela Stuart, who was attempting to win Edgbaston, a Tory seat for as long as anyone could remember. On the train from Euston we gaped incredulously at the front page of the *Sun*, then the top-selling newspaper in the UK, which informed its millions of readers that, for the first time since Margaret Thatcher came to power, it was switching its support to Labour.

That train journey provided me with the perfect opportunity to confide in my friend and colleague, but I didn't. I felt that it would be unfair to burden him with the secret and, if the news leaked out, leave him open to the suspicion that it could have been him who'd blabbed. So neither he nor Gisela knew that I intended at some stage to become a candidate myself, in a more winnable seat, it was to be hoped, than Edgbaston.

I was acutely aware of how lucky I was to be earmarked for

the political equivalent of the Parachute Regiment and dropped into a safe seat. Gisela, like every other candidate, had had to work hard to get selected. The normal route involved wooing party branches, attending numerous meetings and often moving your entire family to the constituency you hoped to represent. Some budding politicians had spent substantial chunks of their lives seeking nomination, relocating from constituency to constituency and fighting unwinnable seats as a necessary precursor to landing a winnable one. They had to put in the effort; all I had to do was wait for a phone call.

We were well into the six-week campaign before I took the initiative and rang Sally Morgan to check that everything was OK. Pontefract had been vacated and filled (by Yvette Cooper), as had other seats. They all required selection by local party members. Indeed, Yvette had defeated my friend Jack Dromey – exactly the fate I was keen to avoid. Fortunately for Jack, he was an appointed official of the Transport and General Workers' Union rather than an elected officer, so his defeat wasn't fatal to his career as it could have been to mine.

Sally told me to relax. The attempt to find a vacancy for me in London had failed but two other seats looked like becoming available even further into the campaign, at a stage when the NEC and not the local members would decide who Labour's candidate should be.

So I continued to trudge the streets of London SE19, delivering election leaflets urging the recipients to 'Vote Wicks' in what was then the Croydon North West constituency, aware that at some stage in this campaign I'd be trudging the streets of some other, as yet unknown constituency asking the electorate to 'Vote Johnson.' My transition would hardly be a major event, leading the news and sending shockwaves around the world. But while I braced myself for the more minor shockwaves to my own world, wrapped in the mystery and uncertainty of it all, I had a dark, preternatural sense of being projected into the unknown.

On the evening of 28 March, eleven days into the campaign, I'd gone with Laura's family to a local Harvester restaurant near the top of Beulah Hill. It was Good Friday and we'd plumped for the only eating place within easy walking distance. The great clay ridge of Beulah Hill is one of the highest areas in London and was used in the eighteenth century as a sighting point to measure the precise distance between the royal observatories of Greenwich and Paris.

On this clear, calm night, as we were walking back from the restaurant, we looked up in astonishment to see the Hale-Bopp comet trailing its tails of blue gas and yellow dust across the evening sky. It was such an amazing event that I spent the next hour or so standing on a bench in our back garden, not wanting to waste a moment of my chance to witness a phenomenon that, until recent months, hadn't been seen by human eye since the days of the ancient Egyptians and wouldn't be seen again until about 4380.

The comet would pass perihelion, where it is nearest to its point of orbit, four days later and would be visible from somewhere on Earth until the end of the year, but few people would have had as clear a view of it as I did on that tranquil evening in south London.

To me it represented something significant but inexplicable. I had none of my mother's religious convictions, still less the belief in mystics and astrologists that she and my sister shared.

But Hale-Bopp affected me as if its gas and dust had entered my veins. I could so easily have spent that evening indoors without a glance towards the north-west sky. And while the magnificent spectacle continued to appear and, like everyone else, we were aware of its existence, to see it on that night, so sharply defined, seemed to me to be a portent; a celestial message that all would be well in the new future that was being shaped for me. Hale-Bopp was searing the sky for me and me alone.

My daughter Emma wrote a poem when she was little that began with the line: 'Everything is go and push.' It was a phrase that neatly encapsulated my three-day metamorphosis from trade-union leader into prospective parliamentary candidate.

Sally Morgan rang Mario, Mario rang me, I rang Sally Morgan. Two Labour-held parliamentary seats had become available, the incumbents having resigned to accept peerages. Candidates must now be found for Dudley North and Hull West and Hessle. It was 9 April and we were halfway through the election campaign. In these circumstances a subcommittee of the NEC would decide who the candidates should be, rather than the local party. As part of my application for the nomination I was to send a CV to Labour headquarters at Millbank Tower.

I'd never drawn up a CV before. Never had to. Nobody asked for one when I left school and began my working life as a post-room boy at Remington Electric Razors at the age of fifteen years and two months. At Tesco and Anthony Jackson supermarkets I'd just turned up, met the manager for a bit of a chat and started work the following Monday. There had been none of these formalities to comply with. At eighteen I'd become a postman, which in those days meant becoming a civil servant, so there was an aptitude test and all kinds of documents to complete and sign, including the Official Secrets Act. But no CV had been requested or submitted. If it had, it would have been a very scanty dossier. Qualifications: none. Educational attainment: zero.

Now at least I could record my rise through the union ranks and in the section dealing with 'education' I could mention the TUC certificates in various subjects acquired through the correspondence courses I'd completed after becoming a union branch official.

Provided I didn't make a total mess of my appearance before the NEC panel, the position of parliamentary candidate was mine. Sally told me that the interview would take place on Friday 11 April. It would consist of a four-minute opening statement from me as to why I thought I was the best applicant, followed by the kind of detailed interrogation normally reserved for candidates at by-elections, where public scrutiny was always more intense. I had a day to prepare.

Sally asked if I had any skeletons in my cupboard. I had a good rummage around while pondering the question but couldn't come up with anything that would interest the media. I certainly hadn't smoked cannabis at university, which seemed to be the subject of most interest to the press, and I figured that being a child smoker of untipped Woodbines required no confession.

I was due to be in Cologne that Friday to participate in a debate on 'job creation in a global economy' at the invitation of a German charity. It was therefore agreed that I would be interviewed first and then hotfoot it to the airport without waiting for the outcome. Sally asked me which of the two seats I wanted to be interviewed for, Dudley North or Hull West and Hessle?

Mario had already briefed me on these two constituencies. I wanted to stand in Hull. It was where my mother's younger sister, my Auntie Dolly, had lived since shortly after the war, having married a Hull soldier by the name of Les Foster.

Lily and Dolly had both worked at the NAAFI in London and Les had been Lily's boyfriend until Dolly enticed him away. It caused a rift so deep that the two sisters didn't communicate for a decade, until my mother, Linda and I visited Hull as part of the peace process and spent a week there with Uncle Les, Auntie Dolly and their expanding family, which eventually produced a cousin count of nine.

Just as I followed the results of Liverpool and Everton in homage to my mother's birthplace, after this visit to Hull in 1955 I began to keep tabs on the fortunes of Hull City. I could still recite the names of players such as Chris Chilton, Andy Davidson and Ken Wagstaff from their glory days of the 1960s (if almost winning promotion from the second division can be so described).

Hull West and Hessle also happened to be the safer Labour seat, so there was no contest, really. It had to be Hull. With a bit of luck, I could rely on a familial block vote.

Once I'd appeared at the selection meeting the secret would be out so I had to use the intervening day to tell my close friends Tony Young, Mike Hogan and Brian Thomson and, of course, my deputy, Derek Hodgson. The next morning, soon after arriving at work, I duly asked Derek to step into my office. He sat on the other side of my desk without the slightest idea why I was engaging him in this solemn conclave. As I broke the news of my imminent departure I watched him struggle to contain his exaltation. Decorum dictated that he appear suitably regretful and he did his very best, pledging eternal allegiance, assuring me that he'd protect my legacy in the union. I admired his self-restraint. Derek's chance to become general secretary, the ambition that had been thwarted by my victory five years before, had just been resuscitated. Given that he was only four years away from the compulsory officers' retirement age of sixty, it would be his last shot, and he could never had dreamed that it would fall into his lap so suddenly and so entirely unexpectedly. To borrow Derek's own indelicate phrase, he was as happy as a dog with two cocks in a forest full of lampposts.

On the Friday morning the local cab I'd ordered was ten minutes late arriving. Thanks to my fast if chatty driver, who happened to have worked in the Post Office for twenty years and insisted on talking me through every one of them, I arrived in time at the headquarters of the Iron and Steel Trades Confederation in Gray's Inn Road, where the interviews were to take place. As I walked up the stairs towards the venue I bumped into my opposite number at the steelworkers' union, Keith Brookman, who was astounded to learn that I would be swapping the top job in my union for the bottom job in the parliamentary Labour party. There were precedents. Ernest Bevin and, twenty years later, Frank Cousins had left their posts at the head of the Transport and General Workers' Union to enter Parliament. But both had been recruited to be government ministers, with seats being found for them only as vehicles for them to perform their ministerial duties in the Commons rather than in the Lords.

Apart from the stature of these men, there was another significant difference between their situation and mine. Bevin and Cousins were seconded to the government. Their position in their union was preserved so that they could return to being general secretary whenever they wanted to. In my case it would mean a complete break. Whether or not I was elected, my career with the CWU would be over.

I joined nine other people in the waiting room, five candidates for each position to be filled. Among those eagerly pursuing the Hull West and Hessle vacancy were Hilary Benn, who at the time was a union official, Ealing councillor Stephen Alambritis, who headed up the Federation of Small Businesses, and a Hull councillor and former mayor, John Black.

Competing for Dudley North was Charlie Falconer who, I knew from Sally, was the other person Tony Blair wanted in Parliament. Charlie was an old friend and former flatmate of Tony's and a QC who was earmarked for the post of solicitor general. We'd never met so I introduced myself and we bonded instantly, like members of a secret sect wishing each other luck. Almost immediately, I was called for my interview. The panel consisted of good friends like Mo Mowlam, Tom Sawyer and Ian McCartney, along with other NEC colleagues. I completed the formalities without mishap and dashed off for London City airport, where a private jet (laid on by the German charity organizing the conference, I should add) would take me to Cologne. I arrived at the venue at 1.30pm and an hour later, having delivered my twenty-minute speech, I took a scheduled flight to Gatwick via Amsterdam and was back in my house in Upper Norwood by 7.30pm.

That evening I was advised by the party that I'd been adopted as the candidate for Hull West and Hessle and that this would be announced formally the following day. The official who'd relayed the news also told me about the various problems the party had experienced with the constituency. 'We call it Hell West and Hassle,' she said cheerily.

Apparently, the MP I was replacing, Stuart Randall (who was not someone I knew at all), had escaped deselection by only one vote. There was open warfare between pro-Randall and anti-Randall supporters, and one branch of the constituency party was suspended. She apologized that nobody had said anything about this prior to my application, but she was sure that I'd be able to sort things out.

John Prescott, who had been the MP for the neighbouring seat of Hull East for twenty-seven years, also rang me that evening. He told me that John Black, the Hull councillor who'd been one of my rivals earlier in the day, shouldn't have applied. He was, it seemed, active in John's constituency. But as the councillor responsible for housing across the city, he'd steered through a controversial public–private partnership to improve conditions on a housing estate in west Hull, which led to a vicious battle between himself and Randall. When Randall agreed to stand down in order to create the vacancy, he did so on the assurance that no Hull councillor would be in the running for the seat. Black had slipped through the net and John Prescott was furious that the deal he'd helped broker had been breached in this way.

From this conversation I felt I could safely predict that when

I got to Hull I'd have a friend in John Prescott but an adversary in John Black.

Having heard nothing about the Dudley North selection, I sought confirmation of what I was sure was the inevitable nomination of Charlie Falconer. To my astonishment, John Prescott told me that no decision had been made. Another panel would be convened in Dudley to decide on a candidate the next day.

I couldn't understand how this had happened. Charlie Falconer was supposed to have been a shoo-in for Dudley North, just as I had been for Hull West and Hessle. I called Mo Mowlam, who was delighted to share the gossip. Charlie, like me, should indeed have been a shoo-in. The snag was that his children were being educated privately.

For a Conservative candidate this would have presented no obstacle to selection. Previous Labour prime ministers, too, had sent their children to public schools without a murmur of rebuke. But times had changed and Labour was now hypersensitive on the subject. One of our principal criticisms of the Tories was that they'd run down public services such as health and education having insulated themselves and their families against the effects through public-school education for their kids and private medical insurance for their nearest and dearest.

Mo told me that the panel's key question was whether, if state education improved under a Labour government, he would send his children to local state schools.

'No, I wouldn't,' Charlie had replied with the honesty and good humour for which he is rightly admired. 'I'd still have them educated privately.' So the NEC subcommittee refused to endorse Charlie Falconer, or anybody else, for Dudley North after the interviews. Instead the party encouraged another lawyer, Ross Cranston, to apply. His nomination would be sealed the next day at a second manufactured selection meeting in Dudley.

Charlie was given a peerage and would participate in governing the country from the House of Lords. And had I not heard the tale from Mo, I would never have known what had happened. There was, though, an interesting codicil to the story.

I remained on the NEC until the next elections in September of that year. In July we had before us for endorsement the minutes of the selection panel that had approved my candidature and failed to approve Charlie's three months earlier. The minutes consisted of no more than the names of the candidates and the outcome. As I glanced at the document prior to its formal adoption, I noticed that my name appeared as one of the candidates for Dudley North as well as for Hull West and Hessle.

I searched in vain for any reference to Charlie Falconer. I was about to raise my hand to point out the error in my own candidacy when a stab of realization struck me. With Charlie's name going unrecorded, the minutes would have been short of the number of candidates required for Dudley North. So it was necessary to present me as a carpetbagger, eagerly applying for both seats, to ensure five names were listed for each. I held my tongue and we moved on to the next business.

In a manoeuvre worthy of the KGB, Charlie Falconer's failed application was to be written out of history.

Chapter 9

ON 14 APRIL 1997, just over two weeks before polling day, I boarded the train to Hull from King's Cross. It was some forty-two years since the last and only other time I'd made this journey, with my mother and sister to visit Auntie Dolly and Uncle Les.

I had a distant recollection of that trip having been made in the winter, all three of us sitting frozen stiff in a compartment with a sliding door on one side that led out on to a corridor linking all the other compartments in the carriage. I remembered a city of bombsites and gangs of kids and a skiffle band playing on a street corner. My most vivid memory was of a magical evening at Spurn Point, where Uncle Les had taken us in his wood-framed Morris Traveller.

On my second train journey to Hull I took a volume of Philip Larkin's collected poems that Laura had bought for me in our early days together. In 'Here', Larkin, perhaps Hull's most famous adopted son, describes the final approach to the city:

And the widening river's slow presence,
The piled gold clouds, the shining gull-marked mud,
Gathers to the surprise of a large town

Speeding past the Humber Bridge and out along the seven-mile expanse of the great tidal estuary, I could see exactly what he meant. It was a clear day and the window of the carriage could hardly contain the vastness of the sky. Travelling alone on an almost empty train, I tried to absorb every scenic detail as we slowed towards the end of the line, Hull Paragon station, past the usual railside tangle of bramble and thorn and houses that had fallen into disrepair. An advertisement for 'Trippet's Gloves and Hosiery' painted on to the gable end of one row looked as if it would have been faded even on my last visit.

I don't know what I was expecting when I got off the train. A welcome committee? A brass band? One thing was for sure: there wouldn't be a media scrum. The political officer of the local CWU branch, Andy Parrish, had called me during my journey and explained that national coverage was virtually irrelevant in a city where people relied predominantly on local media for their news. Stuart Randall's departure had been a major story but there had been little mention of my arrival as the new candidate. As the train passed beneath the station's magnificent five-arch roof, it became clear that what I would be met by was a healthy indifference.

Hull is a city that just gets on with life. It has an aversion to pomp. Three historic incidents illustrate its stubbornly contrarian nature. In 1642, the governor of Hull, Sir John Hotham, refused entry to King Charles I on two separate occasions, depriving the monarch of access to the large arsenal within the city walls, which was instead placed at the disposal of the Parliamentarians. Later in the Civil War, both he and his son were executed for their trouble.

Fast forward to early in the twentieth century, when the Liberal government was placing the nascent telephone services across the country under the umbrella of the GPO. The municipal authority decided, by the casting vote of its chair, to refuse to comply. Hull and the East Riding still has its own telephone service to this day, its cream public call boxes a badge of its BT-free empire.

Even the great Paul McCartney came up against a brick wall in Hull. When he formed Wings in the early 1970s, the band decided to go back to basics. They loaded their gear into a van and travelled the country, simply turning up at venues and taking to the stage, to the delight of audiences in the regions. But on turning up at Hull university, the most famous pop star in the world was told that he couldn't play there because a local country and western band had already been booked.

At least the local CWU branch was mildly excited about my arrival. Andy Parrish was to become a huge support and close friend. The first thing I'd noticed about him in that phone conversation on the train was his accent: a very distinctive Yorkshire variation with flat vowels that made the men sound almost camp. As Maureen Lipman, a noted Hullensian, says, in Hull a pearl is somebody who comes from Poland.

There were, it transpired, two people waiting for me on the station concourse: the chair and the secretary of Hull West and Hessle constituency Labour party (CLP). Trina Peat, a small, feisty Unison official, and John Atkinson, the septuagenarian

CLP secretary, took me to the station café and gave me a fifteen-minute state-of-the-constituency briefing over a cup of tea.

The local party was, as I'd been told, divided into two factions, the pro-Randall camp, which backed my predecessor, and the anti-Randall camp, which didn't. Each camp had a separate election HQ. The party owned its own building but Stuart Randall was refused access to that and denied a key. So he and his supporters had rented their own offices for the duration of the campaign at the other end of the Hessle Road.

The fissure had been opened by the reselection process that Stuart had survived by just one vote. This was solid Labour territory. Hull city council had sixty seats, fifty-nine of which were Labour (one Labour councillor had failed to pay his membership fee on time and was therefore sitting as an independent). With no political opposition, the party had turned against itself.

One of the west Hull wards had been suspended by party HQ because of the threats and allegations being hurled across the divide. That ward had a councillor whose name would have been perfect for a country and western singer: Nadine Fudge. I soon discovered that Nadine was having to deal with far more profound issues than an election – her adult son had gone missing during a night out with friends in Liverpool. I was to learn a lot about coping with personal tragedy while soldiering on in the day job from Nadine.

John Atkinson was my self-appointed agent for the duration of the election campaign, but I was told that we would need to get all the party paraphernalia – balloons, posters, stickers and so on – from a man called John Cherry, who'd been Stuart's agent. I asked John Atkinson to take me over to John Cherry's house to pick up the stuff. He agreed but remained in the car rather than have to make contact with the enemy.

Keen to heal the rift, I assured John Cherry that I'd have been perfectly happy for him to continue in his role. He made it clear he wouldn't have done so, but he did give me some sage advice about the major protagonists in the local party.

I asked him how many voters we'd made contact with, where the phone banks were and how the canvass returns were going. He put a hand on my shoulder and, with a look of indulgence in his twinkling eyes, said: 'We don't worry about things like that in Hull, Alan. Don't fret, lad – you'll win.'

On the evening of my arrival I was due to appear before my constituency party members for the first time at what was rather misleadingly called an adoption meeting. In reality, of course, Hull West and Hessle constituency had no option other than to adopt me as their candidate. Andy Parrish and two other senior officials of the CWU turned up to watch over their general secretary like a detail of the Swiss Guard during a papal audience. As I delivered my carefully prepared speech I saw nothing but friendly faces, on both sides of the Randall divide, among the seventy or so members packed into the party's HQ – the building Stuart wasn't allowed to enter.

One of the principal protagonists in the internal strife I met that night was Colin Inglis, the son of a trawlerman and a local councillor of pin-sharp intelligence. Colin was also openly gay. At that time it was still difficult to be gay anywhere in Britain, where Thatcher's Section 28 – legislation that prohibited local authorities from 'promoting' homosexuality or gay 'pretended family relationships', which was not repealed across the whole of the UK until 2003 – was a notorious representation of the prejudice that still existed. In cities like Hull it could be even harder. Tough working-class communities prized conformity.

While Hull certainly wasn't New Labour territory – to employ the term being used to emphasize the party's more innovative agenda – in the sense that modernity and change were treated with suspicion here, the tensions were about personalities rather than ideology. John Atkinson had apparently been a supporter of Militant Tendency, but the CLP had never fallen to the Trotskyites and nobody else seemed to share his nostalgia for the political chaos of the early eighties.

My most awkward moment of the adoption meeting came when I was asked if I intended to move my family to Hull. It would have been foolish to fudge the issue. Laura had already made it clear that while she was completely supportive of my change of direction, I shouldn't expect her to become some kind of accompanist to my performances on this new stage. She had her own career (she was by this time working at the Institute of Psychiatry at Denmark Hill) and south London was her home. Our house was half an hour's drive from Westminster (only twenty minutes late at night, when the traffic was light). It would be crazy for her to leave her job, move to a strange environment over 200 miles from her close-knit family and live on her own for four or five nights a week, while I was in London trying to rent a place as close to Westminster as the house we would have had to sell.

I explained to the adoption meeting that an MP with a constituency so far from London had to have two residences. Which one he or she determined to be the family home must be a personal decision. It was an argument that seemed to be accepted and the rest of the Q&A passed uneventfully. The fact that I wasn't from Hull certainly didn't count against me. No Hull MP in any constituency had actually been born in the city since William Wilberforce in 1780. John Prescott was from north Wales and Kevin McNamara, who'd been MP for Hull North since 1966, was a Scouser. My trade-union background helped as I set out to win hearts and minds among my party members as a prelude to winning over the electorate.

The problem with taking over the candidacy halfway through the campaign was that the message for over three weeks had been 'Vote Randall' – and indeed this was already being displayed on posters around the constituency. Stuart's predecessor, the MP for Hull West for twenty years, had been the late James Johnson and there were apparently still some 'Vote Johnson' posters knocking around from that time. But it didn't seem like a good idea to be fighting a modern election with material from a distant era.

So we left those posters in the history section and had some new ones printed in record time. Andy Parrish took two weeks of his annual leave in order to drive me around in his pure white people-carrier, which he'd equipped with a loudspeaker connected to the car's cassette-player so that we could blare (and Blair) out D-Ream's 'Things Can Only Get Better' as we toured every street in the constituency.

Andy was a postman, married to Sue, a librarian, with two small children and a mortgage to pay. His decency, modesty and understated spirit of generosity epitomized the values of this working-class city. There were many within and without the Labour party who helped to make me feel welcome in this completely new environment, but Andy's was the most reassuring presence of all throughout that hectic fortnight. He was the bridge between my old life and the one on which I was about to embark.

At 2.30am on 2 May 1997, in the elegant council chamber of the magnificent Guildhall, the chief executive of Hull city council announced the result for the Hull West and Hessle constituency.

In 1992 Stuart Randall had acquired a healthy majority of 10,585. But since then, Hessle, a quiet market town of around 10,000 residents, had been wrenched away from the safe Conservative seat of Beverley and hitched on to Hull West. This was expected to dilute the Labour vote. It didn't. My majority was 15,525. I had been in Hull for seventeen days and taken 58.7 per cent of the vote.

I wasn't foolish enough to think that this emphatic victory had anything to do with my charm and panache. There have been members of Parliament who have believed that their substantial majorities were a personal vote. For a very small number of them this may even be true. I had no such illusions. My vote reflected the popularity of my party and in particular of its leader. Under our awful electoral system, voters are given only one choice. They have no way of differentiating between the MP who represents them in Parliament and the party they want to form the government. In most cases these may well be one and the same, but if they are not, our disempowering first-past-the-post system – as well as being disproportionate, and rendering a vote for one political party in the safe territory of another a futile gesture – doesn't allow for a distinction to be made. I would try to change the system that elected me but I couldn't have been happier with the constituency I was to represent.

The following Saturday a party was held at a local social club to celebrate my win. As we danced the night away, I hoped that the disunity and rancour would disappear as quickly as the booze behind the well-stocked bar. I left at midnight, an hour before the event was due to end, only to be woken by a phone call from Andy in the early hours. After I'd gone there had been a resumption of old hostilities between a few of the attendees. There had been no real violence, thank goodness, but some significant pushing and shoving accompanied by plenty of loud expletives. It was serious enough for complaints to be submitted to Labour's regional HQ and a week later I was asked to write a report for the NEC, of which I remained a member.

Those involved were John Black, John Cherry and Nadine Fudge. As I wrote my report it struck me that this sounded like not so much a fracas as an exotic dessert – Black Cherry Fudge. But even this incident could not detract from the sweetness of my success.

Hull was described in Larkin's 'Bridge for the Living' as:

> Isolate city spread alongside water,
> Posted with white towers, she keeps her face
> Half-turned to Europe, lonely northern daughter,
> Holding through centuries her separate place.

Closer to Rotterdam than to London, its remote position gave Hull access to the North Sea and spawned the livelihood with which it is most closely associated; the livelihood that fed the city and killed its sons. Fishing. This is the industry in which Hull's civic pride is rooted; which provided the riches that largely insulated it against economic depression until that industry collapsed. The wealth and the squalor, the best and worst of Hull, were all linked to fishing, the trade that held the city's separate place through all those centuries.

During my fortnight of getting to know Hull West and Hessle – a kind of political speed-dating – I'd visited factories and schools, offices and shopping centres, and met hundreds of people. But one meeting in particular made a lasting impression and would shape my workload in the strange occupation I had been encouraged to adopt. It gave me a cause to which to nail my colours in a constituency I knew would be weighing me up.

Two days after my arrival in Hull I was asked to meet a delegation of trawlermen from the British Fishermen's Association at the office in north Hull of the member of the European Parliament (MEP) for the area, Peter Crampton. The BFA was an organization the trawlermen had been driven to form themselves, having been abandoned by every other institution that could have helped them: the trawler owners, their trade union and, above all, the government.

These men had left school at fourteen and gone straight to the docks to be 'decky learners', junior deckhands on Arctic trawlers. Each of these ships took its crew of around twenty into the most perilous seas in the world. Once there, the trawler would fish for weeks on end before returning to port, where the men's pay would be calculated according to the size of the catch and its market price. The BFA representatives in Peter Crampton's office that morning, the Hull committee, numbered seven. Most of them, like Ron Bateman, the chairman, and Brian Commander, the treasurer, were short and stocky. I could imagine them braced against a Force 10 gale, shooting the trawl or hauling in the catch; sturdy men whose reliance on one another forged their approach to life – and death. For this was the most dangerous of jobs. One assessment of distant-water trawling put its mortality rate at seventeen times higher than coalmining.

I listened, barely able to comprehend what I was hearing, as Peter Crampton, a former teacher and an eloquent and tireless campaigner for the trawlermen, relayed the horrifying statistics. In 150 years of distant-water trawling, 900 Hull ships had been lost. In the last ninety-two-year period of its history, between the completion of the newest fish dock and the collapse of the industry, 8,000 men were lost from Hull alone.

Hull had been by far the biggest distant-water port. The others – Grimsby, Hull's great rival on the north Lincolnshire coast, just across the Humber, Fleetwood and Aberdeen – all fished in 'near' and 'middle' waters as well. Only Hull's trawlers fished exclusively in 'distant' Arctic waters: the Barents Sea, Bear Island, Spitzbergen.

The industry employed thousands. The men who went to sea were the most numerous, but there were the auxiliary industries, too: engineering, net-making, ship's chandlery, the 'bobbers' who unloaded the catches, ship's husbands, who acted as the owners' agents and managers onshore, runners. All of this activity had been centred on the Hessle Road and all of the BFA committee members had been born in one of the streets leading off this mile-long thoroughfare.

Hessle Road was at the heart of my constituency and these

men and their grievance were my responsibility. As we sat in Peter Crampton's office, drinking mugs of tea, I was still absorbing the catalogue of dangers they endured to bring home 'the silver harvest' as they moved on to the story of how the industry had collapsed and thousands of distant-water trawlermen had been thrown on the scrapheap. I listened with growing incredulity, and then real anger,

There was one simple reason for the demise of distant-water trawling in the early 1970s and it had nothing to do with Britain's membership of the European Economic Community or that institution's Common Fisheries Policy. The collapse had been caused by the British government's agreement to the imposition by Iceland of a 200-mile fishing limit around its coast.

The Icelandic people were almost entirely dependent on the fish that shoaled close to their shores. Fish stocks in the Barents Sea were being systematically destroyed and Iceland had introduced limits in the 1950s and 1960s, first of three miles, then four, then twelve. This final extension was considered by the UK government to be a breach of international law and the Royal Navy was deployed to accompany British trawlers, which cheerfully ignored the latest restrictions.

Iceland had no standing armed forces. The four or five tiny gunboats they did have were, however, fast and highly manoeuvrable. They deployed the effective tactic of towing a wire-cutter across the trawl warps of any vessel found inside the limits, thus chopping the trawlers' gear away.

They also had a major advantage in that NATO had a base at Keflavik, an Icelandic port from which the Americans operated an early-warning defence system. This was an important aspect of the Cold War (here the term took on a literal dimension – humans have rarely inhabited anywhere colder). In exchange for the base facilities the USA had guaranteed to defend Icelandic sovereignty.

Iceland took its case for extended fishing limits to NATO, making a strong case for the preservation of fish stocks. They won the vote but what became known as the Cod Wars (not to be confused with the Cold War) continued, coming to a head when Iceland broke off diplomatic relations with Britain for ignoring the NATO vote. That was when Iceland declared the 200-mile limit. At the same time they issued America with an ultimatum: get British warships out of Icelandic waters or leave Keflavik. Washington leaned on Whitehall and the Navy withdrew.

The British government agreed the 200-mile limit and, at a stroke, made almost all of the distant-water fishing grounds inaccessible.

Generous quotas were offered by Iceland that would have preserved a substantial chunk of the catch. But this offer was rejected by the trawler owners who, unlike the men, had substantial influence in Whitehall. Soon Russia, Norway, Canada and Greenland followed Iceland's example, extending the fishing limits around their own Arctic coasts and imposing quotas until there was nowhere left for the distant-water fleet to fish. The owners received decommissioning grants totalling £15 million. Not a penny was passed on to the trawlermen.

In 1974 a Labour minister announced to Parliament that the trawlermen would be looked after. They would receive compensation, retraining for other jobs, redeployment and relocation. They received nothing. These men, who worked eighteen hours on and six hours off in one of the most dangerous occupations in the world; who had manned the trawlers converted into minesweepers around the British coast during the Second World War and who had been expected to look out for and report sightings of particular Russian warships of interest to the Ministry of Defence, were classified as 'casual' workers and therefore not even entitled to the pittance of statutory redundancy.

The 200-mile limit had been applied from 1 January 1974. These men had been fighting for justice for twenty-three years.

Unlike the dockers in east Hull, the trawlermen were never heavily unionized. It was almost impossible to organize effectively in an industry where the men were split into hundreds of small crews, where naval discipline applied at sea and where pay depended more on the size of the catch than on a negotiated wage structure. The leading lights of the BFA, such as Ron Bateman and Ray Smith, the BFA secretary, had been Transport and General Workers' Union shop stewards but they could never recruit more than a minority of their fellow trawlermen into the union.

Ray was exceptional in more ways than one. For a start, unlike the majority of trawlermen, he was big; huge, even – six foot three, with broad shoulders and hands like shovels. Like Ron, he had the kind of intelligence that, had he been born in different circumstances, could have taken him to university and, in all probability, on to a more lucrative and less dangerous line of work. Ray was studious, fascinated by history and had the clearsightedness to place the struggle of the trawlermen into an historical context. He also had an anti-authoritarian streak which made him a marked man for much of his fishing career.

He once told me how he'd been sent to prison for disobeying

an order at sea. In the middle of a fishing trip during which some of the men had fallen ill, Ray had been instructed to join the filleters – the men who worked on deck in all weathers with sharp knives, skilfully carving the newly caught fish into fillets before packing them in ice, often in the midst of howling gales with fish guts and gore slopping around all over the place. Ray's objection that he was a deckhand with no experience of filleting was rejected and the first mate ordered him to comply. He refused. This impudence was classed as mutiny and he ended up serving a custodial sentence in Strangeways prison.

He explained how the prisoners ranked themselves into a hierarchy according to the crimes they'd committed. Respect was afforded, in descending order, to armed robbers, violent gang members, burglars and so on. Sitting around with his fellow prisoners shortly after his arrival, he was asked what he was in for. He was reluctant to admit that he had been banged up for refusing to fillet fish. In a flash of inspiration, he managed to be truthful without forfeiting respect. He told them he'd been involved in a knife crime.

As the industry wound down after the new fishing limit was imposed, the men waited for the help they'd been promised, relying until then on the greatest defence the fishing community possessed: stoicism. By the early eighties it was clear that compensation from government would never materialize and that most of the trawler owners had taken their decommissioning grants and fled. The TGWU had supported a couple of industrial tribunals where individuals sought to prove that their long service made a nonsense of their designation as 'casual', but when these cases failed the TGWU took the view that they couldn't continue to support a lost cause. It was then that the ex-trawlermen decided to form the British Fishermen's Association.

The BFA constitution set out the four main claims to which the men felt they were entitled, namely: £1,000 a year for each year of service, with a cap of twenty years; no differentiation according to rank – the skippers to get the same as the deckhands; full payment to widows and dependants of the men who'd died and the inclusion of radio officers in the scheme.

With the help of a fine lawyer, Humphrey Forrest, who dedicated much of his time and talent to the ex-trawlermen pro bono through the Humber Law Centre, the BFA began to represent the men at a further series of tribunals. Hull and Grimsby had been devastated by the collapse of distant-water fishing and few of the trawlermen were able to find other work. They would spend their days congregating around the BFA offices (donated free of charge by Hull city council) seeking information. They expected the injustice that had been done to them to be rectified and for some the cause itself became a raison d'être.

Peter Crampton explained to me how men like Ron and Ray, whose formal education had ended in childhood, composed letters to prominent politicians and the media, typing them slowly, the dexterity of their stubby fingers impaired by years of hard manual labour and exposure to temperatures of 40 degrees below freezing. Painstakingly they processed and fought case after case at industrial tribunals, losing time and again. Meanwhile they circulated their demands to parliamentarians at Westminster and in Brussels, working with BFA branches in Fleetwood and Aberdeen as well as Grimsby.

Finally, at their seventeenth industrial tribunal, they were successful and the men were reclassified as employed rather than casual labour. They now had a legal decision to which the government would have to respond. Although fishing wasn't a state enterprise, the government had a responsibility to them because it had been their agreement to Iceland's 200-mile fishing limit that had destroyed the industry.

By now it was the early 1990s. The Major government rejected the BFA's proposals in favour of an ex-gratia compensation scheme which paid out some money but not, in the main, to distant-water trawlermen. The scheme required the applicant to prove a continuous work record for a single employer. A few distant-water trawlermen did work for one employer, but most were taken on to whichever ship was available. If, for whatever reason, a man couldn't sail with one trawler, he couldn't wait three or four weeks until it returned before he could go to work. So they chopped and changed as part of arrangements that suited the trawler owners, providing them with a single pool of labour on which any of them could draw. The ex-gratia scheme was a disaster. The men were no better off and the government was now able to claim that it had complied with its legal obligations.

At the conclusion of my meeting with the BFA delegation Peter Crampton took me to one side and told me how concerned he was that these men had spent the prime of their lives seeking something that might well be unachievable. He was fighting a valiant battle in the European Parliament, but Brussels had little influence on Westminster in cases such as this. The government was facing a whole host of campaigns to right the wrongs of the past: coalminers with emphysema, bus drivers who'd lost their pensions, former prisoners of war in Japan who'd been seeking compensation for many years and the families of Aberfan – where the collapse of a colliery spoil tip on to a school in 1966 had claimed 144 lives – who had watched powerless as the National Coal Board took some of the public donations meant for them and used the money to pay for the clearance of the slurry tips that had killed their children.

He assured me that he would be my staunch ally in this fight but, with no further legal avenues open to the BFA, he was keen to ensure that a sense of realism prevailed in order to protect me and the new government from accusations of betrayal.

It was a sage warning. I had to avoid building false hopes. At the same time, this was an industrial injustice way beyond anything I'd experienced in the Post Office, involving a community I already respected, admired and empathized with in equal measure. There was no one I'd rather have standing shoulder-to-shoulder with me than Ron Bateman, Ray Smith and the trawlermen they represented. If we fought and lost, the struggle would have been worthwhile.

But, as with the battle to defeat Post Office privatization five years earlier, I wasn't interested in the concept of glorious defeat. The only acceptable outcome for these men and their families, who had been treated so appallingly, was the achievement of every dot and comma of the BFA claim.

It was time to put to sea with the trawlermen.

Chapter 10

I DROVE THROUGH the gates of New Palace Yard as the member of Parliament for Hull West and Hessle on a gorgeous May morning the week after Labour's landslide victory in the 1997 general election.

Not counting a milk float and what could almost have been described as a van – from which I helped to deliver milk at the weekends and paraffin two evenings a week as a schoolboy – this was, I calculated, my seventh place of work.

Remington Electric Razors in Kensington High Street; Tesco in King Street, Hammersmith; Anthony Jackson's in the Upper Richmond Road in Sheen, the Royal Mail delivery office on Barnes Green; the sorting office in Wellington Street, Slough, UCW House in Crescent Lane, Clapham . . . and now the Palace of Westminster. I'd been working for almost thirty-two years and had, subject to the wishes of my electorate, reached what I hoped would be my final business premises.

And what fine premises they were. The policeman on the gate had been supplied with a brochure containing photographs of all the new MPs. I wound down my window and he asked for my name, checked it against the photograph of me and nodded me in. That was it: no further checks, no car search, no security arch to walk through. As Big Ben bonged above me, I descended unhindered into the MPs' car park. As I drove into a space, another car pulled in beside me – an open-top, two-seater sports car – out of which unfolded the lean, languorous figure of Alan Clark.

Like me, he'd just been elected to Parliament. Unlike me, he had spent almost twenty years as an MP before losing his Plymouth seat in 1992. He'd just been returned as the Tory member for Kensington and Chelsea. I decided that following him out of the subterranean car park would be the simplest way of ensuring that I ended up in the right place.

From fifteen paces behind I could see from his body language how blasé Clark was about entering Parliament as a fully fledged member. His gait was jaunty, one hand in his pocket; he carried neither briefcase nor papers. Nothing but an air of nonchalance. As I struggled along behind him, weighed down by a huge briefcase full of documents and various bits of office equipment, I was struck by the sense that he belonged here, whereas I wasn't entirely sure whether I did. At the escalator that carries MPs up from the car park to the members' entrance there was then and is now a faint smell of burning rubber. Every time I catch that smell I remember that first day, following Alan Clark into work.

After hanging my coat in the members' cloakroom, on my own coathook, next to the pink fabric loop for my sword (swords, along with suits of armour, have been banned in the Commons chamber for over 700 years because of 'certain persons' having interrupted debates in 1313), I was ready to begin.

It was Wednesday 7 May. The first session of the new

Parliament would begin at 2.30pm. We were to elect a speaker and go through the motions of Prime Minister's Questions and a few other bits and pieces before adjourning again until the Queen's speech a week later.

In the morning the parliamentary Labour party would meet – all 418 of us. We now had a scarcely believable majority of 179. There were far too many of us to be accommodated in even the largest committee room in the Palace of Westminster, so we convened in Church House in Dean's Yard, just across the road from Parliament behind Westminster Abbey. This is where the House of Commons met during the Second World War while the Commons chamber was repaired after taking a direct hit in the Blitz.

We gathered in the enormous tiered central hall, where Tony Blair stood before us – the master of all he surveyed. We'd been in opposition for eighteen years. Indeed, throughout the twentieth century Labour governments had been scarcely more than brief punctuations to Conservative rule. The Tories had been in power in Britain for longer than the Communists in Russia, and the Communists didn't hold elections.

Tony cracked a joke about the Number 10 switchboard operator telling him that morning they had the deputy prime minister on the line. His instinctive reaction had been to wonder what Michael Heseltine wanted to talk to him about. Even our leader was having problems getting used to the change of government. The only sour note at that meeting was struck by Ken Livingstone, who warned Gordon Brown, the new chancellor of the exchequer, that his plan to hand control of interest rates to the Bank of England would be a disaster. Ken looked and sounded like a relic from a different age.

I was standing near the entrance to Church House after the meeting when the famous photograph was taken of Tony Blair surrounded by women MPs looking up to the camera like a field of sunflowers straining to catch the sun. As it happened, what they caught was the *Sun*: my new companions would be patronizingly labelled 'Blair's Babes' in the next morning's edition. The effect of those 101 new women MPs on the chamber of the House of Commons when Parliament met later that afternoon was profound. I had nothing to compare it with, apart from TV transmissions, but old hands told me how grey, male and unrepresentative of the general population the Commons had looked before the influx.

There was, of course, much further to go. Few women sat on the benches opposite and not yet enough on ours, but the riot of colour amid the usual monochrome suits added to the feeling of transformation brought about by our landslide victory, as did the increase in MPs from ethnic minorities and the arrival of Anne Begg, my colleague from Aberdeen, whose wheelchair caused all kinds of problems for the House authorities. They had never had to make permanent provision for a wheelchair before.

I stood below the bar, having arrived too late to get a seat on our benches. There was plenty of room on the opposition side, to the left of the speaker's chair. I hoped never to have to sit there. I wanted to spend all my years in Parliament on the government side. Such chutzpah didn't seem fanciful then, with the Tories sitting huddled together like a threatened species. I've seen happier faces on a fishmonger's slab.

Suddenly, David Blunkett, the newly appointed education secretary, emerged from the doors behind the speaker's chair with his guide dog, Lucy. I watched as Lucy started to lead

David towards the opposition front bench. It seemed to me to be the perfect metaphor for my party. Lucy felt that this was where Labour belonged – in opposition, devising policies that would never be implemented; promoting causes that would never succeed. For some in the Labour party this had been a comfortable berth. They preferred to debate rather than to do; to talk a lot but achieve very little. Opposition was a safe place to be if compromise was to be avoided and purity of principle preserved.

Nobody could blame Lucy for her mistake. Simon Hoggart, in his *Guardian* sketch the next morning, remarked that in any civilized society they'd have allowed Lucy into the chamber before the sitting began so that she could pee on the government front bench to help her find her way back there in the afternoon.

A newly elected MP has no office, no desk and no staff but a backlog of work to do. Constituents don't stop writing to their MPs because there is a general election. From the day the campaign begins, sitting MPs step down to become 'candidates' and are unable to represent constituents for the duration of the contest. For me, replacing somebody who'd resigned, it was worse. MPs seeking re-election at least have the benefit of their staff, who remain on the payroll to open the post and organize it into some kind of order ready for their employer's return. Stuart Randall's staff had gone with him.

CWU members in the House of Commons post office were pleased to see me, mainly because I could relieve them of bundles and bundles of mail they'd had to store since the beginning of the general election campaign. All of it was addressed to Stuart Randall but every sender expected a reply from Alan Johnson.

The House authorities were trying their best to deal with the huge intake of new members by providing help desks. I eventually got an appointment at one and sat down opposite a middle-aged clerk who seemed to be battery-operated. He asked me where I'd like my office to be located. When I suggested Tuscany, he rolled his eyes and patiently explained that offices were situated in the Palace of Westminster itself, number 7 Millbank, Norman Shaw North and South (the original Scotland Yard) and number 1 Parliament Street. Which would I prefer?

I plumped for the palace. The decision on office allocation would be made by government whips, to whom my preference would be passed on, roughly in accordance with members' wishes. However, the more senior you were the better the accommodation. I was very junior. In the meantime, I was given various other pieces of information and a tiny key to open one of the ancient wooden lockers positioned along the corridors around the chamber of the House of Commons. This at least provided storage space for the bundles of mail I was carting around.

Three weeks after the election, I was eventually allocated an airless cupboard of a room with no natural light. It was another week before I managed to recruit anyone to work for me. The airless office didn't last very long but Jane Davies, who became my part-time secretary (on £9,000 a year) would be with me until her retirement in 2015.

Jane knew her way around Parliament, having worked for various MPs for many years before coming to my rescue. Frank Field had recommended her to me, telling me that she was already working part-time for another MP and was looking to extend her hours. In effect, we both had the benefit of a full-time secretary. Such was Jane's skill at managing her workload – typing our letters, keeping our diaries and making phone calls for us from her office in 1 Parliament Street – that we each felt we had her to ourselves.

Thanks to a tip-off from Jane, I managed to nab a spare office close to hers, convincing the whips that the absence of natural light in the one they'd allocated to me was a serious impediment to my good health. Established at last on the fourth floor of 1 Parliament Street, I now had a glorious view of the Thames, Big Ben and St Thomas's Hospital, where Laura had been born.

The view lasted only until the vast edifice of Portcullis House was completed, providing much-needed additional accommodation for MPs and their staff. In the meantime, I continued my quest to complete my own staff. Debbie Eke was recommended to me by a colleague for her sense of humour as much as for her skill. She was indeed very funny, but she was also an excellent researcher in the days before Google helped everyone to do their own research.

I needed one more person: a constituency assistant in Hull. After advertising the post in the *Hull Daily Mail*, I whittled down the fifty-odd applicants to ten for interview. Among those left off the short list were two sitting councillors. I felt that it would be wrong to be too strongly linked to Hull city council when many of the complaints I received from constituents were likely to involve the local authority. Obviously I needed to work closely with the single-party state at the Guildhall, but not so closely that we became intertwined as one institution in the public's mind. Indeed, I soon found out that many members of the public believed their MP was a higher authority, overseeing the council and able to direct it at will.

Having excluded the councillors, I found the ideal constituency assistant in Helen Childs, a Lincolnshire girl who'd just completed her degree at Hull university. She'd given her current place of work, somewhere called 'the Institute', as a reference. It sounded like a worthy Hull academic establishment but when I rang to talk to Helen's boss I found it was a pub where she was working as a barmaid. It was the publican I was speaking to, and he pronounced Helen 'a fine lass'. The team was finally in place and by the summer we were ready to tackle the backlog and begin to properly represent the good citizens of Hull West and Hessle.

I rented a modest ground-floor flat on the marina, paid for by the second-home allowance provided by Parliament. My jovial landlord told me that his contracted decorator would be round to give the place a lick of paint. The decorator duly arrived on a warm, sunny morning, stepping into the flat through the double doors which I'd left open to catch the breeze off the tranquil water.

I recognized his face immediately from the football cards I'd collected as a boy and the *Charles Buchan's Football Monthly* magazines I'd read and treasured. Before he could open his mouth, I exclaimed: 'You're Chris Chilton! The great Hull City centre forward!' And he was. A local sporting legend was decorating my flat. It was like Bobby Charlton arriving to fix the plumbing.

On that glorious morning of 7 May I'd bumped into Alastair Campbell, Tony Blair's press secretary, outside Church House and he'd asked me what I expected to achieve in Parliament. It was a good question. My life had changed completely in a matter of weeks. In a way my almost thirty years in the Post Office had cocooned me. This was a chance to emerge from the chrysalis and take wing.

I had told Alastair rather pompously that while most new MPs were looking to make their mark, I felt I had nothing to prove. I'd get on with representing my constituents and trying to be a good backbench MP. It was an accurate reflection of my outlook. I was not consumed with a burning ambition to be a minister – let alone a Cabinet minister – and I wasn't consumed by politics. I was reasonably well informed, but I didn't scour the print media every day, or devour political biographies, or watch the Sunday-morning political programmes on TV. I certainly hadn't formed 'an opinion' on every issue as proper politicians were meant to do. I had no wide network of contacts and I'd never been to a dinner party in my life.

I may have been a huge admirer of Tony Blair, and for his part, he had created a wonderful opportunity for me, but I was under no illusion that this made us bosom buddies. Collecting friends had never been a hobby of mine. In general, I'd rather avoid a conversation than have one. I'd always been that way – a bit anti-social. Now I found myself in a profession where conversation, dialogue and interaction were crucial to doing the job properly.

The part of my job that did suit me down to the ground was representing the trawlermen. I was happy in Hull but strangely unsettled in Westminster. To some extent my state of mind must have been a natural reaction to veering off in a new direction in my forties, leaving behind a world I understood and where I felt comfortable.

I was invited to say my farewells to the CWU at its annual conference in Jersey the day after my forty-seventh birthday. I spent two days there and was treated to a wonderful dinner by my friends and allies. Some delegates felt that a union somehow owned its general secretary; my enemies, on the other hand, were resentful of the fact that I'd departed of my own accord, thus depriving them of the opportunity to get rid of me. But from the union colleagues I'd worked alongside from youth to middle age there was nothing but warmth and humour. It wasn't as if I'd gone off to become director general of the CBI, after all. And my close colleagues would flourish: Derek Hodgson achieved his ambition to be general secretary and Tony Young became Lord Young of Norwood Green.

I left them with a poem which I recited from the platform of the cavernous conference hall. Housman reflected my feelings of sweet nostalgia.

> Into my heart an air that kills
> From yon far county blows:
> What are those blue remembered hills,
> What spires, what farms are those?
>
> That is the land of lost content,
> I see it shining plain,
> The happy highways where I went
> And cannot come again.

The union had been my life. Now it was part of my past.

Later that year, in September, I visited Linda in Western Australia. Many people take the long-haul flight to Australia on the basis that they'll stay for months; most stay for at least two weeks. I went for the weekend.

The trip came about serendipitously, as an indirect result of the keenness of Ian McCartney, the Department of Trade and Industry minister responsible for the Post Office, that I should put my Post Office experience to good use. I was no less keen to oblige.

Ian was, despite his diminutive stature, an immense figure in this triumphant period of Labour history. A tiny Scot who represented a Wigan seat, he always reminded me of Jimmy Clitheroe, the 'Clitheroe Kid' of radio fame in my childhood. But there was nothing comedic about Ian's incredible work rate or his determination to implement the entire suite of statutory basic minimum standards for workers which he'd helped develop in opposition – chief of which was the national minimum wage.

After being appointed to his ministerial position, Ian contacted me requesting my attendance at a meeting he was having with senior civil servants about postal services. As I headed across to the imposing ministry building at 1 Victoria Street, it was with some trepidation. I'd been to this building many times as a union official, most recently during the battle to defeat Post Office privatization, but as an MP I had yet to make my maiden speech, let alone fully get to grips with how the ancient forum I'd joined actually worked, with its rules and traditions, customs and precedents. I was finding it hard enough to understand all this and catch up with the backlog of constituency work without taking on a quasi-ministerial role to which I hadn't been appointed.

The civil servants gathered around the long table in Ian's office were understandably sniffy about my presence. They worked for the executive, not for Parliament, and they were answerable to ministers, not backbenchers. An MP had no constitutional identity as far as the civil service was concerned until he or she was selected by the prime minister to serve in Her Majesty's government, and I'm not sure if Ian had even consulted his secretary of state, Margaret Beckett, about his decision to have me riding shotgun on his mail coach.

The CWU influence on Labour's Post Office policy had been profound. As general secretary with a seat on the NEC I'd had to fight off a plan from Gordon Brown's team to flog off the parcels division, Parcelforce, before our carefully constructed policy to give the Post Office commercial freedom in the public sector was adopted by Labour and included in the manifesto. Now Ian wanted to discuss how the civil-service machine would turn all of this into legislation.

He also wanted to discuss how to impose the moratorium he'd promised on crown office closures – crown offices were the country's 1,000 or so main post offices, staffed by CWU members – a promise I'd secured while I was still general secretary.

I'm not sure how many civil servants were gathered round that table, all scribbling furiously, as Ian sat among them cheerfully dispatching instructions about what he wanted and when he wanted it. I had been called in to supplement his synopsis of what was needed. His summing-up was already perfect, though his accent – a mixture of Glaswegian and Lancastrian – and his rapid, staccato delivery might have made him difficult to understand.

As I spoke, I was acutely aware of the general feeling in the room that this was an impropriety. I was an unwelcome intruder into a process meant only for the initiated. At the end of the meeting Ian said he wanted all submissions on this issue copied to me.

This was a step too far. It provoked the most senior civil servant present to clear his throat and speak for the institution as a whole. 'Minister, I'm afraid that will not be possible. Government documents of this nature can only be passed to those who have signed the Official Secrets Act.'

There was a pause. Even Ian's exuberance temporarily deserted him.

I suddenly remembered all those documents I'd been asked to sign at the Lavender Hill offices of the Battersea sub-district of the Post Office as an eighteen-year-old recruit to what was then a uniformed arm of the civil service.

'I have signed the Official Secrets Act,' I said quietly, trying not to sound in any way triumphal. 'Almost thirty years ago, when I became a postman.' There is a phrase that describes the way the civil servants' faces fell. It is, I believe, a standard last line to many Victorian jokes. Collapse of stout party. Come to think of it, I don't think I ever did receive copies of those submissions.

Ian felt that the most effective way of placing my knowledge and experience of the Post Office at the government's disposal would be to have me on the Trade and Industry Select Committee. At that time the whips had absolute power over who was chosen for the various select committees which carry out much of the detailed work of parliamentarians. However, ministers were not totally disconnected from the process of allocating positions and Ian probably nudged the whips into appointing me.

And so I joined the select committee. It so happened that a delegation from the committee was scheduled to visit Taiwan in September and, to my delight, I was invited to join it. I accepted immediately. I'd always been fascinated by this small island off the coast of China, where Chiang Kai-shek had fled in late 1949 with his nationalist forces after losing the civil war to Mao's Communists on the mainland.

Chiang designated the island, formerly Formosa, as the seat of the Republic of China, and continued to claim sovereignty over the whole of China. For more than twenty years his government occupied the seat on the UN Security Council reserved for its huge neighbour, which was a bit like the Isle of Wight being accepted as the United Kingdom.

The trip was to take place the week before my sister's fiftieth birthday on 21 September. I worked out that for no extra cost I could fly back to Britain via Western Australia and stop off in Perth for a couple of days. I wouldn't have time to stay any longer, but I had never visited Linda in the fourteen years she had lived in Australia and it was too good an opportunity to miss.

I wanted it to be a surprise. I brought her husband Chas into the conspiracy and, to ensure that she would be at the airport when my flight, from Taiwan via Hong Kong, landed, I concocted a story about sending her a gift by courier which had to be collected from the arrivals hall at midnight on Saturday 20 September.

At the appointed hour Linda duly presented herself outside

the arrivals hall, expecting to be handed a parcel from a courier, only to find her little brother wandering out among the tourists and homecomers. Her astonishment made all the secrecy worthwhile.

It was a strange sensation, seeing my sister in such foreign surroundings. I had studied photographs, of course, of the house and integrated nursery she and Chas had bought outright on their first day in Australia. And as well as sending pictures, she'd described it in those scraps of blue airmail paper we used to write to each other. But none of this prepared me for the reality: the terrace, the swimming pool, the games room and above all just the sheer spaciousness of where she lived now. Armadale was a quiet suburb. It was spring in Australia and when I awoke on the morning after my arrival I drew the curtains to reveal an ordered landscape with sports fields opposite, houses set in neat grids and hills in the distance.

We hardly had a moment to talk, Linda and I, let alone to reflect on the past as her fiftieth birthday dawned. After breakfast a stretch limo pulled up outside to whisk her off to a beauty spa to be pampered for a few hours – the gift of her son, Dean, who had come over from Adelaide, where he lived with his lovely Japanese wife. He was working in computer technology and nursing sick animals in his spare time.

By the time Linda returned, her daughters had arrived to discuss and decide what was to be worn at that evening's birthday party at a restaurant hired exclusively for the evening. Renay, the eldest, had married Shane, an archetypal Aussie male, all barbecued burgers, cold lager and manly outdoor pursuits. His ambition was to head into the outback with

Renay, their few belongings packed into a Land Rover, and live the life of an itinerant farm worker. Not long after this family gathering, he achieved his ambition. Linda has hardly heard from Renay since.

Linda's other daughter, Tara, had, like Dean, moved across this vast country, settling even further away, in Brisbane, over 2,600 miles from Perth on the opposite coast. She had battled drug addiction and courted reckless suitors. Her daughter – Linda's first granddaughter, Jodie – was an amazingly mature and stabilizing influence on Tara. Even as a child, as she was then, her relationship with her exuberant, fun-loving mother was rather like that between Edina and Saffy in the TV comedy *Absolutely Fabulous.*

My nieces and nephew were the children of Linda's first husband, Mike, the kindest, most generous man but one who had for most of his life hidden a dark secret. He had been a functioning alcoholic since his teens and eventually committed suicide at the age of thirty-three. As children, Renay, Tara and Dean seemed to have come through the terrible trauma of their father's death, but such legacies are long and they had all suffered emotional repercussions, to varying degrees, as young adults.

It was after meeting and marrying Chas, whose gentle sensitivity with her children had impressed me from the start, that Linda had come to Australia, in part to bury the past and start again in a new country. At that fiftieth birthday party, surrounded by her family and the many friends she'd made in Armadale, I could see that she'd succeeded.

I almost can't bring myself to mention the male stripper one of her friends commissioned as a birthday surprise. If he imagined that Linda was going to be one of his shyer and more delicate customers, he was in for a shock. Suffice it to say that my extrovert sister relished the show to the extent that the poor man probably quit the next day and applied for a place at a seminary.

My flight back to London was on the Monday evening, which gave me the chance to see Linda's Magic Moon nursery in action. It was separated from her living quarters by a large door off the games room, which was like the entrance to Narnia. It was here, among the thirty or so kids in her charge, that I observed my sister in her element.

Linda had always wanted to work with children, from as far back as I can remember. She must have been only about eight when she was enlisted as babysitter/pram-pusher/errand-runner by a family who lived off the Golborne Road. She went on to become a nursery nurse and then, in her twenties, with three children of her own, a foster parent. Here at the Magic Moon she had four or five girls working for her but she was always in the thick of things, organizing activities in the substantial outdoor play area and ensuring that her charges were properly occupied, nourished and cared for.

I lumbered around trying to look interested and wondering when Chas was going to rescue me by suggesting a lunchtime pint. This was Linda's world: devoting her time to those children who were upset; finding the cause; putting things right. She told me that half of her intake were from single-parent families. Many were Aboriginal, and lived in the poorest parts of Armadale. All would find some comfort in Linda's inexhaustible store of compassion.

It never occurred to her that she was doing anything particularly important or praiseworthy. As I watched her, in her blue apron with its Magic Moon logo, wiping away the tears of a child on her lap, focused entirely on how she could dispense serenity, my heart filled with pride. All my life I had been the beneficiary of her cheery propensity to reassure, her fierce desire to protect. I knew how valuable it would be to these children, to those she'd cared for in the past and to others she would care for in the future. Here, in the lush spaciousness of Western Australia, I could see that if she'd crossed continents to seek fulfilment, she had found it.

I had made my maiden speech before the summer recess. By tradition, an MP's first-ever contribution is uncontroversial, fulsome in its praise of the MP's predecessor and is never interrupted. I was determined to use my maiden speech to highlight the terrible injustice done to the distant-water trawlermen. In that sense only, it would be a break with tradition.

With well over 200 new MPs in the House, there were plenty of maiden speeches to be made and protocol dictated that questions couldn't be submitted, either orally or verbally, by members before they'd undergone this vital initiation. To help the parliamentary authorities and, no doubt, the speaker, who selected which MPs were called in debates, a list of new members was published every week, alongside the whip, with a tick beside the names of those who'd 'bowled their maiden over'. The whip was the document circulated to MPs by the office of the chief whip late on a Thursday which detailed the following week's business.

The job of the whips' office was to ensure that MPs kept to

the policies agreed collectively by their party. There were separate whips for each parliamentary party. If the business to be conducted was underlined once on the document, it was up to individual MPs whether or not they voted on that issue. If it was underlined twice, they could arrange with an opposition MP that they would both be absent, thus cancelling out each other's vote. This option was available only to Labour and Conservative members. If it was underlined three times, MPs would have to attend and vote as instructed or face the wrath of the whips' office and their array of cruel and unusual punishments. Hence the expression 'three-line whip'.

The signal that a vote was about to be taken was the ringing of the division bell. In addition, MPs had monitors in their offices which told them what business was being dealt with and some local pubs and restaurants popular with MPs had their own division bell. We all carried a pager as well, provided by the whips' office, which vibrated when there was a vote. All reinforced the call of the clanging bells across the parliamentary estate, which was hardly necessary as they were so loud it was impossible not to hear them unless one was profoundly deaf.

Once the bell began to clang, MPs had eight minutes to get to the voting lobbies (one for 'aye', the other for 'no'). In our radical mood, stoked by the huge intake of women, who were less inclined to excuse ridiculous procedures because they were 'traditional', there was an attempt to modernize the way we voted so that MPs didn't have to pass through the lobby in person like lambs through a sheep dip.

Although the clerks on their high wooden chairs were no longer marking off our names with quill pens on parchment (they did it with biros on giant pads instead), this was the only concession to modernity that had been made in centuries of parliamentary voting. My great Hull predecessors, the poet Andrew Marvell and philanthropist William Wilberforce, would have been completely familiar with the process, if not with the TV monitors and the pagers.

There was one main reason why it had never been considered necessary to introduce electronic methods of voting that didn't require MPs to gallop towards the lobbies like great herds of wildebeest in order to vote, as our vast army of Labour MPs soon realized. The best place to engage a minister in person, unprotected by a phalanx of civil servants, was in the voting lobby. If there was a school to be saved, a hospital to be built or an injustice to be rectified, the minister responsible would at some stage have to walk through the lobby. They were MPs, too, and subject to the same party whip as backbenchers. And despite our huge majority, the government whips' office, which seemed to consist largely of heavily built Glaswegians, took no risks in ensuring that government policy was secured. Elsewhere one saw very little of colleagues who, once promoted to ministerial office, had been taken off and chained to a treadmill somewhere in Whitehall. So it was in MPs' interests to go to the lobby.

It was on a July evening, in an end-of-session adjournment debate at ten o'clock at night, that I spoke in the House of Commons for the first time.

The Commons is a strange forum in which to speak. I was used to blathering away in all kinds of settings – canteen meetings, conferences, the Executive Council and out in the open air, shouting to make myself heard to striking workers in a

Cartoon from *The Times*, May 1994 – I'm the dog biting Michael Heseltine's leg.

Above: Addressing a Stand By Your Post rally in Manchester.

Right: Me in 1995.

Above: With Laura as the newly elected MP for Hull West and Hessle, 1997.

Below: As a junior minister at the DTI I carried out a review of the Patent Office in Cardiff, and was shown the patent file for the Beatles.

Above: Addressing a mass meeting of Hull trawlermen. Peter Crampton MEP is behind me with his arm on the table. Ron Bateman and Ray Smith are on my left.

Below: Petitioning 10 Downing Street with Ray Smith on my left and Ron Bateman and Brian Commander on my right.

Above: Visiting the Hull docks in 1997. **Below**: With Tony Blair.

Above: With Ara Darzi at the Labour party conference, September 2007.

Below: At a Cabinet meeting in November 2008, with Alistair Darling and Jacqui Smith.

Below: Visiting the Churchill Gardens estate in Pimlico as home secretary – ironically I was badly beaten up there in 1965.

Above: Visiting number 10.

Below: With Gordon Brown in 2009.

Right: With David Miliband and Gordon Brown at the state visit of Jacob Zuma in 2010.

Below: Me and my sister Linda in 2009.

car park somewhere. None was as intimidating as that small chamber where the opposition were literally opposite and indeed the entire layout was confrontational.

Apart from on the front benches, occupied by ministers and their shadow counterparts, where speakers had the benefit of the beautifully crafted dispatch box, there was nowhere to lay notes, no props or devices to assist oratory. There wasn't even anywhere to rest a glass of water. None of this really mattered as far as my speech was concerned because it was short and delivered to a chamber that was almost empty, and thus heard by virtually nobody but a few allies (notably Kevin McNamara and the Grimsby MP Austin Mitchell), the representative from the whips' office, who sat silently observing every debate, the government minister due to reply and a little huddle of civil servants corralled into a snug gallery to the right of the speaker's chair.

Unheralded and largely unnoticed it may have been, but my fifteen minutes of sagacity was recorded for posterity in Hansard and my mission to achieve the objectives of the British Fishermen's Association had been launched.

Chapter 11

A FEW MONTHS later, another huge issue from Hull's fishing history was revived. It concerned the loss of the *Gaul*, a so-called super-trawler, in the 1970s. State of the art in every respect, the *Gaul* had automatic steering, a dual radar system, high-quality radio and telegraph equipment and was the first trawler to be equipped with fifty automatically inflatable life rafts, an overabundance given that the crew numbered thirty-six. She substantially exceeded the minimum recommended stability criteria, was less than two years old and considered to be unsinkable. Comparing the *Gaul* to the old sidewinder trawlers upon which so many men had perished was akin to likening a cruise liner to a rowing boat.

In February 1974, in the vicinity of the North Cape out in the vast expanse of the Barents Sea, the *Gaul* disappeared without trace. There had been no distress calls, no oil had been found on the surface of the water and no wreckage discovered, other than a single lifebuoy, which appeared three months later. Forensic evidence identified a lack of saltwater plankton on the lifebuoy, which suggested that it had been positioned on the water rather than going down with the vessel before being separated from the wreckage and floating to the surface.

An official inquiry into the loss of the vessel had been held in Hull in 1974. There was no evidence, only supposition and theory to guide its conclusions, which were that the *Gaul* had capsized and foundered as a result of being buffeted broadside by heavy seas while attempting a turning manoeuvre against the oncoming awful weather.

All thirty-six men on the *Gaul* were lost. Most of them were from Hull, but six hailed from North Shields, and one, the radio operator, was from Nelson in Lancashire. When an aircraft falls from the sky enormous efforts go into finding the black box to try to determine why lives were lost. There is no such consideration for ships at sea. The bereaved families pleaded with the authorities to search for the *Gaul*. The government refused. The Ministry of Defence stated blithely that 'because of the limited information about the *Gaul*'s position when she went down it would be necessary to search hundreds, probably thousands, of square miles of sea bed'.

All of this taken together fuelled understandable speculation. The *Gaul* had sunk at the height of the Cold War, and the Barents Sea was home to the Russian northern fleet. The government, though, would not admit to using distant-water trawlers to spy on the Russians. Bill Rodgers – who would become one of the Gang of Four that established the Social Democratic Party in the 1980s – was the Labour defence minister in 1974 and wrote to the *Gaul* families: 'I can assure you that the British trawler fleet is not involved in any way in intelligence gathering.' The denial was repeated as recently as 1992, when the Berlin Wall had come down and the Cold War was at an end.

But the trawlermen knew the truth. For years they had been asked to monitor the movements of Soviet warships based at Kildin Island in the Barents Sea. Some skippers took photographs while others were asked to check the identity of Russian ships they'd seen against silhouettes reproduced in a kind of MI6 'I Spy' book. Agents from the security services would occasionally join the crew, posing as trawlermen but in fact pursuing their own trade of espionage and counter-espionage.

Little wonder, then, that books were written, TV programmes made and articles published in newspapers and magazines describing the *Gaul* as a spy ship and suggesting that it had collided with a Russian submarine or that the crew had witnessed something the Russians didn't want them to see. Some of the families believed their loved ones were working in a Siberian salt mine: hardly a pleasant thought, but one which at least gave them hope that their relatives were still alive. And in 1980 a Sunday newspaper carried a two-page story about the *Gaul*'s radio officer being spotted in a bar in Durban, where it just so happened a Russian ship was docked.

The BFA men I worked with in the fight for compensation had told me all about the *Gaul* and how trawlermen knew where the wreck was because they'd snagged their nets on it. Indeed, shortly after the *Gaul* was lost, a Norwegian trawler had reported a sonar reading showing an obstruction on the sea bed some sixty miles off the coast of Norway and not far from the *Gaul*'s last-known location. But the government continued to ignore the families' requests to conduct a search and the many conspiracy theories flourished as a result.

In September 1997 a Channel 4 television crew headed by a TV producer, Norman Fenton, an eloquent Scot who'd long been intrigued by the disappearance of the *Gaul*, found the wreck. Fenton, who had no naval training or seafaring experience, established its likely position from his home, working from naval charts accessible to anyone and from reported sightings. He then hired a former ferry converted into an underwater survey vessel and, in two days, at a total cost of less than £50,000, located what the full might of this maritime nation had apparently been unable to find in almost a quarter of a century. The documentary he made, which showed footage of the *Gaul* lying on the sea bed, was shown on 6 November.

Fenton had taken a couple of Hull people with him on the trip, including an astute trawlerman and skipper, Mason Redfearn, who had been recruited to work for British naval intelligence while skippering a Hull trawler, the *Stella Arcturus*, in March 1963. He was another luminary of the BFA involved in battling for trawlermen's compensation.

To me the two issues were intertwined. The men deprived of work, with the promises made to them of retraining, redeployment and compensation so disgracefully broken, were the very same men who had helped to defend their country, not just in two world wars, when they crewed the minesweepers, but in the Cold War that followed. Bill Rodgers now admitted he'd been misled back in 1974 and a whole series of written parliamentary questions produced candid responses that revealed the longstanding and intense cooperation between the patriotic trawlermen and the security services, for which the men had sought and received no reward whatsoever.

There were now two big catches to land on behalf of the

community I represented and both had been slipping the net for almost twenty-five years: compensation for the men thrown out of work because of government action and a new inquiry into the loss of the *Gaul* and the failure to find the wreck due to government negligence.

The easy bit was bringing up the issue in Parliament, where government ministers had to reply to the points I'd raised and could hardly refuse my request to meet the families to pursue it further. But now that expectations had been raised, it was my duty to ensure that they were fulfilled. That was going to be the hard part.

I still didn't really understand how Parliament worked. The constituency side was more my element: listening to the problems brought to the four constituency surgeries I held every month in different parts of the 'patch'. The surgeries were full. Appointments weren't necessary: constituents just turned up (usually well before the advertised opening time) and waited. Helen and I would sit and listen to heart-rending stories from men and women who were almost apologetic about troubling 'Mr Johnson' over significant issues that they should have drawn to the attention of their elected representative much sooner.

Some of my colleagues are a bit sniffy about constituency work, complaining that it turns them into glorified social workers. It is true that constituency surgeries are a comparatively recent development. In the past, a constituency counted itself fortunate to receive an annual visit from its MP. The job was to represent the constituency in Parliament rather than Parliament in the constituency. In former times MPs had no office staff and often no office. Denis Healey, in his terrific memoir *The Time of My Life*, recalls how he would sit in the House of Commons library composing handwritten replies to every constituency letter he had been sent, right up until he became defence secretary.

Like all MPs then, Denis would have received only a fraction of the correspondence we get today. I can't remember exactly when I opened my first e-mail but it would have been some time around the millennium, and I remember what a novelty it was. Now a deluge of them arrives every day, along with the letters which, as e-mail increasingly becomes the standard method of communication, will no doubt soon achieve the novelty status once held by their electronic counterparts. And for me, as for all MPs, the most important people in my work are my 66,000 constituents. The e-mails and letters given the most prompt and keen attention are those with a Hull West and Hessle postcode.

I have nothing but admiration for colleagues who spend the majority of their time on legislation. That is, after all, our primary function: to examine, scrutinize and approve the bills emanating from the executive; to be present at the daily hour-long sessions where departmental ministers are interrogated; to be on bill committees laboriously poring over legislation in a high-ceilinged room on the committee corridor as the Thames flows on remorselessly below.

My trade-union background was a good apprenticeship for this new occupation. In Parliament Erskine May was the equivalent of Citrine's *ABC of Chairmanship*, the handbook for the trade-union movement, setting out procedures and protocol. But while I could have been a *Mastermind* contestant on Citrine, I've never so much as glanced at Erskine May.

Some MPs arrange for their correspondence to be dealt with by case workers, who filter out and pass on only what their boss needs to see. My failing was an obsession with reading every missive and dealing personally with most of them. And it really was a failing rather than an attribute. For a start, it prevented me from carrying out parliamentary duties. But I couldn't break the habit. It may not have been unrelated to the way I'd been parachuted into Hull. The justifiable need I felt to understand the area and its people had a hint of defensiveness to it; a yearning to belong and a sense that because my family home at that time was in south-east London, I was more vulnerable to accusations of complacency. I wanted to prove my commitment to my constituents through personal involvement with their excessive energy bills, their need for a council house or their inability to get a place at the school they wanted for their child. These were the day-to-day concerns. Other issues raised with me were deeply personal, every one worthy of its own separate chapter.

I soon discovered that my constituents preferred talking to writing. This was apparently to do with Hull having its own telephone system, run by Kingston Communications (KC). In those far-off days when there was a rate for local calls, KC customers could talk to each other all day for 4p. I was told by Kevin McNamara, my avuncular colleague, who'd been a Hull MP for thirty-one years by the time I arrived on the scene, that this was the main reason why it was so difficult to end a phone call with a Hullensian.

I derived a great deal of satisfaction from dealing personally with casework. It put the skills I'd honed as a local union official to good use once more. Because I could raise the problems presented to me with government ministers where required, or instigate debates on the floor of the House of Commons, it was a satisfying combination of being both lay official and national officer. I felt that this modern role of an MP was worthwhile and meaningful. Who else could act for people who had no influence, no powerful networks, no strings to pull? They could queue up at Citizens Advice Bureaux, which did sterling work, but my constituents had elected me to be their specific advocate; to be as articulate and resourceful as I could on their behalf.

An MP has no power but does have influence and status and access to those who do have power, whether that be social services, energy providers, the Child Support Agency, the NHS or the government. The numerous A4 hardcover ruled notebooks I've used to record surgery cases over the years are full of melodrama, tragedy and the occasional comedy. Some cases are a combination of all three, like the smartly dressed woman with the lovely smile who came to one of my very first surgeries.

We chatted away happily in the cramped room of a community centre on that Saturday morning in the summer of 1997. Her name was Joan and she'd evidently regularly visited my predecessor as part of her weekend routine. Having covered the weather, holiday destinations and the Eurovision Song Contest, I decided I ought to move things along and asked what I could do for her.

'I'd like you to have a word with Jack Straw,' she said. The home secretary was at that time doing splendid work to tackle the scourge of anti-social behaviour, which I thought would be the gist of Joan's concerns.

'He's put a camera in my fridge to spy on me, and I'd like him to take it out.'

I looked up from my notebook. Joan was smiling more sweetly than ever.

For a few weeks I spent hours with Joan. In the end I began arranging to meet her for an hour in the Holiday Inn on the marina before my surgeries began to avoid keeping other constituents waiting while I grappled with her charmingly elucidated problems.

I made it a rule that nobody would leave my surgery without at least some hope of assistance. With Joan this was very difficult. Well educated and extremely articulate, it turned out, not surprisingly, that she had a mental illness in which paranoia played a large part. When I reminded Joan of this she took it in her stride, never batting an eyelid.

'Yes, Alan,' she would reply calmly. 'I do have this illness, but these things are actually happening and because of my condition nobody will believe me.'

What she was effectively saying was 'Just because I'm paranoid, it doesn't mean the bastards aren't out to get me.' And it was, of course, unanswerable.

Needless to say, I didn't pass the problem on to Jack Straw. Instead Joan and I continued our regular chats for at least a year.

The biggest chunk of my constituency time, however, was spent with the trawlermen. I met Ron Bateman and Ray Smith on a weekly basis as we marshalled the arguments and prepared the case for compensation. Following the parliamentary debate where I'd raised the issue, responsibility for resolving it ricocheted between the DTI and the Ministry of Agriculture, Farming and Fisheries (MAFF). Given that we were seeking special compensation for enforced redundancy, it was primarily an employment-relations matter – the domain of the Clitheroe Kid, the DTI minister Ian McCartney.

He agreed to meet me and I took a sizeable delegation along with me. It included Ron and Ray, plus representatives from Grimsby, Fleetwood and Aberdeen, the other distant-water ports whose MPs I'd fired up to join me in the battle. Hull was by some way the largest of the four. Austin Mitchell, the MP for Grimsby, the second largest, was an acknowledged expert on the fishing industry. Although Grimsby's variety of fishing grounds had saved their industry from collapsing entirely with the conclusion of the Cod Wars, they had nevertheless lost thousands of jobs and had been equal partners with Hull in setting up the BFA.

At the meeting, tensions between Hull and Grimsby soon became apparent. Ron and Ray were trawlermen, whereas their counterparts from the south bank of the Humber were skippers. While the Hull representatives were arguing strongly for the BFA's constitutional objectives – £1,000 for each year at sea, with a cap of twenty years paid irrespective of rank or position – Grimsby's lead voice, a skipper's widow, wanted the payments to reflect the earnings of job grades, with skippers at the top of the pecking order and deckhands at the bottom.

We'd had this debate already, at a pre-meeting the previous evening where I'd quoted the founding principles of the BFA and had expected the row to end there. Unfortunately, it reared up again at the meeting with Ian and his civil servants. Austin seemed reluctant to rein in his forceful delegation, particularly the skipper's widow, who assumed an air of authority he found hard to contradict.

It meant that the government, which was being asked to re-open an issue over twenty years old, with no legal obligation to do so and no obvious recourse to the substantial funding that settlement would require, was now aware of divisions in the BFA over the nature of the proposed settlement. It was certainly a setback, but not, I hoped, a fatal blow.

As well as regularly seeing Ron, Ray and the BFA committee, every so often I would encounter the ex-trawlermen themselves at what could only be described as mass meetings.

These would be held at venues big enough to accommodate the many hundreds of men and women for whom the BFA's campaign still represented hope: a triumph of faith over cynicism. One of the women, Christine Jensen, was on the BFA committee. It was Chrissie who first told me about the 'triple trawler tragedy', the loss of three Hull trawlers in the space of three terrible weeks early in 1968. She had lost her sixteen-year-old nephew on one ship and her brother on another. What she never told me about, though plenty did, was the heroic role she played with other Hessle Road women in campaigning for safety measures in the wake of that trio of disasters in which fifty-eight men died.

Led by the formidable Lillian Bilocca, known as Big Lil, the women's battle had been a national and international story that succeeded in highlighting the disgraceful conditions the men worked in. Now Chrissie was involved in the battle for compensation. She would be made MBE for her work, although she would not live to see the campaign's conclusion.

Laura and I were invited to one of the trawlermen's reunions, events at which around 1,300 men and women from the Hessle Road diaspora would descend on the Walton Street club or some other enormous venue for four hours of nostalgia, drinking and singing their way back to the fifties, the days before the terraced housing that ran down to the fish dock was demolished; before the families moved out to the huge new estates of Bransholme and Orchard Park, to high-rise flats and maisonettes far from the Humber and the smells and sounds of the sea. Back to when the Hessle Road was known to fishing communities the world over as the place from which a particular breed of fisherman emerged. And not only fishermen, but famous sons such as the actor Tom Courtenay, entertainer Joe Longthorne and Hull FC rugby league legend Johnny Whiteley.

Laura and I sat drinking the rum that one of the trawlermen insisted we tried, listening to the stories of what life had been like when well over 200 sidewinder trawlers vied for space in the fishing docks that brought the vessels right into the city centre, a scene described by Larkin as 'ships up streets'. They told me about the most terrifying experience known to practically every man who'd fished in those 'glory years': 'top ice'.

Temperatures of minus 50 degrees Celsius weren't uncommon in the northern and eastern parts of the Barents Sea and the area around Bear Island. The real danger came when these temperatures were accompanied by wind-driven spray which froze to the masts and rigging. If the weight of the ice was allowed to build up, the trawler would become unstable and capsize, throwing the men into water so cold that it would freeze the blood in their veins within minutes.

The only way to avoid top ice was for some of the crew of twenty to chop the ice away – to climb high into the rigging in raging seas in a race against time to physically remove the ice accretion. Many ships were lost through top ice and many men were killed or injured trying to prevent it. As well as recounting their fear and recalling horrifying tragedies, they talked, too, of their pride in this most distinct of professions.

At a time when most working men never moved beyond their place of work, when miners rarely left the pit village, steel-workers walked to work and shipbuilders saw little beyond the shipyard, these men spent on average 340 days of each year at sea, venturing to the coasts of Newfoundland, Labrador and Novaya Zemlya – as far north as it's possible to go before the Arctic ice barrier blocks any further progress with ice so thick even the most powerful ice-breakers could not penetrate it. They would end their fishing trip 1,500 miles away from the Humber. The best part of the three- or four-week adventure was the luxury of the journey home.

The men told me how different the atmosphere was on board as, with a full catch in the hold, they looked forward to the comforts of home. Trawlermen were known as 'three-day millionaires' because of an alleged propensity to excessive generosity in the pubs of Hessle Road in the short spell onshore before they sailed off again.

These characters were tough. Some were violent. None were saints. But I loved their company. I admired their loyalty, the complete absence of any pretension, the fierce honesty of Ron

Bateman, the tranquil studiousness of Ray Smith, the solid dependability of Brian Commander. The men who had plied their trade beneath the Northern Lights were as exceptional as the industry in which they had laboured.

The chief whip wanted to see me. It was late 1997 and Christmas was approaching, but I felt it was unlikely that Nick Brown wanted to wish me the compliments of the season. His government position wasn't usually associated with compliments; insults perhaps, but rarely compliments.

A parliamentary party is a collection of individuals, their egos, prejudices, obsessions and idiosyncrasies forged into a cohesive unit. Labour candidates had been elected not because of their charm and vivacity but primarily because they were Labour candidates. It wasn't unreasonable, therefore, to expect them, once elected, to pursue Labour's policies and as it was the chief whip's job to ensure that they did, those called for an audience could usually expect a difficult meeting focused on some real or imaginary transgression. It was like being called to the headmaster's study, except that, unlike my visits to see Dr Henry, the headmaster of Sloane Grammar, there was no cane involved. Which is not to say that the whips' office wouldn't welcome the ability to administer corporal punishment if given the opportunity.

On this occasion, however, I knew why I was being summoned. I'd been offered a position as parliamentary private secretary (PPS) to the financial secretary to Her Majesty's Treasury. To put it more plainly, I had been asked to do a very junior semi-ministerial job which brought with it neither status nor salary. My function would be simply to act as the eyes and ears of my minister in Parliament. To be the catcher of moods, discerner of trends, conveyer of comments and criticisms. Ministers toil away somewhere in Whitehall, coming to Parliament only when due to speak from the dispatch box or to vote. They risk being isolated from the daily drama of life in the Palace of Westminster, the gossip and the rumours, without somebody to keep them in touch. Which is why, at minister-of-state level and above, they have a PPS.

Dawn Primarolo's PPS had just resigned over an unpopular decision the government had taken on child benefits. She had rung me to ask if I'd take on the job. I hardly knew Dawn and I'd prevaricated, fearful that this would hamper my efforts to get compensation for the trawlermen and discover the truth about the *Gaul*. She suggested I see the chief whip if I felt it would be helpful. I felt it would.

Nick Brown was a kindly man. In stature and gait he certainly looked like a chief whip, but in personality and demeanour he was more like a local vicar. As I sat in his inner sanctum, accessible only through a series of outer offices just off the Commons lobby, he gently pointed out how stupid I would be to reject this position.

I told Nick about the trawlermen's compensation campaign at greater length than was necessary. He listened intently. When I'd finished he said: 'Alan, where do you think the money for that compensation will come from?'

I hazarded a guess.

'That's right – the Treasury. Now, which government department will you be spending your time in as Dawn's PPS?'

I think I got that one right as well.

Nick leaned back in his chair, mustering fresh supplies of patience. 'So you have the perfect opportunity to be at the heart of government, where all the important decisions are inevitably made, and where any decision to spend taxpayers' money naturally resides, and you're reluctant to accept it?'

'But . . .' I ventured, 'being a PPS means I can no longer speak in Parliament. I'm neither a minister able to speak from the dispatch box nor a backbencher able to speak from there.'

Nick pushed his chair back and sighed, realizing, no doubt, that he was encountering a particularly entrenched level of stupidity. 'Have you decided you never want to serve in government?'

I shook my head. Though I had no yearnings to become a minister, I'd never thought about it for long enough to rule such a prospect in or out.

'Right. Almost all ministerial careers begin like this. Refuse the offer and in all probability you'll never be a minister and you won't be any better off in respect of your trawlermen.'

Quietly, but with feeling, Nick explained that as part of government (albeit a lowly part), it was true that I would not be allowed to speak from the back benches, but I could still represent my constituents. I could send letters, submit written questions, use every parliamentary device except those that required me to speak in the House of Commons chamber. He explained how, as chief whip, he was in exactly the same position, as indeed was the speaker, who chaired debates but couldn't contribute to them. Being part of government gave access to ministers that at the very least restored the balance.

I waved the white flag. I knew when I was beaten. Goodness

knows why Nick bothered, but his little seminar drove a coach and horses through my naïve assumptions. And so I left the room and stepped on to the very bottom rung of the government ladder.

The Treasury was immediately opposite my office in 1 Parliament Street. It was a brooding presence. Clad in Portland stone, it formed its own island that dominated Great George Street, Horse Guards Road and King Charles Street as well as Parliament Street, the short driveway to Whitehall itself.

I crossed the wide road, risking life and limb to dodge between the buses turning off Parliament Square in order to present myself to my new boss. I carried a brand-new ruled A4 notebook with hard covers. I reckoned it was the only tool I'd need.

Dawn Primarolo had been Tony Benn's constituency secretary in Bristol. She had a reputation as a fearsome Bennite who'd led a coup against the moderate sitting MP in Bristol South. Once she'd replaced him, 'Red Dawn', as she'd been labelled by the tabloids, was perceived as posing a threat to the established order with her militant feminism and CND activism. Asked for a comment on my promotion to her PPS, I'd told Kevin Maguire of the *Mirror* that this would be the 'era of a new Dawn'.

If the Red Dawn caricature was ever accurate it certainly didn't match the petite, pretty, smartly dressed woman who welcomed me that winter's afternoon. The new narrative about Dawn, eight months into government, was that she had metamorphosed from Bennite to Brownite under the tutelage of her mentor, now the chancellor of the exchequer.

She ushered me into her big, bright office at the apex of two long, dark Treasury corridors and outlined what was expected of me, which was nothing very onerous. As well as the 'eyes and ears' side of the job, I was to attend the weekly ministers' meeting, the monthly pre-Treasury questions gathering and any parliamentary debate involving my minister.

The most labour-intensive part of Dawn's role, and therefore of mine, would be the Finance Bill, due to be published in the spring, which would bring before Parliament the plans set out by the chancellor in his budget speech. Gordon Brown had introduced an end-of-year equivalent, the Autumn Statement, which would again require some detailed measures to be taken through the House, mainly by Dawn.

I took an immediate liking to Dawn. This was the first time we'd met and I was so relieved that we quickly established a rapport. The first thing that registered was that she was totally devoid of self-importance. Indeed, as I got to know her better, I recognized a trait I later observed in other highly talented female politicians that is best described as self-unimportance. Dawn simply didn't know how good she was. For the next eighteen months or so I underwent a valuable apprenticeship: observing and listening, Trappist-like; soaking up what I needed to know. Learning from a complete professional.

In truth I was useless at the 'eyes and ears' bit. I wasn't a good mixer and rarely visited the watering-holes of Westminster. These were the days before MPs exerted some control over their working hours, so sitting right into (and occasionally right through) the night was not uncommon. I was not a regular in the members' dining room or tea room, where colleagues would wander in to break bread and chat with one another, preferring to sit in my office with something from the canteen spooned into a polystyrene takeaway box. Consequently I was the last person to know what was going on in Parliament, at either the political or the personal level.

In the House, the PPSs sat directly behind their ministers, occasionally being deployed as messengers to and from the little huddle of civil servants seated in 'the box' that ran parallel with and to the right of the speaker's chair. The civil servants were there to provide advice upon request to whoever was speaking for the government – the oracle waiting to be consulted. If somebody asked a question or made a point in the debate that Dawn, as the minister, would be expected to answer at the end, and she couldn't find the information she needed in her voluminous and heavily annotated briefing, I'd be asked to 'go to the box' – to walk along to the civil servants and ask for a note of explanation. Once it had been produced, I'd have to go back with it like a patient who'd collected a prescription.

Fortunately, this was only necessary on rare occasions as Dawn had an encyclopaedic knowledge of her brief and was meticulous in her preparation, particularly when the debate wasn't on the floor of the House but in one of the rooms on the committee corridor, the far smaller stage where political reputations are won and lost. This was where much of Dawn's work was done, both before and after she was promoted to paymaster general following Geoffrey Robinson's enforced resignation over the mortgage he'd given to Peter Mandelson.

Mandelson, trade and industry secretary when all this came to light, was himself forced to resign. Goodness knows why this loan between two friends ended in their resignations from government, but I was pleased that it gave Dawn a well-earned step up to become the first woman paymaster general in the 200-year history of the position. It didn't, however, provide any escape from the hand-to-hand combat that the committee stage of the Finance Bill entailed. In those venerable, high-ceilinged committee rooms, beneath the dark paintings of politicians past, many a politician of the future had come to grief.

The committee stage of any bill is difficult. The legislation is scrutinized line by line by around thirty selected politicians, a majority from the government side. The committee rooms are, in essence, Lilliputian replicas of the Commons chamber. A chair takes on the speaker's role, sitting at a high table with a House of Commons clerk and a stenographer to record the event for posterity. In a distant corner are the civil servants on the bill team, who will have prepared the minister's briefings on the merits of the bill and the failings of the multifarious opposition amendments, designed occasionally to improve the bill but more often to explore the issue, tease out the depth of the minister's knowledge of the subject matter and search for weaknesses in the government's defences. These are known as 'probing' amendments.

The forum is made even more confrontational by the reduced space between government and opposition, who glare at one another across about seven feet of neutral territory.

This is difficult terrain for a government minister in any department, but for a Treasury minister on a Finance Bill, it is a minefield where the need for accuracy and precision is even more pronounced than usual. Every word Dawn uttered about excise duty, double taxation relief, striking the balance between mixer companies and onshore pooling, energy tax, stamp duty – all of it complex and mostly esoteric – would be pored over by tax lawyers and experts from the avoidance industry.

Promising ministers have walked into a committee room convinced that their natural authority and brilliant oratory would carry them through without more than a cursory glance at their brief. Those ministers have usually arrived as up and coming and left as down and going.

An MP for a decade before we gained power in 1997, Dawn had been on Labour's Treasury team in opposition and had crossed the Finance Bill minefield safely year after year. Her calm and courteous approach never wavered and her diligence never diminished. She did, however, make a conscious effort to ease up when Derek Fatchett, a highly effective Foreign Office minister, died from a massive heart attack in May 1999. Dawn made an immediate vow never to take home more than one red box, cutting back on the two or three that her government car service driver customarily loaded into the boot every evening. Presumably, the work that would have been in those extra boxes still had to be done, so the effectiveness of her resolution on reducing her workload was doubtful, but it made her feel better and her husband, Ian, a Unison trade-union official, approved of the attempt.

Being Dawn Primarolo's PPS didn't involve me in very much additional work and it gave me a focus on my parliamentary duties that didn't interfere with my constituency work. Indeed, by the time I left Dawn after a year and a half to take another step up the ministerial ladder, I'd made sure that everyone who mattered in the Treasury was aware of the injustice inflicted on Britain's distant-water trawlermen.

Chapter 12

MY DAUGHTER DIED on 14 July 1999. Natalie was thirty-two and pregnant with her third child.

She'd gone to see her GP the previous morning because she was feeling ill. Her doctor, suspecting a pulmonary embolism, had insisted that she summoned her husband, Lee, from work and went straight to High Wycombe hospital.

Natalie spent the entire day having every kind of test except the one specifically designed to determine whether or not she had an embolism. It was not deemed necessary for her to be kept in overnight for observation.

She died the next morning, alone, on her bathroom floor.

Natalie was fifteen months old when I met Judy, her mother, at a New Year party at my sister's. Judy was unmarried at a time when there was still a stigma attached to having a baby out of wedlock. She had been engaged for three years to Natalie's biological father, Beppe, an Italian student she'd met at teacher training college – until she discovered she was pregnant, news which sent Beppe fleeing back to Italy, never to be seen or heard from again. The sixties may have been a liberalizing decade but the process was slow and, in working-class communities, glacial.

Judy and I married in the summer of 1968 and our second child, Emma, was born on Christmas Eve. Less than a year after our wedding, the four of us moved out of the crumbling grandeur of North Kensington to the one council house offered to us, take it or leave it, on the Britwell estate in Slough. I transferred with the Post Office from Barnes to Slough, where we lived happily for nineteen years.

I'd never considered Natalie to be anything other than my own daughter – indeed, nobody in Slough was aware that, biologically speaking, she wasn't – and she'd never known any other father. I officially adopted her when she was ten, and old enough to understand and give her approval. As the process entitled her to a fresh birth certificate, she got to choose a middle name. Not having one had always rankled with her. For some reason that Judy and I could never fathom, as she didn't know anyone by that name, she chose Anne. And she was adamant that it must be spelled with an 'e'.

In her twenties Natalie decided to track down her birth father. She talked to me about it first and I reassured her that it was a natural desire and that I completely understood. However, I advised her to make sure, given Beppe's radio silence throughout her life, that she was willing to take the risk he might not share her enthusiasm to make contact.

'Oh, don't worry about that, Dad – I'm doing this purely out of curiosity,' she replied. I don't know how she tracked Beppe down, or on what basis it was all arranged, but she went to Italy, met him and came back sad and hurt. She told me he had been cold and distant and that the experience made her sorry she'd sought him out in the first place.

I have to push my pen through these paragraphs because I cannot write about my life without recording the devastating effect of Natalie's death.

We all came together at Natalie and Lee's house in High Wycombe. Judy, who I hadn't seen for over a decade; Emma, who was raising three sons on her own, having decided to split from their father; and Jamie, who was by now working with artists like Paul Weller and Robert Wyatt as a recording engineer and musician. He'd just met Jane, who would become his wife. Lee and his and Natalie's children, Carmel and Jez (aged twelve and four) and a close friend who lived nearby completed the sombre gathering.

Day after day, we met there, making our separate journeys from London and Bracknell and Slough, where Judy still lived, now with her second husband, in the house on the Britwell we'd moved into thirty years before almost to the day. We gravitated to Natalie's home because it was all we could think of to do. To be with one another and spend the day drinking tea and talking in disjointed conversations, punctuated by sobbing and the occasional laughter at the remembrance of some long-forgotten incident that resurfaced as we reminisced.

It was hot and sunny, the height of summer. Somebody had bought me the cassette single of Ricky Martin's 'Livin' La Vida Loca', which I played and replayed on the tape deck in my car, turning up the volume as I drove through the Buckinghamshire countryside towards Natalie's house, waiting for the instrumental break, played on the bass strings of an acoustic guitar, and then joining in at the top of my voice. Music was a comfort but I wanted nothing sombre. Instead I sang along with this hymn to the crazy life. It seemed to help.

At the house we'd sit on the front step, or in the back garden, as if being together would stem the tide of grief. I asked Judy to bring over our old photograph albums. We'd sit turning the pages. The early snapshots were neatly displayed on thick, grey paper and properly captioned: 'First day at Lynch Hill school', 'On holiday at Cobb Cottage, Camelford', 'Britwell Carnival'.

The mountings became less meticulous as the years passed until they petered out altogether. The later photographs, complete with negatives, still in their bright yellow Kodak packs as collected from the chemist's, were shoved unceremoniously into the back of the album.

Of course, there were things to be done, and we'd break away from our reverie to carry out tasks: the grim bureaucracy of death, with its certificates to be collected and funeral arrangements to be made.

For some reason, one Saturday Jamie and I decided to take Carmel to watch a QPR match. Perhaps she'd intimated that she'd like to go; more probably we wanted to take her somewhere and our unimaginative, football-orientated, perverse idea of pleasure drew us to Loftus Road. Carmel's sad beauty reminded us all of the mother she'd lost and made us ache to do things for her. Pathetically, all Jamie and I could come up with was an afternoon at a football match.

The day before Natalie's cremation, we all went to the funeral parlour to say our farewells. She lay in an open coffin, the lid leaning up against the wall near the door.

As we left I glanced at the little silver plaque on the lid recording her married name, Natalie Ann Diggins. The 'e' was missing from the middle name she'd chosen when I'd formally adopted her. The 'e' she had insisted upon. I said nothing, walked on and left it as it was.

I can't help thinking it was a kind of betrayal; that I let my daughter down by neglecting to chase after that missing 'e'; that I didn't loudly protest, insist that the plaque be removed and corrected. But I didn't. Sometimes it's the small things that niggle away, like a dull pain when the agony has passed.

Somehow we all went back to the lives we'd been leading. For me that meant going into Parliament to attend meetings, where I was of little use.

I remember being in one meeting, with Tony Blair, where a number of us electoral reformers were pressing the case for proportional representation following the publication of the Jenkins Report, which the government had commissioned from Roy (now Lord) Jenkins and which had come up with an elegant solution that preserved the important constituency link. I sat quietly, looking on through my dark glasses as my compatriots made the forlorn argument that the government should abandon the voting system that had given them a landslide majority.

Afterwards, Tony asked to speak to me alone. I'd done my best to suppress news of Natalie's death, though of course Dawn and the whips needed to know the reason for my long absence. I considered it to be a very private matter, nobody else's business. To its eternal credit, my constituency newspaper, the *Hull Daily Mail*, having heard of Natalie's death, respected my plea not to report it and only one national newspaper refused to do the same. Tony was kind and considerate, but I hated talking about this to anyone, including the prime minister. When news spread to the parliamentary Labour party I received many lovely letters from colleagues. All were read, but none were answered.

Often, in conversation with strangers, the question of how many children you have arises. When I answer I always include Natalie. Not to do so would be to deny she ever existed. It can be difficult when people go on to ask what my children do. Sometimes I've invented current occupations for Natalie just to avoid having to step back into the black shadow of her death.

Soon after Parliament went into its summer recess I had a call one afternoon from Sally Morgan, the prime minister's political secretary, who had been my go-between during the long gestation period before my rebirth as a member of Parliament. Now she was calling with an invitation from Tony Blair to join his government as parliamentary under-secretary at the Department of Trade and Industry. The prime minister had already reshuffled his Cabinet; Sally was doing the next job on the list: conveying his wishes to the lower orders.

It was another step up but, unlike my PPS role, this was a proper job: as a government minister, bound by the ministerial code, with an office, a salary, red boxes and a government car.

I accepted the offer and she suggested I go straight over to the DTI to meet my private office. Of all the departments, this was the one I knew best. As a union official it had been the scene of my skirmishes with Michael Heseltine and, more recently, of my efforts to assist Ian McCartney.

Ian had been promoted to the Cabinet office and I was now to pick up some of his former responsibilities, including the Post Office and employment relations. It was early evening before I was able to wander across to 1 Victoria Street to begin what was to be an eleven-year stint as a government minister. Waiting for me outside on that soft summer's evening was my private secretary, a young rapscallion by the name of Simon Lancaster.

Simon's wide and encouraging smile was exactly the tonic I needed as I was inducted into the closed order of ministerial life. There is a scene in *Yes, Minister* where Jim Hacker gets his first ministerial job and Bernard, Simon's fictional equivalent, lists the vast array of secretaries in the hierarchy: the permanent secretary, principal private secretary, first secretary, assistant secretary, parliamentary private secretary . . . At the end of this litany, Hacker asks, 'Which one of them does my typing?'

Simon and I went through something similar as he patiently explained who was who at the DTI while I worried about the more prosaic aspects of my job.

The answer to Hacker's question, incidentally, is that none of them did his typing. There wasn't a traditional secretary to take dictation and type letters. Correspondence wasn't something with which ministers engaged, other than to sign the letters that materialized in their name but which had been entirely dealt with by a ghostly hand in something called the 'correspondence unit'.

Simon led me up to the seventh floor, where the secretary of state and his seven ministers resided – ministers who covered trade, science, energy, consumer affairs, equal opportunities, aerospace, biotechnology and every sector of manufacturing industry from cars to textiles, caravans to cardboard boxes.

My affinity with Simon was immediate and lasting. He was as far from the stereotypical *Yes, Minister* version of the civil servant as it was possible to get. Brought up by a single mother on a council estate in Paddington, he'd been expelled from school aged sixteen and had worked in telesales by day and as a pianist at night until he managed to blag his way into the civil service and on to the 'fast stream' reserved for the brightest talents. That's how he ended up as my private secretary at the tender age of twenty-six. Simon, as I was soon to discover, was a fully fledged, late-night-drinking, chain-smoking, woman-chasing 'lad'. An infectious lust for life radiated from him as he soaked up experiences as rapidly as he absorbed the political biographies that obsessed him.

He also displayed a wisdom beyond his years as he took me through the way the department worked. With cheery panache, this handsome young man dispensed advice I've never forgotten and which stood me in good stead in the years to come.

My private office consisted of Simon, an assistant private secretary, a diary secretary and three others, including Mags, an exotic, beautifully spoken, well-dressed woman of a certain age around whom there was always a delicious scent of mystery. Mags was an agency worker and insisted on remaining one so that she could be in control of her own schedule. For long periods she would disappear, giving only vague hints on her return to the office as to what she had been up to. Our guess was that she'd been on a luxury yacht on some sun-kissed sea with a party of prosperous oligarchs. She always came back to the DTI with a lovely tan but no information as to where she'd been.

Simon explained that this office was the conduit through which all my work would flow. 'Remember,' he said as he warmed to his theme, 'we're the only part of this entire operation that's dedicated to you. We'll shield you from those who would do you harm and we'll go into battle on your behalf. No one gets to you without passing through us, and if you want to convey messages to other departments, I'm here to do that for you, no matter how difficult the message or how senior the civil servant it's being delivered to.'

He went on to tell me that someone from my private office would be listening to every incoming call that wasn't personal or confidential and accompanying me on every departmental visit. But their job at all times would be to look after my best interests.

Another member of that formidable team who inducted me into the civil service would, like Simon, play a continuing role after I'd moved on from the DTI. Bron Madson, my press officer, wasn't part of my private office but she might just as well have been. Allocated to me from the press department on the floor below, Bron's outward sweet passivity disguised a warrior within. She was married to an American fighter pilot whom she'd met in her native Suffolk, where he worked at a US airbase, and I always thought she'd be particularly effective at doing her husband's job.

Bron had already achieved notoriety by walking in front of a camera to halt a live interview with the last minister she'd worked for. Now I had her great skill, fearless aggression and quick thinking at my disposal.

Simon advised me that, although I would be spared a red box on my first evening in the job, at least one of these things would be coming home with me to be dealt with every night for the rest of my ministerial life. The entire rhythm of business in Whitehall was focused on getting ministers to read and sign off the 'submissions' the red boxes contained at the end of each working day.

Each box was lead-lined to protect the contents from fire, pestilence and plague. A government car and driver would be allocated to me, mainly for the purpose of conveying these precious red boxes rather than for my personal comfort. I was allowed to cadge a lift with them, but I wouldn't be afforded the same level of protection as the documents. If the car blew up I was dispensable; the red box would safeguard all the classified papers, which weren't.

During the parliamentary recess MPs are considered to be on holiday, although in reality the vast majority use the time to do the work in their constituency that they struggle to complete when they are tied to Westminster for at least four days a week. For ministers there is no recess. I clocked in at the DTI the next morning and every subsequent morning for five years.

My regular routine then was to start the day by jogging twice around an attractive splodge of green, loosely described as a park, off Hermitage Road in Upper Norwood. I'd started jogging as a substitute for the football I'd played as a young postman and the tennis I'd taken up in my mid-thirties. I only ever played tennis against Jamie, who regularly lost to me up to the age of about fourteen but was unbeatable thereafter.

I usually managed to jog every other morning, driving to the park, doing a double circuit, a distance of about three miles – which was as much as I could manage – and getting home again by seven to be showered and dressed by the time George, my government car service (GCS) driver, pulled up outside to take the red box and its minder in to the department.

George Aldred was in his sixties and had been a driver for his entire working life, first in his national-service days with the army and then with another branch of the civil service. He'd joined the GCS just as Labour came to power. Before being seconded to me he had been Peter Mandelson's driver.

Peter had left as secretary of state at the DTI under the cloud of Mortgagegate, the scandal that wasn't. He'd only been at 1 Victoria Street for six months but had revitalized what had become a staid backwater of Whitehall since Michael Heseltine's tenure. Stephen Byers, who had replaced Peter, was now my boss but the department still mourned a departure which had two consequences for me. The first was that I got George as my driver and the second was that I halved my mortgage payments.

It happened like this. Soon after my appointment I received a visit from the permanent secretary at the DTI, Michael Scholar. We junior ministers were rarely honoured with a visit from the the department's Sir Humphrey. He spent most of his time with the secretary of state who, I suppose, could be more accurately described as the temporary secretary. So far the permanent secretary was on his third trade secretary and we'd only been in government for just over two years.

The reason Michael Scholar came to see me was to subject me to a gentle interrogation about my private arrangements. In the wake of the Mandelson affair he wanted to rummage around my cupboard in search of skeletons.

His major concern was my association with the union. As I'd already informed the CWU that I would take not a penny from them, I considered myself to be immune to any allegations of bias.

The CWU, like other affiliated unions, had what were called 'sponsored MPs', that is to say MPs who received financial help from the union to run their offices or employ extra staff. Many Conservative MPs received similar support, usually from businesses but often from individual benefactors. There was nothing corrupt about the system and concerns about the connotations of the word 'sponsored' were being addressed by reorganizing the system to relate it to a constituency agreement which made it clear that none of the money went into the MP's pocket. The misleading term 'sponsored' was to be replaced by 'supported'.

Derek Hodgson had been keen to recruit me to the ranks of CWU-sponsored MPs but even before I became a minister I felt that to take money in this way would dilute the effect of anything I said in support of a publicly owned postal service or the trade-union movement. So I declined the offer.

Since my new role brought ministerial responsibility for the Post Office, it was right for the permanent secretary to probe me further. But now he was suggesting that my very membership of the CWU could be an issue.

We sat on the little armchairs in one corner of my office provided for more intimate conversations. Routine meetings were conducted around the long teak table that took up half the office. Simon, who was usually present at all my meetings, scribbling notes of the proceedings, had not been invited to this one, which Scholar had insisted should be 'one-to-one'.

I refused to contemplate leaving the union, pointing out that most Labour MPs, including the prime minister, were union members. And John Prescott, the deputy PM and my neighbouring Hull MP, was a member of the rail and seafarers' union despite having ministerial responsibility for transport. Thankfully, Scholar backed down and my CWU membership was safe.

'Any other association with the union that I need to know about?' he asked, lifting a bone china cup Mags had managed to procure to his thin lips for a final sip of tea.

'No, I don't think so,' I replied. 'Except for the mortgage.'

I worried he was going to choke as the tea seemed to go down the wrong way and the cup was returned haphazardly to its saucer.

'*Mortgage?* What mortgage?' asked the understandably distraught permanent secretary, still carrying the wounds from the Mandelson affair with a mortgage application at its core. I explained that the CWU was my mortgage-provider but that, far from this being financially advantageous to me, I was repaying it at a fixed high rate of interest and would be doing so until I was seventy-five years old.

As a result I was instructed to change my mortgage arrangements. Like many people, I suspect, I was reluctant to go through the hassle of shopping around for another mortgage-provider. But the permanent secretary followed up our conversation with an official letter and I had no choice. The happy outcome was that I halved my monthly repayments.

Michael Scholar was knighted not long afterwards. Not, I imagine, for his services to my finances, but I will always be grateful to him for those none the less.

Now that I was a government minister with an increased workload I felt that it was even more important to try to stay fit and stick to my regular routine of an early-morning jog at least three times a week.

One morning not long after my elevation I returned, sweating, to my car after a particularly gruelling run, having decided to sprint the final 150 yards. Sitting breathless in the driver's seat, I watched in the wing mirror as a police car pulled up silently behind me. One of its two occupants got out, came over to my car and greeted me through the open window.

'Good morning, sir,' the policeman said pleasantly. 'Is this your car?'

'Yes, officer,' I replied, with my usual cheery deference to authority. 'Why, is there a problem?'

'We've been called to a burglary on the other side of the park,' he told me, tapping the details of my car into a hand-held gizmo. 'A man was seen by the householder running away and as we arrived we spotted you in the vicinity, running very fast. What's your address, sir?'

As he tapped in the address I recited, I suddenly realized that the address for the registered owner of the car wouldn't be the one I'd just given him. Laura's sister had a new company car every few years as one of the perks of her job with Reuters, and was allowed to do what she liked with the old one. I'd bought her Mondeo Ghia, with its electric sunroof and ten-stack CD-player, but hadn't yet completed the change of ownership form (the V something or other) that had to be sent to the DVLA.

I sat there hoping that by some divine intervention the car would be registered at my address. But of course it wasn't.

'This car doesn't appear to belong to you at all, sir,' the policeman said, his tone of polite irony suggesting that the computer had merely confirmed his strong suspicion.

It was then that I made the mistake of seeking refuge in pomposity. I explained the disparity, offering Lisa's address as proof I was telling the truth, but ending with the ill-advised words: 'Anyway, officer, if you care to check, you'll find that I'm a member of Parliament and government minister.'

The policeman paused and gazed across the verdant parkland before leaning down at the window again to deliver his devastating response.

'But that doesn't mean you're a stranger to criminality, does it, sir?'

He turned, gizmo in hand, to walk back to the police car and consult his colleague while I sat bathed in sweat from the run and drowning in the scorn of my interrogator.

They probably left me stewing in my own juice for longer than was strictly necessary before the officer returned to deliver the final blow.

'OK, sir, we've now received a full description of the miscreant. He was young and slim. You can go.'

I would see out the year, the decade, the century, the millennium in a state of acclimatization. Ring binders appeared in my red box on a regular basis so that I could 'read my way into' the multifarious issues for which I was now responsible. Simon commissioned briefings on aerospace, biotechnology and the setting up of the Manufacturing Advisory Service. There was a particularly thick file on the Post Office Bill that I would have to take through its various legislative stages. This bill was designed to give postal services commercial freedom in the public sector – the alternative to privatization that my union had championed in our fight against Heseltine and Major.

Another binder contained details of the new rights for workers, including the minimum wage, that were awaiting introduction after royal assent. At least the summer recess would give me an opportunity to absorb this volume of information before Parliament reconvened in October.

Some new ministers are appointed at noon and expected to take questions on their department, or pilot a bill through its committee stage, an hour or so later. They are accorded little sympathy by their parliamentary colleagues. They have departed from the back benches to join the executive, and those they have left behind on their side of the House may be envious. Those on the other side will already be sharpening their knives, keen to feast on this tender ministerial offering. All of them expect the fledgling minister to acquire instant expertise along with the status and the salary.

Even during the recess I felt I was seeing more of George than I was of Laura. As well as driving me backwards and forwards between my home and Whitehall, George took me on visits to manufacturing plants and to scattered outposts of my empire, such as ACAS and the Patent Office in Cardiff. Being attached exclusively to me often meant dropping me off in the morning and picking me up in the evening with nothing to do in the meantime but occupy the drivers' room, a dark, forbidding place more conducive to sleep than to conversation.

I never sat in the back of the car, preferring the front passenger seat next to George, who'd sit rolling a fag as he waited outside my house in the morning and light it up as we pulled away. Lighting and relighting that slow-burning roll-up seemed to be as much a part of driving the car for him as putting it into gear.

I soon learned that George was the union rep for the government car service. A Transport and General man, he constantly bewailed the fact that long hours of overtime were necessary to earn a living wage. This was a predicament with which I was all too familiar from my days as a postman, and it was such a regular topic of conversation between us that to all intents and purposes I became George's unofficial consultant on union affairs. I had an enormous affection for this squat little man whose posture seemed to have taken on the shape of his driving seat. Born and bred in Tooting, George told me how, as a child, he'd escaped without a scratch when a German doodlebug exploded in Tooting High Street, shattering a huge plate-glass window right beside him.

He was now approaching retirement age but dreaded the thought of being without a routine. 'All my working life I've 'ad instructions to follow,' he said plaintively. 'From the Army to GCS, somebody 'as set a pattern for me to follow.' The discipline of living to a pre-set pattern applied at weekends as well. Every other Sunday George would go for a lunchtime drink and a game of snooker with his son. It was always every other week, never varying or encroaching on the Sundays in between.

The age discrimination legislation formulated by my department, which would end the nonsense of people having to give up their jobs according to an arbitrary date on the calendar, had yet to be enacted. In the meantime, I managed to successfully argue for George to be kept on after the age of sixty-five.

George smoking in the car would be inconceivable today and wasn't entirely acceptable even at the time. He always kept the driver's window open but the fug of tobacco smoke still pervaded the interior. I didn't mind George's filthy habit, principally because I'd reacquired it myself.

During the long hours spent mourning Natalie at her house in High Wycombe I'd accepted a cigarette from somebody and found myself smoking again for the first time in over twenty years.

Having started at the age of twelve, I managed to stop when I was twenty-eight. Through all the traumas of trade-union life, the strikes and disputes and long hours of negotiation, it had never even occurred to me to pick up a cigarette. Now taking up smoking again was my dirty little secret. I never smoked at home and never even revealed my relapse to Laura. Any lingering fragrance on my clothes was easily explained away by George's eternal roll-up.

I wasn't proud of the fact that I'd lapsed but neither could I deny my temporary reliance on the dreaded weed. I'd store my little stock of filter tips, along with a lighter, in the glove compartment of my ministerial car, confident that George would protect the evidence. I'd only ever smoked about ten a day in my youth. Now I was smoking at about the same rate, in snatched moments, in the car or out on the terrace of the House of Commons, or with Simon Lancaster, who could always be depended upon to find somewhere to light up.

At lunchtime, I'd go off alone with my copy of *The Times* to the smoking section of a little Italian sandwich place opposite St James's Park Underground station. After eating my ciabatta with cheese and tomato, I'd have two cigarettes with a cup of tea, just as my mother used to do every morning, her varicose-veined legs at rest, for once, on a kitchen chair as she read her *Daily Sketch*. Lily would cut her cigarettes in half with a razor blade to make them last twice as long. I had no such financial constraints.

There was one other smoking refuge. All government ministers were allocated an office in the Palace of Westminster, so I'd left Jane and my staff in 1 Parliament Street and moved across to an upstairs committee corridor. Unlike my office at the DTI, this one was tiny and useful primarily as somewhere to stash my cigarettes and lighter and enjoy a quick smoke.

It was strange how the urge to smoke had returned so rapidly after all that time, the acrid taste becoming desirable again, the nicotine working its way through the system to make itself indispensable. I can't remember how long this phase lasted – two years at the most, I'd say – before the compulsion left me as suddenly as it had arrived. I cleared out the lighters and fag packets from their secret locations, threw them all away and stopped smoking. I have never been remotely inclined to start again.

The impending millennium cast its spell over everything as the century drew to a close. There was an atmosphere of excitement and optimism; a sense of opportunity. For me the feeling was almost spiritual in its intensity, entwined as it was with a new era in my own life. After a year of us trying for a child, Laura was pregnant.

Having been a father of three at twenty, I was to be a father again at fifty. Standing out among a swirl of emotions was a joyous sense of renewal. The dull ache of Natalie's death would always be with me, but even I, the great unbeliever, found it difficult to deny Linda's conviction, expressed down the phone line from Australia, that there was something deeply symbolic and auspicious about the confluence of events at the end of the twentieth century.

I have no words to describe the profundity of the moment, or to begin to articulate my sense of enrichment, when Oliver Clark Johnson came into this world on 8 June 2000.

When Emma arrived in 1968, a father's attendance at the birth of his child had been more or less prohibited; when Jamie was born at home in 1971, it had still been discouraged. By the time Oliver made his entrance it was virtually compulsory.

I'd been at the Berlin air show, a visit that included a lunch with fellow aerospace ministers (where my traditional French equivalent actually ate his dessert with a spoon in one hand and a Gauloise in the other). Returning on the afternoon of 7 June, I was sitting on the terrace of the House of Commons with Simon on a glorious evening, waiting to vote. Laura was at her parents' house, following the maternity hospital's instructions to time her contractions. Despite Labour's huge majority I hadn't been released from the whip and the vote wasn't due until 10pm. The pairing whip, who decides these things, had rejected my request to absent myself from the vote, arguing that I'd be able to troop through the voting lobby and still have time to be present at the birth. So, inconveniently for us both, while Laura was in labour, I was in Labour.

As always, clipped to my belt was the pager, which vibrated when there was a message to read, invariably a missive from the whips' office telling us that a vote was due. But when the pager buzzed at 9.45pm, it was to alert me to a message from my sister-in-law informing me that Laura had been taken to the Mayday hospital in Croydon. Nevertheless, I hung on for fifteen minutes and voted before rushing off. I'm not sure what that says about the parliamentary system, my priorities or our male-orientated society, but whatever it is, I'm sure it isn't good.

That night I entered a world that had been closed to men for most of the century we'd just left behind and all those preceding it. I witnessed the terrible beauty of childbirth.

In delivery room 4 of the Mayday hospital, staff bustled in and out, sometimes reappearing, often being replaced as shifts changed through the long night. There was one lump of a lad who was apparently being trained and whose presence in this female world I resented. I particularly disliked the way he gazed silently at my wife with a silly smirk on his face. As the labour progressed he constantly parroted a single phrase, something he must have heard a midwife say: 'Keep your chin down.' Having repeated this ad nauseam, to my relief he eventually lurched off, to return, I hoped, to his proper job as a furniture remover.

Some nurses and midwives came in with a smile, bringing a sense of reassurance; others scowled beneath furrowed brows. Instruments were produced, pillows plumped, adjustments made to the medical equipment. In the middle of it all, magnificent in her strength and determination, was Laura.

Occasionally surrounded by people, but somehow always alone.

Having refused even to contemplate an epidural, she went through her ordeal of gas and air, sweat and tears, push and pause, cut and stitch, fighting her own personal battle.

I love the 'The Waste Land' by T. S. Eliot, but I could never explain it. It's the closest parallel I can draw with the awe and mystery of my experience of seeing Oliver enter the world.

What I observed was, in every sense, selfless. Laura would have sacrificed her life, and would have done so happily, if it ensured Oliver's safe delivery. There, on that night in June, as a thoroughly superfluous bystander, I learned more about love and courage and being human than I had ever known or will ever know.

I was perhaps not mature enough to fully enjoy fatherhood the first time round. I loved my kids and was proud of them, but pushing a pram about Ladbroke Grove wasn't what eighteen-year-old boys did. A pram wasn't exactly a Mod accessory.

When Jamie was born I'd had seven weeks' unpaid paternity leave thanks to the Post Office strike of 1971. Back then, as a twenty-year-old postman, it would never have crossed my mind to lend a hand around the house, other than maybe to iron my own shirt before going out with the lads for a Sunday lunchtime drink. In those days it would have seemed to be going against the course of nature for working-class men to change nappies, make beds or scrub floors. I suspect that was as true of other social classes. I only knew about mine. However,

I did read a lot of books, which gave me a window on different kinds of lives, and I found no examples there to suggest that these attitudes were confined to the less advantaged of us.

Thirty years later I was just as self-absorbed, but times had moved on. Now I became an enthusiastic pusher of prams and a rather less enthusiastic changer of nappies. Like everything else, the paraphernalia of infancy had transformed in the thirty years between the births of Jamie and Oliver, significantly reducing the drudgery of childcare. Disposable nappies had replaced terry towelling and muslin squares and the endless buckets and bleaching needed to launder them. Ready-made baby food filled the shelves of supermarkets and there was a variety of helpful gadgets on the market designed to assist in the business of bringing up a baby.

As for prams, they were a rarer sight than vintage cars. Every self-respecting parent pushed their child around in a 'buggy'. I would take Oliver out in his at every opportunity, making a ritual of walking him up to Crystal Palace on a Sunday morning to buy the papers. On the way I would cast envious glances towards some of the slicker buggies we passed, noting the brand in case we ever wanted to trade up, which we did several times.

Having more money made a difference, of course. We had all the household appliances – washing machine, tumble-dryer, vacuum cleaner, dishwasher, fridge – that Judy and I could only dream of in the early 1970s. We had a car, too, enabling us to experience the intellectual challenge of fitting a baby's car seat. We also had enough disposable income to indulge in luxuries like the video camera I purchased soon after Oliver was born.

There is just one photograph each in existence of Linda and me as babies. Thereafter it was only thanks to the primary-school photographer that a pictorial record of our childhood development was made. In the new millennium, every stage of Oliver's young life was captured on that camera, the completed tapes meticulously stored, in date order, and transferred to DVD as digital technology developed alongside him.

In one early tape Oliver is crawling around our front room. It's his first birthday and the television in the background is reporting the news of Labour's second landslide victory in the general election of June 2001.

Chapter 13

My own re-election as MP for Hull West and Hessle wasn't ever in much doubt, although I never took it for granted. Hull had elected Labour MPs for many years. The only novelty was for those MPs to be representing the party of government.

Labour had never in their 101-year history won two full terms in office. As we'd celebrated the fiftieth anniversary of the National Health Service in 1998, I'd reflected on the sobering fact that in those fifty years Labour, the party that created the NHS, had been in power for just fifteen and the Conservatives for the other thirty-five. But in 2001, our majority for our second term was again huge, slightly smaller than in 1997 but reduced only from 179 to 167.

In Hull West and Hessle, my agent in this election was Kath Lavery. I'd appointed Kath when John Atkinson stepped aside. The switch was nothing personal. Despite being on different wings of the party, John and I developed a close friendship. He was into his eighties by then and simply felt it was time to hand over the baton. MPs have sole discretion in appointing an agent, a role which is really only an active one during a general election, when the agent takes responsibility for dealing with all the necessary paperwork and keeping control of the election finances.

I liked and trusted Kath, with whom I shared a passion for T. S. Eliot. She may well have been the only agent in the country who knew 'The Love Song of J. Alfred Prufrock' by heart and could quote whole chunks from *Four Quartets*.

We worked hard throughout the campaign, approaching the election as if we were fighting a marginal seat. We were out door-knocking on the night my neighbouring MP John Prescott made the headlines for punching an egg-thrower in Rhyl. The most profound comment on this incident came from a middle-aged man – evidently a rugby league fan (rivalry between Hull FC in the west and Hull Kingston Rovers in the east is fierce) – who came to the door in his vest and trousers. He pronounced that you could tell Prescott was from east Hull, because 'If 'e'd been from west 'Ull 'e'd have nootted 'im.'

On the June night when I was re-elected with a handsome 58 per cent of the vote, Kath had the team kitted out in red T-shirts with 'Election 2001' emblazoned across them.

There were a lot of good things happening in Hull. The maternity hospital, housed in a Victorian former workhouse some six miles from the general hospital, was at last to be replaced by a brand-new mother-and-baby unit attached to Hull Royal Infirmary. An eye hospital was also under construction. A terrific millennium attraction, the Deep (which insists on calling itself a submarium rather than an aquarium), was about to open. There were more police and fewer crimes, a new road to ease the congestion east of the River Hull and more jobs in a growing economy.

But paramount among all the improvements under a Labour government was the issue that attracted hardly any attention at all in the national media: we had secured the compensation scheme the trawlermen had been pursuing for twenty-five years.

Ever since that first meeting with Ian McCartney at the Department of Trade and Industry we had lobbied, rallied, petitioned and argued. Twice we'd lobbied Parliament, decanting coachloads of trawlermen, mostly from Hull, on to the prosperous streets of Westminster. In Hull we'd held mass meetings in whatever premises could be found that were big enough: the Trades club in Beverley Road, the Walton Street community centre and, for the final meeting, where victory was declared, the Methodist central hall in King Edward Street. Such was the energy and enthusiasm these men, most of them elderly by this stage, had devoted to the campaign, I feared that now it had ended, now the just cause which had brought meaning to their lives and kept them going no longer had to be fought for, they might struggle to fill the vacuum.

The agreement didn't take much explaining. The BFA had achieved precisely the objectives laid down in their constitution at the outset. For every man who lost his job after 1 January 1974, when the 200-mile fishing limit around Iceland had been imposed, £1,000 for each year of service, irrespective of rank, capped at twenty years, and full payment to widows and dependants.

For a long time, while the DTI were claiming it was an issue for MAFF, and MAFF claimed it was the province of the DTI, we had known that the final decision would rest not with either department but with the Treasury.

When we'd met the chief secretary to the Treasury, Andrew Smith, in his dark, forbidding office, he'd asked if we were prepared to compromise: to limit payments to ten years rather than twenty, and/or to reduce the £1,000-a-year figure. There had been some internal debates about whether we should or shouldn't; whether half a loaf was better than no bread at all. I was unusually implacable. All my experience of negotiation had taught me that compromise was necessary to secure a deal, but this wasn't like a pay claim, with a union seeking more than it expected and prepared to settle for less.

The people I was negotiating for this time weren't decently paid union members asking for a pay rise. Many of the trawlermen and their families had been thrown into destitution. Even now, no amount of money could reset their lives in the way that an immediate package of compensation, retraining and redeployment could have done.

Andrew Smith asked how much we estimated this would cost. We said £10 million, peanuts in terms of government finances. He countered that the Treasury estimate was double our figure. Bigger peanuts, we retorted, but still peanuts. Finally the deal was sanctioned by the prime minister and announced just before recess in the summer of 2000. It ended up costing over £40 million and would have been justified at twice that amount.

There would be issues relating to the administration of the scheme to be dealt with that would keep me occupied on trawlermen's compensation for another decade. And it would be four more years before the quest for the truth about the fate of the *Gaul* was re-examined in what was described as a 'reopened formal investigation' into its loss.

Since the original, hurriedly convened inquiry in 1974, which had had no evidence to guide its conclusions, there had been a full survey of the wreck. John Prescott, as the minister responsible, authorized two major projects that gleaned much information from what was, in effect, the disturbance of a tomb. The reopened investigation, held in Hull thirty years after the first inquiry, would find in December 2004 that the *Gaul* sank in terrible weather because of 'a sudden and rapid accumulation of water on the factory deck'. This confirmed what the Hull trawlermen had always suspected, though some of the families continue to believe that there were more sinister reasons for the tragedy that dominated their lives.

For now what mattered was that the compensation scheme was established and that, for most affected families, substantial sums would begin arriving quickly. Ron Bateman and Ray Smith, who had led their men to victory, were a perfect leadership combination but I had soon realized that they didn't actually get on. Like many double acts, they suppressed their mutual loathing for the greater good. I loved them both, their lack of airs and graces, their humour, their profound good-heartedness.

Little Ron and Big Ray insisted that we embarked on a celebratory pub crawl down the Hessle Road. It was arranged for a Saturday lunchtime. We visited every single boozer before settling at Rayner's, officially called the Star and Garter, but known to everyone by the name of its legendary landlord of bygone days, Henry Rayner.

While the industry that sustained the community had gone, the culture had changed little since Rayner ran the pub in the 1950s. The men tried to maintain their Teddy boy quiffs despite their thinning hair. The women were as tough and brash as they'd had to be as matriarchs of the distant-water fishing families. They still sang the songs of Elvis, Cliff and Connie Francis and told tales of Hessle Road in its heyday.

There was no false romanticism about the hard lives they'd endured, but they were real and vivid and loyal and proud. We came from different backgrounds, separated by accent and geography, but being in their company was nevertheless like returning to Southam Street and the Golborne Road in the fifties and sixties, where there was a boozer on every corner and a piano in the corner of every boozer.

As the blue curl of tobacco smoke drifted towards the ceiling of whichever pub we were in, small tumblers of the obligatory rum would be placed in front of me by ex-fishermen who, if they said anything at all, merely grunted, 'Get that down yer.'

And on that occasion, get it down me I did – far too much of it, unfortunately. But the respect of these special people seemed to me to be the most important accolade I could have earned in my political career. It felt that day like my crowning achievement. It still does.

The weekend after the election I waited to hear from number 10. Was I to be promoted, sacked or re-employed in the same position? All the cards were in play, which I suppose made it a shuffle rather than a reshuffle. The prime minister was busy appointing a new government and as always the Cabinet was chosen first. My driver, George, had been keeping me abreast of developments during his nightly visits to bring me my red box.

It contained very little, just the stuff that had to be processed through the civil-service machine. The country still has to be governed during an election and in its immediate aftermath, and so ministers continue in their government positions throughout the campaign and beyond, until they are sacked, elevated or entrenched.

The government car service was always a reliable source of information because the drivers would take ministers to 10 Downing Street when the call came and collect them after they'd seen the PM. They were therefore the first to hear the news when their minister emerged. They were also inveterate gossips.

George told me there was a problem with the foreign secretary. Robin Cook had been driven to Downing Street but had not emerged, which meant that, as George put it, ''E ain't 'appy wiv what 'e's been offered. And if 'e ain't 'appy, it means 'e's being moved.'

My former boss Dawn Primarolo, my old friend Kate Hoey and I formed an anxious little trio as we rang one another constantly to check if any of us had been told our fate. Certainly none of us expected promotion to the Cabinet. We were functionaries further down the chain of command, waiting and worrying about whether we still had our government jobs, Dawn as paymaster general, Kate as minister for sport and me as parliamentary under-secretary at the DTI.

Eventually, on Sunday, we found out. Of the three possible eventualities, between us we'd collected the full set. I was promoted, Dawn remained as paymaster general and poor Kate was sacked.

An athlete in her youth and profoundly interested in every

aspect of sport, Kate seemed to me to be a square peg that fitted perfectly into a square hole but she had fallen victim to the curse of the Millennium Dome. Intended to be the crowning glory of the millennium celebrations, the dome had turned out to be one of the mishaps of our first term.

I visited the 'millennium experience' twice, once as a DTI minister with Simon before it was opened to the public and again with my daughter Emma on a private visit when it was in full swing. It wasn't bad but it was hardly Epcot and it didn't much resemble the 'beacon to the world' of which Tony Blair had boasted. It just lacked the 'wow factor' that was understandably expected of it. The dome had been the scene of a rather lacklustre televised celebration to see in the new millennium, which the newspapers had hammered mercilessly – mainly because their proprietors and editors had been forced to queue for ages to get in.

The Department for Culture, Media and Sport (otherwise known as the Ministry of Fun) had to carry the can and in the reshuffle all its ministers were sacked. Kate was dreadfully upset. The public humiliation of a ministerial sacking is devastating enough, but what made it worse for Kate was that she had been doing a job she loved. Losing it added bitter resentment to deep disappointment.

My new minister of state position at the DTI carried roughly the same responsibilities as I'd had before. Patricia Hewitt, who'd been a junior minister with me, was promoted to replace Stephen Byers as secretary of state. Stephen had gradually earned my respect in the two years I'd worked for him. He was a quiet, studious sort of guy who, I suspect, was incredibly shy. He and Alan Milburn were often talked up as the next Blair and Brown but I didn't think Stephen had either the aptitude or the ambition. In that regard we were kindred spirits. I liked his understated leadership style. In his office, with its picture window looking out on to the façade of Westminster Abbey, he was never to be found at his desk, preferring to sit with his laptop at one end of the long meeting table doing his work from there.

I was impressed by the way he took full responsibility during the crisis at Longbridge, when the Rover group folded leaving thousands of jobs at risk. He could have sent the issue up to the PM or down to me, his junior minister, but made no attempt to pass the buck. He also found a viable solution although, as things turned out, it was only a temporary one.

The money for the trawlermen's compensation scheme came from the DTI budget, with DTI officials administering it. While I wasn't allowed to have any ministerial involvement in the matter because of the conflict of interest, I knew that Stephen Byers would have had a major say in whether the scheme was sanctioned. He was himself an MP for a fishing port and I knew he was empathetic. For that I would always be grateful.

Now Stephen was off to head up the department responsible for transport and local government, which changed its title so often that I can't remember what it was called at the time. Patricia, his replacement, was intelligent and personable. Her problem was something she could do nothing about. She sounded patronizing. She wasn't, but she sounded as if she were. She spoke slowly and precisely, like the lady who presented *Listen with Mother* on the wireless when I was a kid.

I liked her a lot and dubbed her the Kylie Minogue of the

Cabinet, partly because she had been born and raised in Australia and partly because of the prime minister's tendency to refer to her in speeches simply as 'Patricia'. Just like Kylie, it seemed she needed no surname.

In fact I liked most of the ministerial team, which included several of the old members, such as Brian Wilson, the trade minister, a roughish free spirit whose passions were literature and Celtic football club.

Brian and I were allies in resisting some of Patricia's managerial obsessions. Sometimes we'd win, more often we lost. For instance, she was concerned that we were the only members of her vast ministerial team who didn't communicate via e-mail and insisted that we take a course in mastering it.

We dug our heels in and eventually she gave up. One skirmish we lost was over a daft self-awareness initiative. Each member of the team was forced to pick a group of colleagues who would then have to fill in endless forms detailing our strengths and weaknesses. We were shown the results, but not told who had said what. At least, I think that was how it worked.

It was a complete waste of everybody's time, but it pleased Patricia, who refused to be daunted or discouraged by the little nest of laddishness in her DTI tree occupied by Johnson and Wilson.

One minister I didn't like was the junior minister Nigel Griffiths, who was given the task of overseeing the administration of the trawlermen's compensation scheme. He'd taken root in the office earmarked for me on my promotion. Office allocation was based on rank. I was now due an upgrade and Nigel, as an under-secretary, was supposed to be taking my old office.

But before the move could be arranged he had occupied the office I had chosen.

It was in that office that we met, at his request, so that he could gain a better understanding of the trawlermen's scheme. We sat opposite one another, sipping tea and exchanging pleasantries, before getting on to the main business. He listened carefully as I explained some of the administrative issues the BFA and I felt were important. The sun shone through the huge windows of the lovely office, with its views of the abbey and Big Ben, its comfortable armchairs, in which we now reposed, its long sofa, attractive carpet and huge mahogany desk for the minister to sit behind.

After I'd finished, Nigel Griffiths leaned forward and said, 'Well, Alan, that's very interesting. I can see how important this scheme is to you and I'd love to get on with sorting out some of the issues so that these families can begin to receive their money.

'The problem is this. I'm having to move out of here and my staff have to pack all the files away. After I've moved into my new office I'm not sure where this file will be. It may well be stuck at the bottom of a box which will mean it will be a while before it gets processed.'

He leaned back in his chair and sipped his tea. Spoons rattled, Big Ben chimed. I could hardly believe what I'd heard. My ire was beginning to rise.

'Let me get this right,' I said. 'Are you actually telling me that if I don't allow you to stay in this office, payments to my trawlermen will be delayed?'

He pondered the question, a pained expression on his pinched face, but said nothing.

I may have misinterpreted his silence but I don't think so.

As extortion goes it was hardly in the *House of Cards* category, but to me it was equally despicable. I'm afraid that, once the expletives are deleted, there is nothing much to record of what was said next. Suffice to say I got my allocated office and the trawlermen got their money on time.

In September I went to Brighton for the TUC's annual congress. It was part of my job as the minister responsible for employment relations to spend at least a day there, as well as at the CBI conference. The government was interested in engaging both sides of industry in the kind of social-partnership mentality that was such a prevalent part of industrial relations in the rest of Europe.

After four years in power we had introduced the national minimum wage, taking advice on the rate from the Low Pay Commission, a body made up of an equal number of trade unionists and business people, along with a few academics, one of whom, Professor George Bain, was its brilliantly effective chair.

Labour had ended Britain's opt-out from the Social Chapter, an EU protocol setting out broad policy objectives on improving living and working conditions, thus introducing the requirement for employers to pay part-time workers the same hourly rate as full-timers, and staff on temporary contracts the same as regular staff.

The Working Time Directive (which was never part of the Social Chapter, although the Major government had wasted money on an expensive court case trying to claim it was) came into force, giving workers the right to rest breaks, at least four weeks' paid holiday a year and a day off every week. We'd legislated to legalize whistleblowing in the Public Disclosure Act, to outlaw the blacklisting of trade-union activists and for employers to be required to recognize a trade union where that union had recruited 50 per cent plus one of the workforce. Our anti-discrimination legislation had enshrined the right of workers not to be dismissed on the grounds of race, religion, disability or sexual orientation.

Now I was preparing to take a bill through Parliament increasing maternity leave from sixteen weeks to six months and, for the first time, introducing the right to paternity leave, as well as giving adopting couples the same rights to maternity and paternity leave as biological parents.

All this and more represented the most substantial package of workers' rights ever introduced in the UK. The Blair government had done more than any other to construct a framework of decent minimum standards to ensure that British workers were treated fairly.

In the public sector, where most union members worked, there was a huge push to bring investment in health and education up to the European average. Schools and hospitals were being built, doctors, nurses, teachers and teaching assistants recruited. Wages were rising, especially in the NHS, where a ten-year plan principally designed to reduce the scandal of long waiting times for treatment was also establishing higher pay rates, particularly for nurses and paramedics.

Labour politicians should have been able to look forward to a rapturous reception from the brothers and sisters of the TUC, but we were anticipating nothing of the kind. To quote Thunderclap Newman, there was 'something in the air'.

Part of it was a genuine sense of disconnection. The trade unions, having formed the Labour party, had always expected to be closely involved in the deliberations of a Labour government. Now, through the virtual elimination of the block vote and the introduction of a policy-making process that was more considered, their power over the party had diminished.

The internal dynamic within the unions had long been shifting. In the past, union leaders had had strong central control; now they were more susceptible to the whims of local activists, many of whom were far to the left of their general secretaries and contemptuous of the Labour party. There was also a sense that Labour was trying to distance itself from the unions – understandable because it was true. The John Smith reforms and (bizarrely) the changes to Clause IV were seen as part of that estrangement but there was more substantial evidence of it.

The party under Blair and Brown was as determined to ditch its reputation as being anti-business as it was to prove that Labour could run a successful economy. To some it seemed as if in order to be pro-business the party had to sound anti-union.

My friend John Monks summed up the genuine sense of discord when he said that the Blair government treated the trade unions as if they were embarrassing elderly relatives. Tony Blair was mystified by the criticism. For sure, he didn't understand the trade-union perspective. I would occasionally try to explain some arcane aspect of trade-union thinking on a particular issue and watch his eyes glaze over.

He certainly wasn't going to concede to the demand that we should repeal 'Thatcher's anti-trade union laws' because that would deny trade unionists the right to be balloted before strike action and to re-elect their leader every five years. It would also bring back the closed shop, meaning workers could be sacked for refusing to join the union.

The TUC had in any case long since accepted that these aspects of trade-union reform from the early 1980s were here to stay. Much of the subsequent Tory legislation, which had become more and more vindictive through their eighteen years in power, had already been repealed – indeed, it was the Blair government that removed the employers' freedom to sack their entire workforce on day one of a strike, which had been legal since the birth of trade unionism.

For Tony, the unions' attitude was a variation on the famous scene in Monty Python's *Life of Brian* where the Judaean People's Front (or was it the People's Front of Judaea?) sit around moaning, 'What have the Romans ever done for us?' and the answer gradually emerges as a great deal, actually.

My own view had always been that if a Labour government was perceived as being in the pocket of the trade unions it was damaging to both the party and the unions. The Labour party needed to have a broader swathe of support and trade unions needed to have a strong voice in society, irrespective of which party was in power.

The prime minister was due to come to Brighton on Tuesday 11 September to make his speech at the start of the afternoon session of congress. I went down to the Sussex coast as the advance guard. The media had billed this as a showdown, although I struggle to recall precisely what the showdown was about. There was a general air of grumpiness.

At lunchtime I did the media round, trailing after John Edmonds, the general secretary of the GMB, who seemed to be the morose mouthpiece of whatever discontent was fomenting at the time. I was due to join Tony Blair in his suite at the Grand hotel for a final run-through of the speech when the course of history changed.

News was breaking that there had been a terrible disaster in New York. A passenger plane had collided with one of the Twin Towers of the World Trade Center. Watching the live pictures from across the Atlantic in the media room at the conference, waiting to do another interview, I stood transfixed, like millions around the world, as a second plane smashed into the second tower and it became clear that this was no accident.

Everybody around me was rooted to the spot. What we were witnessing was unthinkable, so unbelievably horrific it was hard to process. Embargoed copies of the speech Tony was due to deliver had just been circulated to the media, but nobody was reading it. That speech about the mundane issues of jobs and prosperity and workers' rights would never be delivered.

I wasn't needed in the PM's suite as he prepared a very different speech; one which tried to pre-empt the new world order we would be entering after the event that would become known simply by its date: 9/11. It was the finest speech I ever heard him make.

Congress was abandoned. The TUC dinner that evening was cancelled. I went back to my hotel room, switched on the TV and sat on the edge of my bed, glued to the screen, feeling disorientated and afraid. People were throwing themselves out of windows high in the towers, flames blocking any chance of escape or rescue; first one or two, and then so many that they looked like birds cresting the airflow, chests pumped out, arms outstretched behind them, falling to certain death defiantly, gracefully, nightmarishly.

The Tom Petty track 'Free Fallin'' plays in my head whenever I recall this indelible image, as if it had been playing as a soundtrack to the TV coverage at the time. I can't listen to it now without being taken back to that day of sun and death in America.

How could there be people so crazed, so evil, so inhumane that they would use passenger airliners full of innocent men, women and children as guided missiles and be happy to kill themselves in the process?

When the Twin Towers crumbled it felt like Armageddon. It wasn't over yet. Another plane crashed into the Pentagon in Arlington County, Virginia; a fourth, being steered towards Washington, DC, came down in a Pennsylvania field. As all this unfolded there was no sense it would ever end. Horror piled on to more horror. Whoever was responsible for this atrocity seemed to have a thirst for death that was unquenchable.

Irrationally, I worried about Laura and Oliver. Laura was in the back garden. Yes, she and Oliver were fine. She'd seen some of the coverage, though she wished she hadn't. All was tranquil in Upper Norwood but I felt an impulse to take them away from London to a remote island somewhere, the Outer Hebrides, perhaps. Somewhere – anywhere – far away from what had previously been known as civilization.

I suppose war was inevitable. The terrible events in New York had been, in effect, a declaration of it. Within weeks US and

UK forces had launched Operation Enduring Freedom against the base in Afghanistan of al-Qaeda, the global Islamist terrorist group responsible for the US attacks. They were joined by forty-nine other countries. Al-Qaeda's training camps were destroyed, the Taliban government fell and the Islamic Republic of Afghanistan was established. The war, however, continued and Osama bin Laden, the leader of al-Qaeda, who'd been wanted by the United Nations since 1999, remained at large.

In an address to a joint session of Congress in the aftermath of 9/11, President George W. Bush had vowed that 'our "war on terror" begins with Al-Qaeda, but it does not end there. It will not end until every terrorist group of global reach has been found, stopped and defeated.'

There was no obvious connection between Saddam Hussein, the tyrannical president of Iraq, and the attack on the Twin Towers, but by 2002 the focus of the wide-ranging 'war on terror' had moved there. Saddam had spent eleven years ignoring a whole series of UN resolutions. He'd committed the two most serious international crimes – genocide against his own people and the invasion of neighbouring countries – not once, but twice during his brutal dictatorship. All of this, together with his refusal to allow UN weapons inspectors full access to search for 'weapons of mass destruction', had made him public enemy number two in the aftermath of 9/11.

And so it was that on Tuesday 18 March 2003 I stood below the bar in the House of Commons, observing the debate that would send British troops back into a second war with Iraq to resume the conflict begun with the Gulf War of 1991.

Government ministers occupy the front bench to the speaker's right, known as the Treasury bench, but ministers of state like me had no chance of parking our posteriors there on big parliamentary occasions. It could only just accommodate the most senior members of the Cabinet as it was (along with the government whip, who always has to be perched at the end nearest the doors).

Unable, by tradition, to sit on the back benches (where, in any case, there was not enough room that day even for those non-ministers fully entitled to a seat there), we junior ministers had no alternative but to stand just inside the huge oak doors, facing the speaker's chair, a vantage point from which we could observe but not participate. Government ministers couldn't enter into debates anyway, unless they were speaking for Her Majesty's government, and the only place they could do that was from the dispatch box.

This was the first time Parliament had been given the authority to make such a decision. All other hostilities had been subject to royal prerogative – war by decree, the prime minister and (perhaps) the Cabinet having made up their minds without consulting Parliament.

I'm sure that no whip had been issued for this debate. That is to say that Labour MPs did not receive any notification from the whips' office instructing them to vote in favour of the government motion to commit British forces to war. If there was a whip, it would have been futile. On issues such as this, MPs would be disinclined to follow anything other than their consciences.

The debate had been preceded by huge marches and demonstrations against going to war. Whether or not Parliament had the final say, the main protagonists for war in Iraq were the president of the United States, George W. Bush, and the prime minister of the United Kingdom of Britain and Northern Ireland, Anthony Lynton Blair.

Tony had aged visibly since that awful day in September 2001 when we'd been due to meet at the TUC in Brighton. I'd seen his gaunt features only on television, at Prime Minister's Questions or in the parliamentary Labour party meetings in Room 14 of the committee corridor. Those meetings had been given reports on his efforts to secure a UN Security Council resolution, culminating in Resolution 1441, which had been adopted unanimously on 8 November 2002. This had given Saddam Hussein 'a final opportunity to comply with its disarmament obligations', which dated back through ten other similar resolutions to the end of the Gulf War and threatened 'serious consequences' if he didn't.

The debate within the party – and indeed the country – was whether those 'serious consequences' for Saddam, if he didn't cooperate fully with UN weapons inspectors, meant that Iraq would be invaded without a further UN resolution.

Nobody doubted that he possessed so-called weapons of mass destruction. My colleagues who opposed the government motion in the March debate believed Saddam had them; so did the countries that opposed a second, unambiguous UN resolution being put to the Security Council after he'd failed to comply with 1441, France and Russia. They did not argue that Saddam had no weapons. Leaving aside the fact that he'd definitely had such weapons in the past and had indeed used them against his own people; ignoring for a moment the evidence of one of Saddam's relatives who'd fled to the West and revealed what he knew about the existence of such weapons (before being lured back to Iraq and murdered), we had the report of the weapons inspectors themselves, published eleven days before the debate.

On being evicted by Saddam in 1998, in contravention of yet another UN resolution, the UN inspectors had reported that 10,000 litres of anthrax, up to 6,500 chemical munitions, at least 80 tonnes of mustard gas and unquantifiable supplies (possibly more than ten times that amount) of sarin, botulism toxin and a host of other biological poisons, an entire Scud missile programme and a far-reaching VX nerve-agent programme were unaccounted for.

On 7 March, their latest report, 173 pages long, listed twenty-nine different areas where they'd been unable to obtain information on this stockpile of ghastly weaponry. Regarding anthrax, for instance, they said that, on all the available evidence, there was not only a strong presumption that the 10,000 litres listed in 1998 had not been destroyed, but that the potential production of the stuff might now have more than doubled.

Let others who were there that day claim that they were misled, lied to or entranced by the compelling oratory. It's my belief that if any random group of 650 citizens had been asked to debate and decide this issue, the majority would have voted to insist that the 'serious consequences' mentioned in UN Resolution 1441 were implemented; that Saddam and his murderous regime, which had been ignoring and humiliating the UN for over a decade, should not be allowed yet again to disregard the international community.

My political hero, Robin Cook, took a different view. The previous evening, once again standing below the bar in a packed Commons chamber, I watched Robin electrify the

House with his 'personal statement' and resign from the Cabinet. It was a brilliant speech. There was no rancour, no bile. Robin praised Tony Blair, stating that he had no sympathy with, and would give no comfort to, those who wanted to attack 'the most successful leader of my lifetime'.

Robin felt that we needed a second UN resolution to justify invasion. But France and Russia, having agreed to the 'serious consequences' in Resolution 1441, had vetoed any attempt to define what those consequences would be when their use became necessary. My own feeling was that a second resolution was desirable but not essential. The prime minister had tried hard to get one but failed. The decision had to be taken on the basis of what we had before us and, in my view, could be delayed no longer.

These were honest disagreements, pursued openly in serious debate. Tony Blair didn't lie; neither did he break the law.

Robin Cook spent much of the time remaining to him reassuring Muslim Labour supporters and convincing them that they should not desert the party. Less than two and a half years later, in 2005, he died suddenly of a heart attack. An epitaph on his headstone in the Grange cemetery in Edinburgh reads: 'I may not have succeeded in halting the war, but I did secure the right of Parliament to decide on war.'

I was one of those who decided and I would, in the same circumstances, make the same decision again.

Chapter 14

After four years I was nicely settled at the DTI. The personnel in my private office had changed. Traditionally, positions here attracted young high-flyers who wanted the experience of working closely with a minister. Apart from anything else, it was a good grounding for a future civil-service career. They rarely stayed in that hothouse environment for more than a few years. The long hours and stressful atmosphere increasingly discouraged applicants as 'work–life balance' became more of a consideration in every occupation.

That dreadful phrase was a mantra we at the DTI chanted often and may well have invented. As employment relations minister, it was my job to give it meaning. I took legislation through the House which gave a right to parents to request flexible working (and placed a legal obligation on employers to give such requests serious consideration), as well as the bill extending parental leave.

Simon Lancaster had moved on elsewhere in the department and Giles Smith, a quiet, unassuming West Ham supporter, was his latest successor. Giles made an immediate impression on me by revealing that his father had written a 'B' side for a

Pretty Things single back in the sixties. I'd seen the Pretty Things with a schoolfriend in the days when, as fourteen-year-olds, we used to brazen our way into clubs like the Marquee and the 100 Club in Soho.

The 'Things' were as big as the Stones in their early years and Giles told me that his dad still received an annual royalty cheque for that 'B' side, albeit nowadays for only a couple of quid.

Giles's number two in the private office was a young lesbian with a dazzling smile. Justine Jeffries was determined to persuade the world to become more tolerant by speaking to the population one at a time. Unlike Giles (and me), she'd fall into conversation with anyone as we travelled the country on ministerial business, invariably steering the conversation towards her favourite subjects of tolerance and equality.

Giles may have been quiet but he was a natural diplomat. Once, on an old train with compartments and corridors, he left me working on the speech I was on my way to give somewhere to go and fetch the coffees. All of a sudden, a woman in the next compartment began to scream.

I rushed in to find a man and a woman in their thirties who'd obviously been involved in some sort of physical altercation, which they'd stopped as soon as I appeared. I told the man that if he attacked his girlfriend again I'd be back in to protect her. Just then Giles came back along the corridor. He shooed me into our compartment while he sorted things out.

When he rejoined me ten minutes later he politely requested that I desist from making interventions like that again. He would be in trouble with his line manager, he said, if it was known that he'd let his minister get involved in a fight.

'But Giles,' I protested, 'I will not sit here while a woman is being attacked in the next carriage.'

'That's not what happened,' Giles explained patiently. 'She was attacking him.'

Giles and Justine were fine ambassadors for their generation. Decency radiated from them like heat from a fire. Both from modest backgrounds, they were also good examples of the diversity that was gradually permeating the civil service. There was still an old guard whose progression was probably linked to whichever public school they'd attended. I often thought they must have been as bemused by having somebody like me in their midst as we postmen used to be when the student casuals came into the sorting office to help with the Christmas rush. It was a collision of two worlds: they knew little about ours, and theirs was beyond the understanding of most of us postal workers, for whom going to university would have been as realistic as visiting Pluto. There was no animosity, just mutual incomprehension.

All of the civil servants, including Simon, Giles and Justine, refused to address me as anything other than 'Minister' and, uncomfortable though I found it at first, I understood and accepted the need for such protocol. What I couldn't accept was the old guard's insistence on standing when I entered a room. Fortunately, that practice died out somewhere around the millennium.

I never felt that those *Yes, Minister* caricatures of civil servants viewing ministers as temporary irritants interfering in their governance of the country were entirely accurate. In my experience, civil servants liked nothing better than a decisive minister who knew what he or she wanted to do.

It was a bit like driving a car with dual controls. If the minister just sat behind the steering wheel admiring the dashboard, then at some stage the civil service would put the car into gear and drive it forwards, always being careful to give the impression that the minister was in control. But the minister was always the preferred driver, even if his L-plates were still attached.

Much of my work involved implementing manifesto commitments or initiatives originated by my boss, the secretary of state, but I did have the occasional idea I was keen to pursue as minister of state. One was a proposal I devised to provide every workplace in the country with a simple four-step procedure to deal with grievances and other disciplinary matters. It allowed for a worker and an employer to exchange information, for a meeting to be held to decide the facts, for a disciplinary or grievance hearing and for an appeal against any punishment.

Among the many measures we'd introduced to set decent minimum standards in the workplace was the so-called 'right to be accompanied', which gave any worker in any workplace the right to have a union representative with them at disciplinary or grievance hearings, whether or not the worker was a member of a trade union and regardless of whether the employer recognized a trade union. It had struck me as being anomalous that workers had a right to be accompanied but no corresponding right to actually have a discipline or grievance procedure to be accompanied to. Moreover, the number of expensive tribunal cases was increasing and many of them involved simple issues that should have been nipped in the bud through a workplace process rather than allowed to clog up the courts.

I convinced Patricia Hewitt of the merits of my scheme and the special advisers from 10 Downing Street that it was a better way forward than charging for tribunal hearings, which had been suggested as an alternative way of reducing the number of cases being brought to court.

The civil servants didn't much like the idea and raised important questions. How could we effectively ensure that every business employing just one or two people had sufficient resources to administer such a scheme? How could we guarantee its availability in hundreds of thousands of workplaces throughout the country?

They presented a submission listing the pros and cons but in the end completely accepted my decision to press ahead. The legislation was drafted, the bill went through the Commons and the Lords, received royal assent, became an act of Parliament and was a complete and utter disaster.

I had moved on by the time I heard that my precious act was being repealed. The civil servants had been right: it seems it was widely ignored and therefore never made a dent in the number of tribunals. All the help to make it work came from the civil service. The failure was mine alone.

My final engagement as a DTI minister was at Bishop Burton college in the East Riding of Yorkshire, close to my constituency. I'd gone there to deliver a government speech. I can't remember what about.

It was the summer of 2003 and there was a reshuffle going on. As usual, the Cabinet was reshuffled first. I wasn't expecting to be moved, even though Patricia Hewitt had made a point of telling me that she'd been singing my praises to the prime minister.

In those days the government car service had drivers in every region. When ministers had a long journey to make our designated Whitehall driver would take us to the station and a regional driver would meet us at the other end. My London driver now was Frank Rose, George having by this time finally left for the retirement he dreaded. Frank, who would be with me for five years, was the coolest guy in the GCS. He had the looks of an American soul singer and a calm temperament that was pure Zen.

Frank drove as if he were enjoying a leisurely spell on PlayStation. The connection between driver and steering wheel was more of a gentle caress than a grip. Often he'd have just two fingers of each hand lightly applied to the part of the steering wheel nearest to his lap. Other drivers would blast their horns, gesture and scream abuse, but nothing disturbed the serene expression on Frank's face. To him, road rage was incomprehensible. Road relaxation, perhaps, but never rage.

That day he'd dropped me off at King's Cross in the Rover 75 all DTI ministers had been allocated. At the other end, waiting to pick me up from Brough, just outside Hull, was the GCS driver for Yorkshire and the Humber in a dark red Jaguar with cream upholstery. I sank into the plush interior, admiring its walnut trim and the integrated telephone positioned between the two front seats.

After I'd finished my speech at Bishop Burton and we were heading across the Humber Bridge to my next engagement, in north Lincolnshire, the car telephone rang. The official who was with me – that day it was neither Giles nor Justine, for some reason – answered it and told me it was the number 10 switchboard. The prime minister wanted to speak to me. The conversation went something like this:

'Alan, I want you to take on a really important job that only you can do.'

'Of course, Tony. What is it?'

'I'd like you to be the minister for higher education.'

There was a pause while I tried to take this in.

'But Tony, you know that I never went to university.'

'Precisely.'

I allowed this succinct comment to sink in before accepting the sideways move. I knew I was being pitched into a fierce battle.

The government had refocused its attention on the Dearing Commission on Higher Education, set up by the Major government but supported by us in opposition. By the time it reported, Blair had replaced Major and Labour were in power.

Ron Dearing had been chairman of the Post Office when I was a union official, and while it held no significance for me personally at the time, I knew he'd been born in Hull. His father, a docks clerk, had been a civilian casualty of the Second World War. Ron had been entirely educated in his home city, eventually attending Hull university as an adult after joining the civil service as a sixteen-year-old clerical officer. He had risen through the ranks to become one of the most senior and distinguished of mandarins before taking on the Post Office chairmanship. Unlike those who succeeded him, he hadn't been an advocate of privatization and was hugely respected throughout the business and beyond.

Since leaving the Post Office, Dearing had been asked to review various aspects of our education system, culminating in the comprehensive report on higher education (HE) published in 1998. I had found his arguments compelling from the start. There was a significant funding gap in HE, along with a disgraceful social-class division that had widened rather than narrowed since the introduction of student grants in the wake of the last major review of HE, the Robbins report, in 1963.

If the Blair government wanted to meet its goal of 50 per cent of eighteen- to thirty-year-olds accessing higher education, it couldn't continue with a funding structure designed to give the benefits of a university degree to a privileged élite.

There was a growing awareness across the world of the importance of tertiary education to a country's ability to compete in what was at that time referred to as the knowledge economy. China and India were building new universities at an incredible rate. Against our target of 50 per cent, Australia already had a participation rate of 65 per cent, the Netherlands 54 per cent, Norway 64 and Sweden 69. The average among member countries of the Organization for Economic Co-operation and Development (OECD) was 47 per cent. We'd just got to around 40.

Dearing was a fierce advocate of widening educational opportunity and argued that those who benefited from higher education should make a contribution. Society benefited, so the taxpayer should contribute; business benefited, so they should contribute over and above the taxes they paid. But graduates themselves also benefited, and they should therefore make a contribution, too – not when they were students, but once they were earning a reasonable salary, defined by his commission as £15,000 a year.

Graduates who never reached that income level would pay nothing back; if their income dropped below the threshold, they'd cease to pay. The graduate contribution would be defined, deducted from pay by the Treasury as if it were a tax, with no real rate of interest, and the amount to be repaid each week would be 9 per cent of earnings above the threshold, so that it would be fair, manageable and nothing remotely like the credit-card debts many students were already incurring. Maintenance loans, accessed by 85 per cent of students, would be repaid on the same advantageous basis.

This was a graduate tax in all but name. Indeed, as Dearing pointed out, it had all the advantages with none of the drawbacks (such as an open-ended sum rather than a defined contribution).

I agreed with him: the existing system of funding higher education was regressive. Working- and lower-middle-class people were paying through their taxes for upper-middle-class people to reinforce their already privileged position in society. Not only would some of the extra money from fees be used to reintroduce grants for poorer students, there would be a drive to encourage children from all backgrounds not to feel that a university education was beyond them.

Of course, we needed to promote good vocational education as well. The new two-year vocational foundation degrees were part of our 50 per cent target but, in my experience, the people who complained that we needed plumbers, not graduates, never envisaged their kids being the plumbers.

Back in 1998, the Labour government had responded to the Dearing Commission by introducing an up-front fee of £1,000 a year. It was applied to students, not graduates, and was therefore not contingent on income. Neither was the money raised sufficient to close the funding gap or reintroduce maintenance grants for poorer students, who would instead be exempted from some or all of the fee.

At that stage the full Dearing package was unaffordable and considered to be undeliverable. Unaffordable in that Dearing envisaged the higher fees being paid immediately to universities by the Treasury, which would wait many years to recoup the money from graduates; undeliverable because Dearing had kicked off a fierce debate about the principle of charging for what many considered to be a sacred right to free higher education.

In fact the majority of university students paid for their courses. Overseas students paid, adults paid, part-time students paid, postgraduate students paid. Dearing's supporters argued that education should be free up to the level where an individual no longer had the right to be educated by the state. Entering higher education was a choice that not every student was qualified to make.

Such was the political controversy around the issue, and the suspicion that Labour intended to ramp up the £1,000 a year already applied, that our 2001 election manifesto had specifically committed us to not introducing 'top-up' fees – in other words, we would not allow universities to raise the £1,000 to whatever sum they thought appropriate.

Since the election, the Department for Education had published a White Paper proposing to implement Dearing's original plan. The fee would be £3,000 a year, paid by graduates under the Dearing formula, with students from poorer families receiving a discount.

It was into this maelstrom that I was to be tipped.

When I arrived in my new ministerial office at Sanctuary Buildings in Great Smith Street, I was told that my official title would be minister for higher education and lifelong learning. I pointed out that the initials would make me minister for Hell. Printing of the letterhead immediately ceased and my title was changed to minister for lifelong learning, further education and higher education.

My boss, as secretary of state for education, was Charles Clarke. I'd known Charles since his days as Neil Kinnock's chief of staff. Exceptionally talented, he also happened to be terrific company – a fascinating combination of intellect, bonhomie and aggression. A big man, Charles relished discussion and debate. The more heated it became, the more he enjoyed it. With many in the parliamentary Labour party fiercely opposed to the White Paper, I suggested that Charles and I should go on a charm offensive which would involve me being charming and Charles being offensive.

There was no one better to go into battle with. We certainly had a job on our hands. It wasn't helped by the other two main political parties neatly adopting the only two alternative policies to the Dearing recommendations. The Tories, under Michael Howard, opposed us by arguing that student numbers should be cut. The Liberal Democrats, under Charles Kennedy, accepted that expansion was a good thing, but argued that the cost should be met entirely by increasing income tax.

I couldn't have been more committed to our cause, but I was respectful of the many colleagues for whom this was a deeply personal issue. Apart from all the other arguments, most of them had benefited from the free higher education and generous grants introduced in the 1960s and were sensitive to the accusation that they were now engaged in pulling up the ladder after them.

Tony Blair had obviously had this in mind when he'd given his cryptic 'precisely' response in that Humber Bridge conversation. It was possibly one of the few occasions when somebody qualified for a senior position because of their lack of qualifications.

Pulling up the ladder, then, was an accusation to which I was immune, although, to my amazement, *Newsnight*'s fearless inquisitor-in-chief Jeremy Paxman tried to make it. The programme was going out live when he opened an interview with me by asking: 'Now, Mr Johnson, presumably you had the benefit of a free university education – why are you trying to stop today's kids from having the same opportunities you enjoyed?'

Two things struck me about that interview. The first was the assumption that a government minister must have gone to university. Plenty hadn't, including two previous prime ministers, James Callaghan and John Major. The second was Paxman's evident lapse in not having checked out this simple fact. I'd been in *Who's Who* for some time, although it's fair to say that I'd also have qualified for *Who the Hell is He?* had such a book existed.

Unfortunately for Paxman, as he had based his whole interview on this false premise, it proved irrecoverable. I'd got through a Paxman grilling unblemished.

Many detractors, such as Tony Benn, rooted their arguments in the fact that they'd enjoyed a university education in a postwar period of austerity. Yet when I was born, in 1950, only 5 per cent of young people progressed to higher education, and less than 10 per cent by the time I left school. Of course free higher education was affordable when it was the preserve of a tiny élite. The odd working-class kid would get through, but they were the exceptions, succeeding in spite of the system, not because of it. Many more qualified, but never managed to gain a university place because the policy in force (known as 'norm-referencing') prevented any expansion of numbers by shifting the goalposts and admitted only those with the highest marks. Those who were successful were generally students from public schools who had been coached and trained specifically for the entrance exams.

A number of the Labour colleagues who opposed our plans wondered why the hell we were courting such unpopularity with students and their parents, not to mention party members, when there was no pressing need to go further than the £1,000 up-front fees we'd already introduced, to the great consternation of our supporters. But Ron Dearing, the university vice-chancellors and various distinguished educationalists argued that the need was indeed pressing. We'd grasped only a tiny bit of the HE nettle. I admired Tony Blair all the more for doing something that was necessary but unpopular.

All the universities were supportive, as were newspapers and magazines on the left such as the *Guardian* and the *New Statesman*. HE funding per student had already fallen by 36 per cent between 1989 and 1997. The substantial shortfall identified by the Dearing Commission had hardly been touched by the £1,000 fee.

If there was any extra money from taxpayers available beyond the considerable sums already pledged by government to higher education, it would be better spent on the state education to which all children were entitled, and particularly on early intervention through Sure Start children's centres.

As we prepared the ground for the bill that would carry our controversial plans into legislation, there was one other significant opponent: Gordon Brown, the chancellor of the exchequer. With the Second Reading approaching it was unclear how many Labour rebels there were. Despite our majority of 167, with the other parties against the bill, if eighty or more colleagues also voted in the 'no' lobby, it would be lost. If we could get past the Second Reading, we calculated that we'd be home and dry.

I spoke personally to virtually every potential rebel, explaining the detail; emphasizing that a youngster from a poor family would no longer have to ask his or her parents for money. The fees wouldn't be payable until graduates were earning over £15,000 a year and they'd receive a grant as well as the student maintenance loan to keep body and soul together in their three years of study. Yes, the annual fee was rising from £1,000 to £3,000, but it was no longer payable up-front. I even went to a Socialist Campaign Group meeting to try to persuade my hard-left colleagues, such as Tony Benn and Dennis Skinner, of what I regarded as the progressive course. I got a good hearing, but made no converts.

As for students, by and large, once they understood the deal, they responded with only muted opposition and there was little venom in the demonstrations organized by the National Union of Students.

If one aspect would swing the vote our way, it was the decision Charles and I made, after much deliberation, not to give a discount on the fee to poorer students. Instead, that money would be used to boost their maintenance grants to a substantial £2,700 a year. We also insisted that universities provide a minimum bursary, ensuring that the grant would match the £3,000 fee.

The argument was impeccable. Why give a discount based on the family income of the student when repayment was based entirely on the earnings of the graduate? The income threshold of £15,000 before repayments began applied to everyone, and by definition it meant that repayment would be affordable, regardless of family background.

The discount on the existing fee had been introduced because the £1,000 a year had to be paid as an entry charge to university. As our system contained no such barrier, poorer students wouldn't be put off by the fees but they might be discouraged by the prospect of not being able to rely on their parents for income while they studied. This was where the discount money should be spent. It was the bold move many of the waverers were looking for.

Yet while a government policy was being courageously promoted by number 10 Downing Street, next door, at number 11, the chancellor and his acolytes were busily trying to undermine it. Charles told me he'd had a blazing row with Gordon and gave me a blow-by-blow account of it. It was my first proper experience of the so-called TB-GBs. In fact, such was my naïveté that when the press harped on about it in our early days of government I actually believed it had been manufactured by Blair and Brown to introduce some creative tension. I would tell journalists about my hunch that Tony and Gordon would end most days sipping whisky together, smiling about the stories of division while they plotted the next episode. I was now finding out how wrong I'd been.

The Second Reading of the Higher Education Bill came on 27 January 2004. It is a day etched vividly on my memory. The efforts Charles and I were making to convert enough of our colleagues had been reinforced by the prime minister, who had seen a whole stream of Labour MPs the previous evening. We still didn't know if we'd done it and the whips, whose job it was to crunch these difficult numbers, were telling us that while it was too close to call, they were veering on the side of pessimism.

A last-minute deal with Gordon to introduce some independent commission or other to monitor the implementation of the policy was supposed to have closed off that area of vulnerability, but it had been concluded only on the morning of the debate and we couldn't be sure that it would swing the 'Brownites' to our side. Such were the calculations required in a government with two competing polar stars.

The debate raged on through the afternoon and into the evening. The concerns of MPs on all sides were genuine, unlike the position of Her Majesty's loyal opposition, which was opportunistic. Their proposed solution of reducing the student population by 400,000 was ludicrous and their abhorrence at the introduction of variable fees short-lived.

One Tory backbencher, Robert Jackson, a predecessor as higher education minister, spoke against his own front bench, voted with us and later crossed the floor of the House to sit as a Labour MP, so strongly did he feel on the issue. But other backbenchers on our side worried about the variability of the fees and how that might lead to a market in higher education. Of greater concern was how thick the opposite end of the £3,000-a-year wedge might become. In the bill we had screwed down this figure as tightly as we could, making it virtually impossible for it to be increased before 2010, and even then only through further primary legislation.

I had the job of replying to the debate at the very end. I stood up to speak to a packed House at 6.38pm and at 6.39pm stood on the paw of David Blunkett's guide dog, who had stretched herself out in an apparent attempt to turn herself into a hearth-rug in front of the dispatch box.

The poor dog wasn't hurt and I made a weak joke about postmen usually being on the receiving end of such abuse, which at least punctured the tension in that rarefied atmosphere.

At 7pm precisely the question was put: that the Higher Education Bill be read a second time. Such was the uncertainty surrounding the vote that as Tony Blair, Charles Clarke and I sat on the Treasury bench waiting for the tellers to declare the outcome we were discussing who needed to do what if the motion was defeated.

We solicited the advice of the leader of the House, Peter Hain. In that hurried consultation it was agreed that we should immediately announce a confidence motion to take place the following day. We were still talking about who should handle this when the chief whip, Hilary Armstrong, came over to whisper that we'd won – by just five votes.

~

It emerged from my red box like a rose bush from a turgid swamp. An invitation to attend the graduation ceremony of the Liverpool Institute for Performing Arts – and to meet its patron and co-founder, Sir Paul McCartney. Jo Ware, my wonderful private secretary in the man-free zone that was my private office at Education, had written on the submission that I 'may be interested' in attending. I was invited to make a speech about how institutions such as LIPA and the BRIT performing arts and technology school in south London were important symbols of the growing diversity of our education system.

'May be interested'? Yes, I may be, Jo, in the same way that a lottery winner may be interested in the cheque that has plopped through the letterbox. The Beatles had been one of the lodestars of my life since I was twelve. One of my clearest memories is of sitting alone late one night in our damp, dilapidated front room in North Kensington, listening to their second LP, *With the Beatles*, on our Dansette record-player. I was thirteen and had saved up the money from my milk and paraffin rounds to buy the record. I played it three times without pause.

The Dansette was used to playing singles. The only other LP we had was a Bachelors record that Linda had bought for our mother. There had been very little interest in the long-playing record before the Beatles. There had been little international interest, either, in British pop stars or in the music written for them in Tin Pan Alley by professional songwriters. The Beatles consigned all that to history, bringing an end to a kind of musical ice age that thawed over the course of seven years and ten Beatles albums. For me, throughout my life, they have towered over all successors, all imitators.

By the time album number six was released, in December

1965, I was fifteen, working at Tesco in Hammersmith, and in my first proper band, the Area. I wanted so much to be Paul McCartney. And if I couldn't be him, I wanted at least to look like him. At home – by then the council flat in Battersea where I lived with Linda after our mother died in 1964 – I would pose in front of the built-in mirror over the mantelpiece, with Linda's old school hockey stick standing in for Paul's Höfner bass guitar, miming to his lead vocals on songs like 'Can't Buy Me Love'. I would spend hours trying to dry my long but naturally wavy hair into my hero's resolutely straight mop-top – not easy when we didn't possess a hairdryer.

Beatles albums were entering their rhapsody phase, each one shifting the musicality of 'pop' to a new and higher plane. It was an amazing year for the band. In the summer they had played Shea stadium in New York in front of 55,000 people and that autumn all four of them had been presented with MBEs by the Queen, in the days when awarding such an honour to pop stars was unheard of. But the UK tour that winter on the back of the acclaimed new album, *Rubber Soul*, would turn out to be their last in this country.

I remember first hearing *Rubber Soul* in the bedroom an old schoolfriend, Clive Llewellyn, shared with his two brothers in a high-rise block on the Churchill Gardens estate in Westminster, where a disparate bunch of teenagers had gathered to listen to it. Clive and his friends were all still at school and studying feverishly for their O levels. They envied me my apparently sophisticated lifestyle, sharing a council flat with my sister, unconstrained by parental diktat.

I arrived at Clive's temporarily short of the cash to buy the album myself, but as somebody who considered himself to be an authority on and, I hoped, a doppelgänger for the winsome bass guitarist of the most sensational band in the world. There were about six of us squeezed into the small bedroom. I'd grabbed the top bunk, hoping that a girl I fancied would join me. She didn't, but once George Harrison's introduction to 'Drive My Car' began, all else was of peripheral interest and would remain so until the fade-out of 'Run For Your Life'. Then we played the record again, and again, stopping only to turn it over and debate the relative merits of each side. All were agreed that we were listening to the best album ever made by anyone.

Not long after that I was badly beaten up on the Churchill Gardens estate. I acknowledged the irony of having grown up in an area of London so violent that the police would only patrol in threes yet receiving my worst-ever beating in Pimlico. I never went back to Clive Llewellyn's flat, or saw anyone who'd been in that bedroom ever again. Now, almost forty years later, I was being invited to meet one of the men whose genius had brought us all together on that magical *Rubber Soul* evening, just as he'd brought together so many other young people the world over.

The girls in my private office must have been bored to tears by my eulogies on the Beatles. Only one of the six of them, Karen Warren, the diary secretary, was old enough to possibly remember the time before they broke up. There was talk of her accompanying me to Liverpool on those grounds but in the end the lucky winner was Jenny Poole, who qualifed on two counts: it emerged that not only was she a fan, but she had been born in Liverpool. This was a revelation: previously she had been known chiefly for her American accent (she'd been brought up there) and a nut allergy. At our previous Christmas staff lunch I had seen at first hand the perils of restaurateurs giving false information to customers with nut allergies about the ingredients in their food. Jenny had left the restaurant in an ambulance.

It was at Jenny's suggestion that we arrived early in Liverpool on the great day and asked our driver to take us on a quick tour of Strawberry Fields, Penny Lane and the childhood homes of Paul and John Lennon before heading to the magnificent Philharmonic Hall for the graduation ceremony.

I was listed on the programme near the end: 'Alan Johnson, minister of state for Lifelong Learning, Further and Higher Education, delivers his address.' Underneath were printed two other important words: 'Receives applause.' I had with me a speech prepared by my civil servants, full of facts and figures about the importance of further education and the success of LIPA. It was worthy but dull as a concrete slab.

My host for the afternoon was the principal and co-founder (with Paul McCartney) of LIPA, a wonderfully garrulous and charming man, aptly named Mark Featherstone-Witty, who had also helped to found the BRIT school. He took Jenny and me to the green room, where we mingled with the other guests: the choreographer Arlene Phillips, the playwright Willy Russell, Jon Webster, who ran Virgin Records, dramatist Tim Firth and the American pop-rock group the Bangles, all of whom were to be awarded 'companionships' (LIPA's equivalent of honorary degrees) during the course of the afternoon .

I had a cup of tea in one hand and a cheese and pickle sandwich in the other when, without warning, Mark brought Paul McCartney over to me.

I'd entertained the hope that I might get a quick introduction but I'd never dreamed Paul would make his way to where I was standing, look into my eyes and engage me in conversation. I would have crawled across a field of upturned drawing pins to prostrate myself before my lifelong hero. At least then I'd have had time to think of something to say. As it was, I was caught unprepared and totally and utterly speechless.

The cheese sandwich went down the wrong way and the cup slopped tea into the saucer as I hastily put it down to cling too tightly to Paul's outstretched hand.

He smiled and asked cheerily, 'How's it going?'

I so wanted to tell him how 'This Boy' had been the song I'd sung at my failed audition with Peter Jay and the Jaywalkers – the only time I came close to rock stardom. How I'd actually wanted to be a paperback writer at the time that song was released. How 'Eleanor Rigby' had inspired me and 'For No One' made me cry.

But all I could do, eventually, was mouth platitudes so meaningless that I can't recall a single garbled word of any of them.

At the appointed time we all left the green room to take our allocated seats on the vast stage, where we participants were ranged in a long row with Paul at the centre. There were enthusiastic students behind me, proud parents in front of me and rock legends alongside me. My civil-service speech was all wrong for this audience. As the moment for my contribution approached, I decided to ditch most of it.

I was on. I walked to the lectern to one side of the platform and saw Paul swivel in his seat to focus his attention on me, as if he were really, really interested in what I was about to say.

Now I loved him for his courtesy as well as for the lifelong joy he'd brought me.

I told the assembled gathering about how I'd always wanted to be a musician and a songwriter. My ministerial position, I assured them, was just an interlude until I had the chance to further that ambition.

As an example of my talent, I recited some lines from a song I'd written called 'Bad Skin', about a kid who suffered from that teenage affliction.

> I've got acne, I've got eczema, I've got every skin disease
> Gives me pimples I can pick, it gives me blackheads I can squeeze.

The middle eight was the *pièce de résistance.* I quoted it with pride:

> How can a girl want to be wiv ya,
> When every kiss she gets just tastes of Nivea.

I left the platform to 'Receives applause'. Paul didn't say anything but I could tell that he recognized a genius in the mould of his own.

That year, 2004, I had another brush with greatness, although the brush in this case was more literal.

It came when I was appointed to the Privy Council, the formal body of advisers to the sovereign, which predates the legislative pre-eminence of Parliament itself, having existed in one form or another since Norman times. In the sixteenth century it was composed of forty members, with the monarch relying for advice on a smaller committee of privy counsellors which eventually evolved into the Cabinet.

Nowadays the Privy Council consists of all current and former Cabinet ministers (membership is for life), plus a few other more junior ministers like me, the country's three senior bishops and some high-ranking judges. It is membership of the Privy Council that confers the title 'Right Honourable'.

The oath I had to swear dates back to around 1570 and is written in the language of the time. The whole initiation ceremony is a sixteenth-century concept and involves leaning one knee on a stool before the Queen, swearing the oath and then leaning your knee on another stool closer to Her Majesty, this time taking her proffered hand and lightly kissing it, according to my written instructions, with 'no more than a touch of the lips'. At the rehearsal several days before the ceremony proper, the gesture was described to me as 'brushing Her Majesty's hand lightly with your lips'.

Four of us were to be sworn in at the ceremony, which took place in an ornate chamber at Buckingham palace, entered through double doors inlaid with gold. Three more privy counsellors stood waiting for us to join them afterwards – nobody but Her Majesty sits down at Privy Council meetings, and even she does so only to sign the documents we are there to approve (acts of Parliament and papers regulating public institutions and certain judicial functions).

The ritual entry into this sect of the four new privy counsellors was the first item on the agenda and I was the last to go. I was grateful for the chance to watch how my three colleagues handled it before my turn came.

When it did, all went well with the kneeling and the swearing and the kneeling again. It was the 'brushing Her Majesty's hand lightly with your lips' bit I had trouble with.

I blame Oliver. By now he was almost four years old and the recipient of many kisses, invariably audible ones. I blush to think of it now, but not as severely as I did at the time, when my lips insisted on making that tight squelching sound that represents a proper kiss – like pulling a wet sink-plunger off a glass pane.

In that Privy Council chamber the noise sounded appreciably louder than it did when I kissed Oliver; even worse, it then seemed to me to echo round the room. I retreated (as one must), making sure not to turn my back on the monarch, who was therefore treated to the sight of her newest privy counsellor's beetroot face all the way back to my allotted position at the end of the line.

Keeping participants on their feet is an excellent way of ensuring that meetings don't drag on and Privy Council proceedings are very short indeed. They are ended when the Queen presses a discreet button on the side of her desk which rings a bell outside, prompting the finely dressed functionaries waiting there to fling open the splendid double doors and escort us out.

Before thus dismissing her privy counsellors, Her Majesty always walks across to engage them in a bit of a natter about this and that. When she reached me she asked how I was enjoying my job. I'd met her once before when she made a royal visit to Hull but, disappointingly, I hadn't had the opportunity to tell her how Linda and I had celebrated her coronation at the bombsite in Southam Street that we knew as the Debry (we thought this was the name of our particular bombsite/playground, having never heard of the word 'debris'), which had been cleared specially for our street party in her honour.

But it didn't seem appropriate to bring up the coronation now, either, so I answered her question and chatted on about nothing in particular. I found it a bit disconcerting when she backed away, just as I was getting into my stride, and reached for the button to end the meeting and save herself from any further contact with the blushing idiot she'd just recruited to be one of her advisers.

Chapter 15

TONY BLAIR REVEALED at our party conference in 2004 that he would be going into hospital for a minor heart operation. (I made a stupid joke at a Young Fabians rally the same evening, commenting that Tony Blair had a dicky heart but with Bill Clinton it was the other way round. Nobody laughed.) He went on to announce that the 2005 general election would be his last as leader.

I think his aim was to reassure the electorate (and the party) that his heart complaint wasn't serious; that he'd be at the helm for a while longer but that he had no intention of going on for ever. Whatever his intention, the result was destabilizing for the party, not least because Gordon Brown was waiting in the wings to take over the role of leading man.

A few weeks earlier, during yet another reshuffle, I'd been summoned to 10 Downing Street and promoted to the Cabinet as secretary of state for work and pensions. Tony Blair and I sat on a sofa in his office as he emphasized the importance of the pensions review led by Adair Turner (the former director general of the CBI) and of stemming the numbers flowing on to Incapacity Benefit. They had tripled under the Tories, who had shepherded redundant workers from the steelworks, coalmines and shipyards of the north into a workless ghetto that had the virtue of not registering on the unemployment statistics.

At the end of our discussion I accepted the position but, in an attempt at self-deprecation, said I hoped Tony knew what he was doing by appointing me. This was the prime minister's opportunity to say how confident he was in my abilities and what a good job I'd done at Education. Instead, to his eternal credit, as he stood to indicate that the interview was over, he uttered just three words: 'So do I.'

The promotion wasn't entirely unexpected. My stint in Education had strengthened any credentials I had but nevertheless I was daunted by the prospect of actually running a government department; of becoming a general rather than a lieutenant.

What followed was a six-year tour of Whitehall taking in five different departments.

I have fond memories of twice, as a child, taking advantage of a London Transport Red Rover ticket. For two shillings and sixpence (12½p), a child could travel anywhere on any red bus from dawn till dusk on a Saturday, Sunday or Bank Holiday Monday.

I made my first trip with my sister Linda, on my mother's insistence. She did not want me travelling alone. By the time of the second Red Rover tour my mother was in hospital and teenage Linda had better things to do with her weekends than be saddled with me. I think she paid for my ticket, probably to get rid of me for the day.

I walked down Latimer Road to Shepherd's Bush Green, stepped on to the first bus I fancied and took it to the end of the line before swapping to another one. On each bus I'd make for the front seat on the top deck. I had no plan whatsoever, no idea of where I wanted to go or what I wanted to see. I just enjoyed the ride and the sense of freedom, uninhibited by anything other than the distant borders of London Transport's network, where red buses were replaced by green London Country buses, on which my Red Rover was invalid. It was liberating to be able to chop and change routes whenever I liked.

In my time as a Cabinet minister I felt as if I'd been handed a kind of ministerial Red Rover, enabling me to travel anywhere in Whitehall, albeit on the whim of the PM and without ever really knowing where the hell I was going. A bunch of fellow travellers accompanied me from department to department.

At Work and Pensions I took the unusual step of re-recruiting my predecessor's special advisers, Chris Norton and Tom Clark. SPADs, as they are known, tend to arrive and leave with the Cabinet minister who hired them. It is very much a personal appointment, the relationship between minister and SPAD being much closer than any other in Whitehall, and the only appointment entirely in the gift of the secretary of state. The permanent civil service, including the private office, is, of course, at the minister's disposal, but they are an impersonal resource with one major defect: they are apolitical.

Economists like to joke that being in their profession is like being a heterosexual man who knows a hundred different sexual positions but has never actually met a woman. It is a bit like that with civil servants, who help to formulate policy but never deal with the constituents affected by it. There is a political heart beating away somewhere in these exceptionally bright men and women, but its desires must never be revealed. The civil service knows little of the profoundly political world we ministers occupy and, upon appointment, we know very little about how government policy is drawn up and applied. A good SPAD helps minister and civil servants by crossing between the two worlds, political and technocratic. The best SPADs are able to do their minister's bidding without alienating those whose job it is to make sure the machinery of government runs smoothly, whoever is in charge.

Chris and Tom were very good SPADs who'd been employed by my predecessor, Andrew Smith, for their expertise in the subject matter (Tom) and in the art of government communications (Chris). Having had their farewell bash at the DWP the previous evening, they'd come into the office, nursing hangovers, to pick up their leaving presents. Susan Park, my PPS, who always referred to them collectively as 'the boys', suggested I invited them into my office for a cup of tea.

We clicked straight away and, to my enormous relief, Chris and Tom agreed to stay on. I don't think they ever did return their leaving presents.

My spell at the DWP was little more than a kind of 'introduction to government' – seven months in which we made progress in tackling poverty at both ends of the age scale, among children and pensioners, but none whatsoever on the most troublesome part of the empire, the Child Support Agency. We stemmed the flow of people on to Incapacity Benefit and were engaged in helping those trapped on it to escape when, in July 2005, the country went to the polls again, returning the Labour government for another term.

Our majority was significantly reduced from the landslides of 1997 and 2001 but remained comfortable. Tuition fees cost us a number of university-town seats. They went to the Liberal Democrats, who pledged to get rid of the fees altogether without expecting ever to be in a position to put that policy into practice.

The day after the general election, I took a call from Tony Blair. There was no need for me to come into 10 Downing Street, he said. I was being reshuffled over the phone. Tony asked me to return to the Department of Trade and Industry. I was delighted. Having been a parliamentary under-secretary and minister of state at 1 Victoria Street, I could now complete the ministerial three-card trick by going back as the secretary of state.

At the end of the conversation, Tony mentioned in passing that the name of the department was to be changed but he couldn't remember what to. He said that my PPS would fill me in when he rang the next day.

I had a pen and paper ready by the phone when Matthew, my PPS, called as promised and carefully unveiled the new title.

'It's the Department of Productivity . . .' I grimaced as I recorded a capital 'P' on my notepad. A noble cause but an ugly word to include in a departmental name. ' . . . Energy . . .' Matthew continued, as I took down the usual abbreviation, 'En', '. . . Industry and Science.'

I looked down at my pad.

'Matthew,' I said. 'This means that we're the Department for Penis.'

I can't be certain, but I'm pretty sure that Matthew actually replied, 'Yes, Minister.'

Four days later I was due to meet the prime minister for the traditional one-to-one chat about his expectations for the department now under my control. As I left 1 Victoria Street to walk to Downing Street on a gloriously sunny day, I noticed that the 'Department of Trade and Industry' nameplate had been unscrewed and removed from the marble plinth at the front of the building. Mercifully, its replacement had yet to materialize.

At number 10 I found Tony Blair on the rose-garden terrace, soaking up the sun. He was surrounded by a battalion of advisers in wicker chairs, arranged in a 'U' shape of fearsome combined intellectual might.

We chatted about the biggest challenge I faced: committing to rebuilding our ageing stock of nuclear power stations. The government had tiptoed around the issue for a couple of years, aware of the fierce opposition to nuclear fuel in some quarters of the Labour party but also of the fact that it accounted for around 20 per cent of electricity generation, which couldn't possibly be replaced by renewable energy before the existing nuclear plants were due to be decommissioned. If we did nothing, the country would lose a large chunk of its electricity supply.

The chinwag moved on to assorted other matters, with various number 10 SPADs, policy advisers and senior civil servants chipping in as the honey bees gently fumbled at the rose petals and the perfect summer afternoon meandered towards evening.

'Anything else?' Tony asked as he prepared to call it a day.

'Yes, there was one other thing,' I said boldly. 'Why has the name of my department been changed to Penis?'

There was silence. Tony took in a breath as if preparing to speak but nothing came out. Instead he looked quizzically at the Cabinet secretary, sitting on his left, who, in turn, cast a searching glance at the person next to him. The unspoken question was passed round all ten or so people seated on the terrace and left hanging in the balmy air.

'That's a dreadful name,' said Tony eventually. 'Can't we change it back again?' I informed him that the old sign had been removed but that the new one hadn't yet been erected. The absence of a Penis erection was the cause of great merriment and Tony ordered that my department revert to its original name forthwith. A press release was prepared and my victory recorded on the front page of the *Financial Times* the next day.

I never did find out who was responsible for that daft name but civil servants had a gift for proposing silly acronyms, as I'd learned to my cost from my 'minister for Hell' experience at Education. I was faced with another one later at Health, where a perfectly sensible submission to set up an expert panel to guide our response to concerns about the rise in sexually transmitted diseases was rather spoiled by the recommendation that it should be known as the Sexual Health Advisory Group. Shag would go the same way as Penis and the dignity of government was preserved.

I did a deal with the prime minister's office over the phone as I was walking through Hull city centre.

Just before the general election, and at the eleventh hour,

we'd managed to avoid a strike by 3 million civil servants, nurses and teachers who were understandably concerned about a Cabinet office proposal to raise their traditional pension age from sixty to sixty-five. I'd met the various unions and royal colleges concerned and succeeded in getting them to abandon plans for an industrial-action ballot in favour of a series of negotiating meetings that I would chair.

After our rose-garden meeting, where it must have slipped Tony's mind, his office contacted me to ask me to continue with this project even though I'd now moved from the DWP back to the DTI.

I said I'd do it if I was allocated an extra SPAD. Chris and Tom had come with me to the DTI but with such a vast and diverse department to run I felt we needed extra help on the SPAD front anyway. This new task gave me the opportunity to recruit Mario Dunn, who'd impressed me so much in my union days.

So the wheels on the bus went round and round, but occasionally one fell off. The deal I eventually negotiated with Brendan Barber (John Monks' equally talented successor at the TUC) preserved the pension age at sixty for all 3 million in-post employees who had been recruited with this contractual expectation.

In return, it was agreed that the threshold would rise to sixty-five for all new entrants. With additional employer contributions and an innovative 'cap and share' arrangement that covered future liabilities, this settlement remained within the cost envelope handed to me by the Treasury. Long lead-in times for the new arrangements had already been part of the planning. It should have been a triumph, and it would have been if the CBI hadn't cut up rough, portraying it as a cave-in to the unions.

Civil servants had retained the contractual right to a pension at sixty since Napoleonic times. Increasing this by five years to the level of the normal state pension age by means of negotiation without any industrial action whatsoever was a good outcome. The prime minister was happy with the deal, even if the chancellor was less enthusiastic. But the CBI director general, Digby Jones, went on the warpath and twenty captains of industry wrote a vitriolic letter to a national newspaper. The TUC discovered that every signatory had a retirement age of sixty and vastly superior pension arrangements to any found among nurses, teachers or civil servants. The fuss soon died down and the bus moved on.

The passengers changed a bit. Mario had hopped aboard, while Tom left to become a leader-writer for the *Guardian* after heroically withstanding the wrath of Shriti Vadera, appointed by Gordon Brown to do the Treasury's bidding at the DTI.

Shriti was a brilliant former investment banker who spent eight years as Gordon's economic adviser. She was determined that we shouldn't close off the option of privatizing Royal Mail. I was equally determined that we should, and as quickly as possible. Shriti's style could best be described as combative, but she got nowhere with Tom, who had to deal with her on a daily basis. His youth and general air of slightly bemused cordiality neutralized her shouty aggression.

Shriti, not a woman to be scorned, tried to convince me that Tom should be sacked. That was a very short telephone conversation. She and the Treasury were left in no doubt that the only way to get rid of Tom was to get rid of me. In the end he left of his own accord for that better job in Fleet Street and Royal Mail remained in the public sector, although I never realized my ambition to turn it into a company wholly owned by its workforce.

Tom's replacement as my SPAD was Clare Montague. She was recommended by Chris and Tom, who had known her since their early days at the DWP, when she had been their link at number 10. Clare had left Downing Street to run a Sure Start children's centre in Essex, a move typical of her disregard for status and ambition.

We lured her back into Spadsville in 2006, just as I returned to Education after a year at the DTI. By the time the government Red Rover took me back to Great Smith Street there were seven of us on board. In addition to myself, there were the three SPADs, Bron Madson, who I'd reappointed as my press secretary upon my return to the DTI, and Simon Lancaster, by now a mature married man. Simon had transformed himself into a speech writer for Patricia Hewitt at the DTI and found his forte. An innovative and imaginative exponent of his craft, he once wrote a speech for me to deliver at the City of London lord mayor's banquet with twenty references to Beatles tracks buried in the text. To my amazement, the lord mayor of London replied with ten more.

Last but not least of the Magnificent Seven was Suzanne Bullock, who'd joined the civil service from school twenty years earlier and had worked at 10 Downing Street, the Cabinet office and the whips' office before ending up in my private office at the DTI. Her sweet smile was never soured by the pressures of running a Cabinet minister's diary and needing to know precisely where I should be every minute of the day. She was so good at controlling my ministerial life that I couldn't bear to lose her.

The DTI permanent secretary agreed that the civil servants who wanted to follow me could do so, and thus I arrived at Education (and subsequently at Health and the Home Office) insulated against vicissitude.

It was harder for my team to change departments than it was for me. Bron had to work with a completely new team in the press office; Suzanne sat among strangers in an unfamiliar private office. Simon managed to get himself a berth with Chris, Mario and Clare in a cramped office close to mine, but still had to adapt his speech-writing skills to entirely different terrain.

And what exactly were we there to do? It was easy to treat ministerial life as purely managerial, to simply ensure that the department was well run, but that was the permanent secretary's job, not mine. Ours was a democratic socialist government with two straightforward objectives: the eradication of poverty and the attainment of greater equality. Never before had any Labour government won more than a single term in government. Now, with three successive election victories, we'd been given the opportunity to fundamentally change Britain in the direction of those objectives.

The department of which I was now in charge was central to the cause of greater equality. From the early intervention of Sure Start children's centres, through the introduction of the Educational Maintenance Allowance, which helped kids from poorer families to remain in education, to the expansion of HE, Education was the engine room of social change.

A new secretary of state could set out merely to avoid controversy and get through his or her period in each particular department without any major gaffes. To be, as the saying goes, 'a safe pair of hands'. But whereas avoiding controversy might have been just about manageable at the DTI, it was a complete impossibility at Education. My predecessor, Ruth Kelly, had become enmeshed in a tangled web over List 99, a register of people barred from working with children that had been kept secret for eighty years. There were also tensions over academy schools, reform of A levels and admissions criteria, as well as the continuing arguments about variable university tuition fees.

There was (as usual) a bill to take through the House, but much of the sting had been extracted from it when the government decided, before my arrival, to withdraw plans for trust schools to set their own admission arrangements. We succeeded in reinjecting some drama by attempting to amend the bill to stipulate that all new faith schools had to make at least 20 per cent of places available to children of other faiths and no faith at all. Having tabled that amendment, we were forced to make what was described as the fastest U-turn in history.

We planned to introduce the change to our bill in the Lords, where there seemed to be support for it, a similar amendment having been proposed by Ken Baker, education secretary under Mrs Thatcher. The amendment was published on a Friday and by the Sunday it was being denounced from the pulpit of every Catholic church in the country. By Monday, Labour MPs had summoned me to a meeting in the Commons, where I was left in no doubt as to my foolishness in trying to sneak in an amendment to a bill that had already passed through the Commons and which would be totally unacceptable to a whole swathe of the parliamentary Labour party. I could only admire the political thoroughbred that was the Catholic Church.

We did the arithmetic. The amendment, if it were carried in the Lords, would be defeated in the Commons. The handbrake was applied, there was a screech of clashing metal, a smell of burning rubber and the amendment was withdrawn.

I'd cooked up the doomed idea with my schools minister, Lord Adonis. I'd known of Andrew Adonis well before I first met him. His father, Nikos, was a UCW representative at a sorting office in north London. Nik had come to London from Cyprus in the late 1950s and fathered a son with an Englishwoman who had left them when the child – Andrew – was three years old. She never made contact again.

Nik couldn't manage by himself and Andrew was brought up in a council children's home until he was eleven, when he was awarded a local education authority grant to attend a boarding school in Oxfordshire. He went on to graduate with a first-class Bachelor of Arts degree from Oxford university.

Nik had often regaled me at union conferences with news of his journalist son, of whom he was immensely proud, and gave me worthy books Andrew had written on Parliament and Britain's electoral system. Eventually, at Nik's insistence, I met Andrew, who was by that time writing for the *Financial Times*. We remained in touch as he moved to the *Observer* and, after the 1997 election, on to 10 Downing Street as Tony Blair's adviser on education. Andrew never spoke to me about his childhood and I never talked about mine, but we brought to the Department of Education a distinction of sorts. He was probably the first schools minister to have grown up in a children's home and I was probably the first education secretary to have been a consumer of free school meals.

During our time at Education we tried to improve the life

chances of children in care, working with an equally determined children's minister, Beverley Hughes. At the time children in care represented only about 0.5 per cent of the country's population of minors. However, as adults, individuals who had been in care as children made up 27 per cent of the prison population. Kids were pushed into care too easily, moved around too often and kicked out too early – at just sixteen years of age.

The White Paper Beverley and I produced contained radical proposals that were incorporated into legislation after I'd left the department. I'd hoped it would improve the situation for these children but the statistics suggest that nothing much has changed.

I also began the process of raising the education leaving age from sixteen to eighteen and tried to pay more attention to those forgotten backwaters of our education system, further education and sixth-form colleges. Oh, and for two months of my spell at Sanctuary House, I tried to become deputy leader of the Labour party.

After Tony Blair had announced in 2004 that he would not be contesting a fourth general election as leader, his deputy, my Hull colleague John Prescott, said he would step down with Tony to enable the party to elect a new leadership duo. I'd decided then that I'd take a crack at deputy leader. I liked the idea of passing this important position across the River Hull from east to west. There were already more MPs from Hull in

Cabinet (two) than there were from London (one), and the continuity appealed to me.

I didn't believe I possessed the qualities required to be leader (as I was to admit publicly on *Desert Island Discs*, to the frustration of my SPADs, who wanted me to keep my options open) but felt I could make a fist of deputy leader.

There was little doubt as to whose deputy I would have been. Gordon's impatience to take over had led to the relationship between him and Tony Blair deteriorating even further. In Cabinet I observed it at first hand. Gordon's body language was a conspicuous manifestation of his chagrin. He would sit directly opposite Tony, head down, scratching out notes in the thick, black marker pen he always used (because of his poor eyesight), holding his head with the other hand, eyes averted from the man in front of him, hair ruffled and reruffled. He looked like a schoolboy who'd been rebuked by the head teacher and forced to stay behind to write lines.

It wasn't only Gordon who had a sense of entitlement. The parliamentary Labour party and the media had decided long ago to anoint him as the chosen one: Tony Blair's natural successor as prime minister and leader of the party. By September 2006, Tony had yet to fix a date for his departure, pressure on him was mounting, speculation was rife and the atmosphere was febrile. A number of Labour MPs, including a government minister, had signed a letter calling for Tony to go. The suspicion was that it had been composed with the support of the chancellor. This was descending to a level where it damaged the credibility of a Labour government that had only just won an election and had plenty of life in it yet.

I was due to join Tony on a visit to a school in St John's Wood on 7 September. Invited to a pre-meeting the day before to discuss it, I arrived at number 10 to be told that the PM was having a one-to-one in the rose garden. I was asked to wait in the Cabinet room, from where I could see him in animated conversation with Gordon. Actually it was Gordon who was animated, pacing the terrace before sitting down again, hands gesturing in demented semaphore, while Tony sat quietly as if waiting for someone to fetch him an iced drink. They went on for so long that my meeting was abandoned.

The next day I sat with Tony in the back of his car as we headed to St John's Wood with a Sky TV helicopter tracking the journey on live television. The interest wasn't in the visit to Quintin Kynaston school but in the expected coup against the prime minister.

As the motorcycle outriders smoothed our journey we chatted about the succession as if we were exchanging holiday anecdotes. Tony told me that he would have liked to stay on into 2008, giving Gordon a good two-year run-up to the next election, but had concluded that for the sake of the party it was best to bring that timetable forward. He wouldn't set a date, as Gordon wanted him to, because that would be fatal to good governance, but he would tell the press on this school visit that the Labour party conference in a couple of weeks' time would be his last as leader.

And he did just that, making a speech at the school that was funny and light-hearted (describing me as a friend, he said how good it was that he still had one) and then giving an impromptu press conference, one hand in his pocket – relaxed, articulate, but certainly not demob happy.

~

Tony Blair formally resigned eight months later, on 10 May 2007. John Prescott announced his resignation as deputy leader at the same time. The elections for their replacements would therefore be held concurrently. There were six candidates for deputy but only one for leader. Nevertheless, for some reason it was decided that Gordon would do 'hustings', going around the country speaking to activists in his lonely procession towards the prize he'd been waiting to collect for so many years.

It would probably have been better for him if some poor sucker had challenged him; thrown themselves across the track for Gordon the tank engine to run over. He had been a hugely successful chancellor of the exchequer, presiding over forty-seven successive quarters of growth in the UK economy, and his elevation to leader had been seen as a foregone conclusion for so long that nobody much fancied the ritual humiliation that awaited any other contestant. But it would have enabled Gordon to emerge from an election rather than a coronation.

We six hopeful deputies followed the sheriff around the country, waiting for him to do his solo in the spotlight before crowding on to the stage. The election seemed to go on for ever and by the end we all knew each other's lines. If one of us – my fellow candidates were Hilary Benn, Hazel Blears, Jon Cruddas, Peter Hain and Harriet Harman – had failed to turn up, the rest of us could easily have given their speech for them.

My campaigning skills were non-existent and whereas rivals like Jon Cruddas knew exactly what they wanted to do in the post I was vague and dissembling. I knew little of party structures and had nothing new to offer. Nevertheless, I'm told that I was responsible for the first-ever political tweet. My campaign manager, Gerry Sutcliffe (a Bradford MP and soon to be sports minister), set up our headquarters in Leeds and hired a guy called Stuart for his skills in social media. It was Stuart who sent out this revolutionary message on my behalf but, as I guess very few other people were on Twitter at the time, I'm not sure how effective it would have been.

The election culminated in a conference in Manchester on 24 June 2007, where the result would be announced. I was the favourite and actually thought I'd won. I'd even prepared an acceptance speech, finalized at the conference centre, where Clare Montague stuck some make-up on my face for the TV cameras and worked out a simple code so that I could alert her, Chris and Mario to how I'd fared. I would text Chris a surreptitious 'Y' if I'd won and 'N' if I'd lost.

I was to be incarcerated with the other candidates in a room behind the stage where we'd be told the result and released only when it was time to be paraded to our seats as the conference was taken through the various rounds of voting. We were under strict instructions – no phone calls, no texts. But my loyal SPADs had put so much effort into trying to get me elected that they deserved to know at least whether or not I'd been successful before the endless voting rounds were relayed on the giant screen of the conference hall.

I was taken to the room where my five fellow candidates were gathered. The general secretary of the Labour party immediately congratulated the winner and I duly texted 'N'. After a while we were led back into the auditorium and shepherded to our seats, the lights were dimmed and the show commenced.

Up on to the screen came the first round results: Jon Cruddas first, me second and Hazel Blears eliminated. In round two, with Hazel's second preferences distributed to other candidates, I came top and Peter Hain was eliminated. I was top again in rounds three and four, but as Jon Cruddas dropped out and his second preferences were distributed, there came a forlorn shout from behind me in the second row: 'Oh fuck! It's Harriet!' It was unmistakably Clare Montague, who was genetically incapable of saying anything sotto voce.

It quickly became a YouTube sensation for which Clare is rightly famous. In her defence, it was a cry of surprise rather than consternation.

So, although Harriet hadn't been among the front runners, she had pipped me to the position. While I felt bad for my supporters, I wasn't at all distraught myself. I told the media that I had always thought I was the best man for the job but, as is so often the case, there was a better woman.

The membership got it absolutely right. I would have been a poor deputy leader whereas Harriet would perform her role with huge distinction for the next eight years.

Chapter 16

TONY BLAIR AND John Prescott had already attended their final Cabinet meeting three days before that Manchester conference. On conclusion of business Gordon, now prime minister designate, had made an eloquent speech telling Tony that, whatever Labour achieved in the future, it would be 'on giants' shoulders'.

Tony's last PMQs came the following Wednesday. He left the chamber to a standing ovation, initiated by the leader of the opposition, David Cameron. I sat on the front bench, a few places away from the outgoing prime minister, reflecting on the fact that without him I wouldn't have become a member of Parliament, let alone a Cabinet minister.

I'd never been part of any political circle. Neither Blairite nor Brownite, I tended to drift along with the current, making a few friends along the way but avoiding cliques and factions. My closest friend was still Ernie Sheers, a postman at Slough sorting office. These days we hardly had any contact, except on our birthdays. Every year we still exchanged a £20 note: he would send one to me on my birthday in May and I'd return the favour on his birthday in August. That note had gone back and forth for over twenty-five years.

In the end Tony Blair had just about gone at the time of his choosing, and with an orderly handover of the baton to Gordon, who now embarked on a reshuffle of his own. He called me into his House of Commons office at 9.30 that same evening, 27 June – his first as prime minister – and gave me a choice. I could stay at Education, but I needed to be aware of his intention to move further and higher education to a different department. Alternatively, I could go to Health, which would be his absolute priority up to the next election.

I chose Health.

The big question was when that next general election would be. There was speculation that Gordon would call it early in order to acquire a mandate from the electorate for his premiership. That Saturday, I accompanied him on a visit to Kingston hospital. He wanted to use his first weekend in office to stress his commitment to the NHS.

I was asked to be at 10 Downing Street by 8.30am. Gordon was in his office. I couldn't help noticing that the sofa in the corner, where Tony used to sit to discuss issues with his inner circle, often with his shoes off, feet perched on the adjacent coffee table, had vanished. It was obviously a deliberate statement. Gordon would not be engaging in 'sofa government'.

We left for Kingston upon Thames at 9.10, plenty of time to get there with the police outriders clearing our path. But I suddenly realized that there were no outriders. They had gone the same way as the sofa. Gordon said he couldn't be doing with motorcades and that we must plough through the traffic like mere mortals.

As a result, we were late arriving. The motorcade was soon back on duty, the security services having told the new prime minister in no uncertain terms that it was their job to keep him safe and the purpose of the outriders wasn't to make travelling more convenient but to avoid the PM becoming a sitting target in slow-moving traffic.

As we crawled towards Kingston hospital that Saturday I asked Gordon whether he would go for an early election and he told me that his instinct was not to put the country through an unnecessary ballot and all the resultant uncertainty.

I had been frustrated at having to stay in London for this visit because I wanted to get to my constituency, where two months' worth of rain had fallen in six hours. Other parts of the country had been similarly devastated.

That same afternoon, following our hospital visit, there was an attempted suicide attack on Glasgow airport, in which two men tried to drive a Jeep loaded with propane canisters into the terminal. The previous night a bomb had been found in a car parked outside a London nightclub. Natural disasters and terrorist attacks all happening at once. Gordon appeared on the ten o'clock news that evening from Downing Street, his hair unkempt, his comments serious and devoid of soundbites. His style was in marked contrast to the slick performances of his predecessor and it seemed to work. By the time we got to a special political Cabinet at Chequers at the end of July, we had a 13-point lead in the polls.

Gordon unspun had captured the public's trust. There was an authenticity about him that people took to; an honest dedication to duty that attracted public admiration and confidence.

But he still hadn't decided whether or not to hold a snap election. By September, and the end of a successful Labour conference, the poll lead had held and the Tories were preparing for their conference the week after ours in a glum and pessimistic mood.

Only one man, to my knowledge, saw what was coming. David Miliband stopped me as we walked back to our hotel in Bournemouth at the end of our conference. 'Why doesn't Gordon say something now? Either announce a general election or, more wisely, say there won't be one because he refuses to put personal ambition above the national interest?' I couldn't quite grasp David's point. The sun was shining, we'd had a reasonably successful conference and Gordon's personal rating was sky-high. What could possibly go wrong?

In hindsight I'm sure Gordon recognizes that missed opportunity. Had he ended the speculation about an impending election that weekend, he would have continued to occupy the moral high ground. The Tories were bound to see a bounce in their poll rating following their week in the media spotlight. As it happened, they had a higher bounce than usual because of a George Osborne pledge to lift the threshold for inheritance tax.

While very few citizens qualify to pay inheritance tax, most people believe they could be liable and the announcement was therefore shrewd and effective. Our poll lead slipped back a bit and when Gordon announced that there would be no early election the perception was that he wasn't calling one because he now felt he might lose.

Whether or not that was true, the effect was understandable. The reputation for honesty and straight dealing that Gordon had secured just by being himself evaporated overnight and was never recaptured.

~

I was secretary of state for health for two years. Having stayed for between seven months and a year at my previous stopping points, this seemed like an eternity.

I was back in Richmond House, opposite Downing Street, where I'd arrived for my first Cabinet post at the DWP. By now the DWP had moved elsewhere and the entire building was controlled by the third-biggest employer in the world, behind the Chinese Red Army and the Indian railways. My empire stretched across 1.3 million employees and my spending settlement would, at the end of its three-year period, take the NHS budget to £110 billion – roughly 9 per cent of our national wealth, the average percentage allocated to health services across Europe. In thirteen years we'd gone from spending about £460 per head of the population on health to £1,600.

Part of a secretary of state's duties is to negotiate the spending settlement for his or her department. Having once been an annual ritual, this now took place once every three years. I enjoyed these encounters because they involved the kind of proper negotiation I was used to from my union days. I'd just completed the three-year deal for Education before being moved. Now, at Health, the Treasury (who, as always, sat on the other side of the negotiating table) were attempting to introduce a system which would give them, rather than my department, control of a proportion of the spend.

We saw them off, but Treasury interference was a constant irritant in government. I encountered the most ludicrous example when I ended a barbaric practice that had existed in the National Health Service since its foundation. Where a drug wasn't available on the NHS and patients decided to pay for it themselves, all NHS care would be withdrawn. The patients trapped by this Catch 22 were almost always those with terminal cancer, whose families were desperate to extend their lives, if only by a few weeks, through the purchase of such drugs.

I asked one of my array of talented professional clinical advisers, Mike Richards, a cancer specialist, to examine how we could end this heartless edict. His report confirmed my suspicion that abolishing it, far from posing a risk of taking us down the path towards a two-tier NHS, would in fact reinforce the founding principle of this magnificent organization to provide a comprehensive service available to all. There were marginal costs involved, which we would meet by reducing costs elsewhere. But the Treasury objected on the nit-picking grounds that we might not be able to absorb these costs in the next spending review, which was almost three years away. Fortunately, it was only the Treasury that objected, and a shibboleth that had been around for almost sixty years was removed quickly, quietly and with no public revolt.

Health was unique in that the secretary of state, while having ultimate control, had not just one but three senior civil servants to work with. This triumvirate – the permanent secretary, the NHS chief executive and the chief medical officer (CMO) – all ranked as highly as one another and there was no first among equals. Indeed, Liam Donaldson, the CMO, operated in an enclosed world where his annual report wasn't even shared with me ahead of publication, let alone the other two. Given that its content was integral to the way the health service worked, this was unhelpful. The permanent secretary, Hugh Taylor, and I drew up secret plans, to be implemented after the next general election, to force the CMO to become a team player rather than a lone wolf.

It was fortunate that I had a good relationship with Hugh, David Nicholson, the NHS chief executive, and Liam and that they were complete professionals who collaborated successfully with one another. What could have been a messy and confused leadership worked satisfactorily because of the determination of the office-holders to make it work.

Another potentially tricky relationship was introduced with the appointment of a renowned colorectal surgeon, Professor Sir Ara Darzi, as a junior minister in my department. The role was Gordon's idea, and it was a brilliant one. Ara was given a peerage so that he could serve in government and was asked to conduct an inclusive review of how we could improve quality of care and the patient experience within the NHS.

Consultants aren't noted for their self-effacement. In general they do not wear their status lightly. So bringing one of the most eminent of the species into the hierarchy of the NHS was fraught with risks. The medical expert might well have overlooked the 'junior' part of his job description and sought to control the NHS from this position, along with the entire department. The fact that Ara had prime-ministerial patronage added to our concern.

We needn't have worried. Ara Darzi was one of the least self-important people I'd ever worked with. Born in Baghdad into the Armenian community, he had trained at the Royal College of Surgeons in Ireland, where he had acquired his Irish accent, and practised in England for twenty-six years, pioneering minimally invasive and robot-assisted surgery. Once, at St Mary's hospital, where such was his eminence as an honorary consultant surgeon that other clinicians would step back and bow to him as he entered a lift or walked down a corridor, Ara worked for a day as a hospital porter, just to find out whether it was true, as some NHS staff in less skilled jobs claimed, that they were treated differently by their colleagues from NHS staff in more senior roles. He told me that none of his fellow clinicians recognized him because nobody looked at him or noticed him at all. The importance of respecting every health-service worker became a major theme in his lectures.

News of the Darzi review was well received (although in view of his colorectal speciality, it was probably foolish of me to describe it as 'bottom-up' on the *Today* programme). Having been focused for so long on structures and finance, NHS workers were given free rein to prioritize quality, which Ara wanted to establish as the organizing principle of the NHS in place of regulation.

As soon as I was appointed, I'd announced that there would be no further top-down reorganizations of the NHS for the foreseeable future. David Nicholson, whose cooperation was essential and who could have made life difficult for Ara, bought into the concept with wholehearted enthusiasm.

David was a Communist. Many have been seduced by the cause in their youth, but for him it was no mere brief flirtation at university. He'd carried the hammer and sickle into middle age. Portraits of Marx and Lenin hung on his office wall. Sadly for the revolutionary zealots of my younger years, Communism had become an interesting character trait rather than something to be feared by the Establishment.

David was just one of the engaging personalities among the most fascinating bunch of people I ever worked alongside in Whitehall. The ministerial team were all exceptionally talented and easy to cooperate with. Ben Bradshaw, effectively my number two, was Cabinet material, as I pointed out to the PM. Dawn Primarolo, my old boss and the woman who taught me so much about the craft of being a minister, became my public health minister, taking the lead on the crucial and extremely sensitive Human Fertilization and Embryology Bill. Having spent a decade at the Treasury, Dawn never seemed even to be considered for the Cabinet position her abilities deserved.

Ivan Lewis was a thoughtful minister and utterly determined to solve the growing problem of adult social care. The ageing population was leading to acute hardships for those who needed essential care outside the NHS, which was neither universal nor free at the point of use. Since it was administered by local authorities, it was subject to differing levels of care dependent on where patients lived. Ivan was the first person to propose that the two services be integrated, although we couldn't convince number 10 or number 11 Downing Street of the urgency. Neither would they face up to the difficult funding implications.

So it was a diverse team. We even had a former nurse, Ann Keen, to deal with nursing issues, as well as Ara, who continued to practise as a surgeon at weekends.

There had been changes among my faithful band of fellow travellers. Chris Norton had gone into public affairs, but not before 10 Downing Street had tried to poach him, recognizing that Whitehall would be losing its best communications adviser. Jo Revill, a journalist and health correspondent for the *Observer*, replaced him. Jo had once written a book on bird flu and just after her appointment, right on cue, a new strain, H1N1, appeared. It was a wholly new virus that had jumped the species barrier and begun spreading from human to human.

Thankfully, it didn't become the kind of full-blown pandemic that was last experienced in 1969 and which the world had been dreading ever since.

Simon Lancaster had left to start his own speech-writing business, which became a huge success, as did the two books he has written on the subject. And Frank Rose, my cool, laid-back driver, had also moved on. In his place came one of an increasing number of women entering the macho world of the government car service.

Louise Harradine had been obsessed with cars all her life. A vivaciously positive person, she was the perfect travelling companion and had come to the GCS from a coach company. I think she only wanted to work for me to get behind the wheel of the sleek black Jaguar with cream upholstery that was now my designated vehicle.

The Darzi review was published in two stages. It set out a new accountability in clinical practice which put the patient at the centre of every decision. Ara proposed moving care from hospitals to GP-led health centres, centralizing stroke, trauma and cardiac services into specialized units and making primary care more accessible in the evenings and at weekends. He invited NHS staff to take a hand in designing their own targets and, with David Nicholson, established the NHS constitution, laying down in one document all the guiding principles of this great public service.

As our minister in the Lords, Ara had to take health legislation through the second chamber. It wasn't his favourite part of the job, but the peers found his company literally life-enhancing. One evening, in the ornate, gold-plated, red-cushioned splendour of the Upper House, Ara was waiting to reply to a debate when Lord Brennan, who'd just delivered a passionate speech, collapsed. Ara leaped across, calling for a defibrillator, which was duly provided. So serious was Lord Brennan's condition that the Archbishop of York, John Sentamu, was already beside him intoning the prayers for the dying.

As the stricken peer's eyes opened and his body stirred into life, Ara turned to the archbishop and observed, in his Irish lilt, 'I got to him first.'

It wasn't the only time Ara's medical skills were called upon down at the red-carpeted end of the Palace of Westminster. Indeed, it was said that when he was in the Lords chamber attendance trebled, as elderly peers realized that it was the safest place they could be.

In 2008 we celebrated the sixtieth anniversary of the NHS. With waiting lists at an historic low, funding at a record high and public satisfaction greater than it had ever been, this inspirational organization was entitled to bask in the admiration of a grateful country. But if anybody was in danger of losing sight of its occasional failings (and, given what had happened to my daughter, I wasn't one of them), along came the scandal at Stafford general hospital as a sobering reminder.

Despite the fact that we were pouring money into the NHS, the chief executive of the hospital was convinced that the way to improve the status of his trust was to cut staff. He had decimated nursing and clinical personnel, particularly in A & E, where a receptionist with no medical training whatsoever was engaged in triage nursing.

When a report by the Healthcare Commission was published, the dreadful level of care that was the natural outcome of this financial masochism became apparent. I went to talk to affected families. The most prominent campaigning group, called Cure the NHS, was led by Julie Bailey, a woman whose mother had died in the hospital and who had long been convinced that poor nursing had been a contributory factor. She had been primarily responsible for alerting the Healthcare Commission to what was going on at Stafford.

There was another group of families, which refused to have anything to do with Julie's organization. I met them separately first. Then I took Mario with me to the café in the main street where Cure the NHS based themselves.

A sign on the door read 'NHS Staff Not Welcome Here'. I entered to find a lively group of campaigners with Julie in their midst. She was personable and committed but obsessed to a degree where she found it difficult to put what had happened into any kind of reasonable perspective. I liked her but it was clear to me that whatever was done wouldn't be enough. A visceral antipathy to the NHS was reflected in that sign on the café door.

Julie believed there had been some kind of conspiracy of silence, but that wasn't remotely possible in an organization like the NHS. Yet there was certainly silence – a deafening silence, suggesting not malevolent intent but ignorance of the scale of the problems, or perhaps fear of the consequences for anyone who exposed them.

It's worth mentioning here that we had set up the Healthcare Commission precisely because there had been no neutral body with the power and authority to explore how hospitals were run. Prior to its introduction, any complaint against a particular hospital was dealt with by the hospital that was being complained about.

I ordered a series of reports to complement the one we already had from the Healthcare Commission. The primary concern (after restoring the correct levels of staffing) was to determine whether any deaths had been caused by the substandard care provided in some parts of Stafford hospital. In a completely independent process, neutral clinicians from outside Stafford would, at the request of affected families, examine all the medical case notes and conclude whether or not this was a factor in the loss of their relatives.

While some hysterical elements of the media suggested that hundreds if not thousands of patients were being killed by poor NHS care at Stafford, the review, which carried out its work meticulously over a three-year period, found only one case of premature death – and that had been caused by misdiagnosis rather than poor care. That's not to say that inadequate nursing hadn't led to appallingly low standards of care at Stafford, only that there was no evidence of anyone dying as a result.

Critics of the NHS were desperate to portray Stafford as representative of the service as a whole. But it was an aberration, as the example of the A & E triage demonstrated. I was urged to set up a formal commission of inquiry but I could see no need to bog Stafford down in a long, expensive procedure that was likely to end up confirming what we already knew. Besides, it was crucially important to restore public trust at Stafford. Nobody wanted the hospital to close. With new leadership and appropriate staffing, Stafford general hospital needed to move on rather than become petrified as an institution incapable of escaping the long shadow of the Healthcare Commission report. Local MPs were keen for some kind of formal inquiry. I was still pondering this matter when I was moved for a final time.

~

In early June 2009, I caught the 7.14am train from King's Cross to Hull. It was a Friday, the day I usually managed to keep free for constituency work.

It is one of the better aspects of our system of government that ministers (apart from the few in the House of Lords) remain anchored to their constituencies. Throughout my years in Whitehall I managed to deal personally with most of the letters I received from constituents, usually by going into the office very early in the morning.

Jane Davies was still at the helm of my parliamentary office on the fourth floor of 1 Parliament Street. All government ministers are obliged to have an office in the Palace of Westminster itself, rather than its annexed outposts. Those in the lower echelons are scattered across the estate, with the secretaries of state bunched together on a 'ministerial corridor' which is more like a school dormitory.

I evaded this echo of *Tom Brown's Schooldays* by holding on to the office I'd been allocated after the 2001 election when I first became a minister of state. It was at ground level, off the colonnade – the long walkway that leads from Star Chamber Court along the back of New Palace Yard, parallel with the Thames, right up to the escalators that carry the worker ants, as well as the MPs for whom they toil, to and from the contemporary accommodation of Portcullis House.

My large office was isolated from the rest of the House of Commons and accessed through its own ancient door under an arch between New Palace Yard and Speaker's Court. The windows were set high above the colonnade and through them I could hear the constant footsteps and chatter of passing parliamentary pedestrians.

When I became a member of the Cabinet the last thing I wanted to cope with was shifting my accumulated rubbish from one House of Commons office to another, and so I ignored every request to move to the cramped, uniform ministerial corridor above the House of Commons chamber. After a while the accommodation whips gave up and I continued to reside untroubled in my bolthole. I'd spend the day slaving away in whichever ministry I'd been appointed to, knowing that when the division bell rang to announce an early vote, I had eight minutes to get to the voting lobbies. In the evenings, when those votes were more likely to occur, we ministers would migrate to our Commons offices, where the 'aye' and 'no' lobbies were within easy reach.

I've always been fascinated by Samuel Pepys' diaries and devoured Claire Tomalin's wonderful 2002 biography of the great man, *Samuel Pepys: The Unequalled Self*, which informed me that Pepys had once lived in New Palace Yard, close to Westminster Hall. I calculated that my office could well have been on that precise spot.

When I'd worked in Great Smith Street at Education I'd almost enjoyed the rush to the voting lobbies when the bells rang, feeling that Pepys must at some stage have taken the same walk from there to New Palace Yard. I imagined him shuffling between Westminster Abbey on one side and St Margaret's church, where he had been married, on the other, then across the road into Parliament and through the mediaeval glory of Westminster Hall, where he had witnessed in 1661 the arrival of the newly crowned Charles II, 'with his Crowne on and his sceptre in his hand – under a Canopy borne up by six silver staves', having failed to get a decent view of the coronation at the abbey. After the vote I'd go to the spot that Pepys called home and I called my office.

Poor Jane had to troop backwards and forwards between her office in far-flung 1 Parliament Street and mine, carrying letters for signature in one direction and tapes full of dictation in the other.

Awaiting my arrival in Hull that day was another mainstay of my working life, Tracy Windle, who'd joined me as my constituency assistant six years earlier. I'd headhunted Tracy after she lost her seat on Hull city council, insisting that her contract contained a break clause to be invoked if she were ever tempted to stand again as a councillor. Thankfully, that never happened. It would have been difficult to find anyone as perfect for the job as this talented local woman. My constituency assistant had to work alone and unsupervised most of the time, while I was at Westminster. Not only was Tracy utterly trustworthy and reliable, she had one of the sunniest dispositions I've ever encountered. My constituents could get a suntan just from standing too close to her.

It was Tracy's welcoming smile that greeted every visitor to my constituency surgeries as we sat together on those Friday nights and Saturday mornings when I held surgeries, notebooks at the ready, waiting to bring help and solace and sagacity to the good people of Hull West and Hessle. They didn't necessarily know or particularly care what ministerial job I was doing. Why should they? Once a woman came to my surgery with a complaint about the NHS and asked if I could write to the secretary of state for health. I told her that would be no trouble at all. I didn't bother burdening her with the information that I was the secretary of state for health.

And that was the position I still held when I boarded the train for Hull on that overcast June morning. I was still secretary of state for health at Grantham, and at Doncaster, where the carriage, always sparsely occupied at that time of day, emptied completely. Just as we pulled out of the station my phone rang. Gordon wanted to speak to me. By the time we reached Selby I was home secretary. I celebrated alone with a cup of Hull Trains tea.

My predecessor, Jacqui Smith, had resigned. She was one of the most talented ministers to emerge in Labour's period of government and had become the first woman home secretary in the 225-year history of the department. She had decided to step down because, in her own words, she'd become the 'poster girl' of the parliamentary expenses scandal that had erupted after the disclosure of misuse of MPs' allowances and expenses, and which had caused widespread public anger. Jacqui had a marginal seat and wanted to dedicate her time to trying to win it again at the election that would have to be held by June 2010, just a year away.

As my train passed the spot approaching Hull where, according to Larkin, 'sky and Lincolnshire and water meet', I felt a strange mixture of elation and apprehension. I knew enough about my new position to be aware of its notoriety as the graveyard of political reputations.

When I alighted from the train in Hull news cameras were already waiting to get background shots for the lunchtime and evening bulletins.

My main task that day was to hold a meeting with ex-trawlermen in a room above Ye Olde Blue Bell, their favoured haunt in the city centre, near the impressive, gilded statue of 'King Billy' – William of Orange – on horseback. I was to be joined there by my friend Gloria De Piero, the television journalist, who was doing a feature on me for the *New Statesman*, and planned to interview me on the train back to London.

After their victory in the fight for compensation, Ron Bateman and Ray Smith of the BFA had alerted me to their suspicion that there was another battle to be waged on behalf of the trawlermen. They wondered why so many of them couldn't recall ever seeing their pension money. Having paid sixpence a week into an occupational scheme introduced in the early 1960s, very few of them had seen evidence that payments had been received. Hardly any of the trawlermen had had bank accounts back then, so it was difficult to be sure. Cheques would be cashed in Rayner's and other Hessle Road pubs (none of which issued monthly statements). I traced the remnants of the pension scheme to Norwich Union, which was in the process of changing its name to Aviva.

What I uncovered was a catastrophic failure of responsibility. The only details held about scheme members were surname, initials and date of birth. There were no addresses, no telephone numbers and no next of kin. The trawler owners had relied on the Fishermen's Mission to distribute pension money and after the main mission leader in Hull died, the entire system atrophied. Even before then the scheme had been deeply flawed. The men had been expected to apply for their money via the trawler owners, who were going out of business anyway. The trawler owners were then meant to contact the insurance company, who would send the cheque to the Fishermen's Mission, which was supposed to pass it on to the pensioner.

I discovered that a staggering 6,000 distant-water trawlermen from Hull, Grimsby, Fleetwood and Aberdeen had never received the pension to which they'd contributed.

We set up a 'Find the Fisherman' campaign, and for three years it managed, through the media, local libraries and council records, to track down 2,000 of the unpaid pensioners. But many of those who Aviva claimed had been given their money, and who were therefore not on the list, insisted that they had not, and Aviva had no way of proving what had happened either way. To be fair, having inherited the core scheme, Aviva had had no involvement in its original dysfunction. Given the disgracefully lax way the scheme had been operated, I argued that these men should be given the benefit of the doubt. There weren't huge amounts of cash involved. It was a modest pension plan but, whatever the sums, the money belonged with the trawlermen and their families.

It was yet another example of the appalling way these people had been treated. Not only had they been thrown out of work, wrongly classified as casual workers, denied the help they were promised and abandoned by their employers, now they'd been robbed of their pensions, too. But there was surprisingly little anger in evidence as we discussed a plan for resolving the situation, fortified by pints of best bitter and plates of meat pies. After all they'd been through, the men seemed resigned to ill-treatment.

On the return journey to London, Gloria, who'd added a dash of TV glamour to the occasion at the Blue Bell as she chatted to the trawlermen in her Bradford accent, conducted her interview over a celebratory glass of Chardonnay.

As the train pulled into King's Cross I glimpsed what was in store for me on the platform. There were four policemen with sniffer dogs, five plainclothes protection officers and sundry others – reporters, station staff and commuters caught up in the mêlée. It was like one of those old war films where the hero, having broken out of a prison camp and travelled across most of Europe disguised as a peasant, is faced, only hours from safety, with recapture as the train enters the terminus. He searches for an escape route before finally surrendering to the inevitable. Gloria said: 'I'll see you when you're free,' stepped off the train and disappeared into the crowd while I was taken into custody.

The cheery face of Louise greeted me from the driving seat of a different black Jaguar from the one that had brought me to the station. This one was armour-plated. The protection officers, holding open the rear doors, told me where to sit in order to avoid assassination. One officer got into the front passenger seat, where I was no longer permitted to ride, and four more travelled in two accompanying vehicles.

When we reached the underground car park of the Home Office, a film crew was waiting. Michael Cockerell, the award-winning political documentary-maker who'd told the story of the

UCW's successful campaign against Post Office privatization over a decade previously, was shooting another film. This one was about the great offices of state. The Home Office was the Methuselah of government departments. Alongside the Foreign Office, it was the very first to have been created, in 1782. Together with the Foreign Office, 10 Downing Street and the Treasury, my department completed the quartet of ministries that were the subject of Cockerell's documentary. Thus my startled arrival at the pinnacle of my political career was recorded for posterity.

I soon discovered it was like no other department I'd served in. My remit now would be immigration, counter-terrorism and law and order, which meant responsibility for the police and MI5. Much of what the Home Office did I would never be able to talk about to anybody for the rest of my life. While I was in office, anywhere I intended to go would have to be checked out in advance by a security detail. I could never go out alone. Whether I was making a speech somewhere or popping down the road to buy the Sunday papers from my local newsagent, I would be accompanied by armed men and women.

If I went jogging they'd jog with me. When I walked 600 yards to my in-laws' house for lunch I would be protected. If I sat in a restaurant with family or friends, my protectors would be watching out for me from a nearby table.

All of this was explained to me over the weekend in a series of meetings with various representatives of the police and the security services in our house, which had been immediately fitted with security devices and alarms. By the time I arrived at the Home Office again on Monday morning for my first full day as home secretary, I knew that this would be the most demanding job I'd ever do; that there would be a higher level of intensity and that I must be permanently on call.

I'd spent the weekend telling myself that the Home Office was just the latest in a long line of workplaces stretching back to Remington Electric Razors in 1965. The trick was confidence. Just the same sort of self-belief demonstrated by the kids who used to ride their bikes without touching the handlebars around our streets when I was a child. The boys who were confident cycled for miles with their hands in their pockets; the boys who weren't fell off.

David Normington, the permanent secretary at the Home Office, had arranged for the staff to gather in the huge atrium at our Marsham Street headquarters to welcome me that Monday morning. As I walked in a doorkeeper stepped forward to wish me well. 'Congratulations, Mr Milburn,' he said, confusing me with another Alan who'd served in a Labour Cabinet. I smiled, ruminating on the fact that it would be a long while before I became a household name; probably longer still where he lived.

A pale yellow light permeated the atrium as I looked up at the staff crowded on to balconies, up and up, tier upon tier. Clare and Mario, Jo, Bron and Suzanne were standing near the spot I was to speak from, a reassuring collective presence as we entered yet another new department.

I wanted to be able to consider this my workplace for several years but would we remain in government? Another general election was only twelve months away and Gordon had never recovered his early popularity. And he was receiving little credit in Britain for the gargantuan efforts he made through the G20 to prevent the global recession, which had begun the previous year with the collapse of Lehman Brothers in America, from becoming a depression of the kind not seen since the 1930s.

The documentary cameras were rolling as I stood dry-mouthed, waiting to address the assembled throng. They thought we were at the beginning of something but I knew, with absolute certainty, that it was an ending. The road would soon run out and a different journey would begin.

Epilogue

In 2004, just as I was appointed to my first Cabinet position, I had a call from Linda to tell me that our father had died. He'd breathed his last in Dulwich, a couple of miles from where I lived, yet the news came from Australia. Sandra, our half-sister, had called Linda, and Linda rang me.

Nothing much stirred inside me. A man I didn't know had lived into his eighties, longer than both his wives. Twice as long in fact as his first wife, my mother.

Linda wouldn't be going to the funeral and neither would I.

Sandra told Linda that Steve had been happy in his old age, doing the things he'd always done. Going out every morning to the bookies' to put on a bet, armed with the *Mirror*, popping into the pub for a lunchtime pint, coming home to sit at his piano – 'tickling the ivories', as he always put it.

When I closed my eyes I was back in the crumbling, squalid dystopia of London W10. Steve, Lily, Linda and me in our two gaslit rooms in Southam Street. Then I thought of Lily's final days in Hammersmith hospital, her hopes of a happy future with Steve long gone.

I can't remember if Lily was still alive when I saw an early episode of *Coronation Street* in which Ena Sharples and Elsie Tanner argued fiercely in the street. Ena, in her overcoat and hairnet, shouted at Elsie: 'There's something wrong with a woman who can't hang on to her man!' At the time, I was infuriated on my mother's behalf. Now I realize how much that statement encapsulated the attitudes of the time in working-class communities; attitudes Lily was forced to suffer after her abusive husband ran off with another woman.

Linda and I were all that remained of the love they'd shared. I pictured Lily confronting her heart condition with a fragile bravery. An abandoned woman.

Linda had sat with her in intensive care after her operation. A tracheotomy had been performed to help Lily breathe and she was in an induced coma, but the nurse said she would know Linda was there and would be able to hear her. So Linda talked about how successful the surgery had been and how Lily would now be able to look forward to a brighter future, out of the slums and in better health. We both knew, my sister and I, that if our mother had come round, if she had been able to think at all, the only thing she would have been thinking about was what would become of us.

If only Lily could have glimpsed what the future held for the other three occupants of those two dank, condemned rooms into which I'd been born. Steve had a happy second marriage. Even at the end, his life was contented. As for Linda and me, thanks to my sister, we battled through the dreadful aftermath of our mother's death to lead fulfilling lives and never forgot the values she'd instilled in us.

I so wish our mother could have been reassured in those final hours of her life. Everything will be all right, Lily, all right for all of us. Really, it will.

Acknowledgements

My grateful thanks to:

My wife, Carolyn Johnson, for her unceasing support and encouragement and for her skill in converting my handwritten scribble into a computerized text.

My agent, Clare Alexander, a constant source of wisdom.

Larry Finlay, Doug Young, Patsy Irwin and all the wonderful people at Transworld.

Caroline North, the finest editor in the business.

I am also indebted to the following publications for providing invaluable information on the fishing industry:

The Headscarf Revolutionaries: Lillian Bilocca and the Hull Triple-Trawler Disaster, Brian W. Lavery (Barbican Press, 2015)

The First Casualty, Bert Wyatt (The Memoir Club, 2006)

Fishing Explorer: The Final Visit to the Gaul, Ernest Suddaby (Maritime Info UK Ltd, 2006)

Trawling with the Lid Off, John Nicklin (Aurora Publishing, 1996)

Picture Acknowledgements

All photos from the author's collection except: p. 1 Richard Willson/News Syndication; p. 2 (*below*) Getty Images; p. 3 (*above*) Hull News & Pictures; p. 5 (*above*) Rex Features/John Voos, (*below*) Getty Images/Adrian Dennis; p. 6 (*above*) Rex Features/Paul Grover, (*below*) Carl Court/PA Archive/Press Association Images; p. 7 (*above left*) Rex Features, (*above right*) Stefan Rousseau/PA Archive/Press Association Images, (*below*) Getty Images/WPA Pool; p. 8 (*top*) Getty Images/Mark Cuthbert.

Index